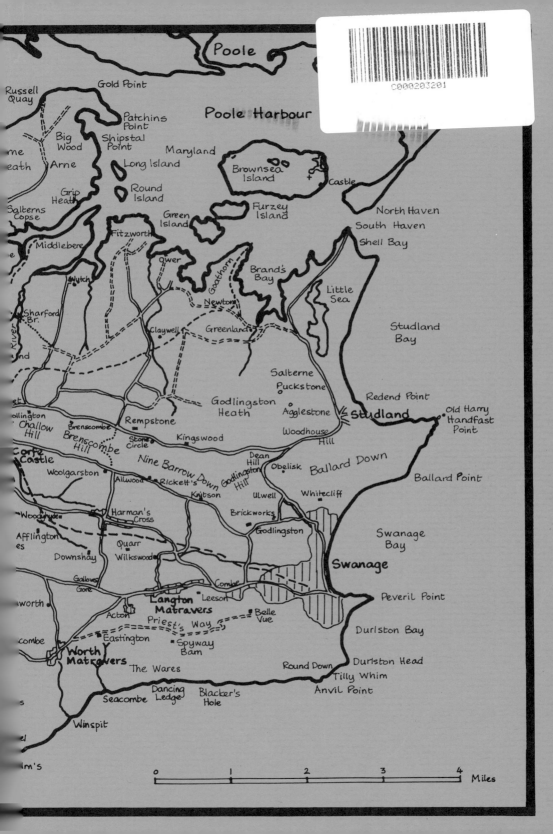

Poole

Poole Harbour

Russell
Quay

Gold Point

Patchins
Point

Maryland

me
eath

Big
Wood

Shipstal
Point

Brownsea
Island

Castle

Arne

Long Island

North Haven

Grip
Heath

Round
Island

Furzey
Island

South Haven

Shell Bay

Salterns
Copse

Green
Island

Little
Sea

Fitzworth

Middlebere

Qwer

Goathorn

Brand's
Bay

Studland
Bay

Wytch

Newton

Sharford
Br.

Claywell

Greenland

River

Salterne

Puckstone

Redend Point

nd

Godlingston
Heath

Agglestone

Old Harry
Handfast
Point

ollington
Challow
Hill

Rempstone

Woodhouse

Studland

Brenscombe

Brenscombe
Hill

Stone
Circle

Kingswood

Hill

Ballard Down

Ballard Point

Corfe
Castle

Woolgarston

Nine Barrow Down

Dean
Hill

Obelisk

Godlingston
Hill

Ailwood

Rickett's

Knitson

Ulwell

Whitecliff

Woodryde

Harman's
Cross

Brickworks

Afflington
es

Quarr

Godlingston

Swanage
Bay

Downshay

Wilkswood

Gallows
Gore

Combe

Swanage

aworth

Leeson

Langton
Matravers

Peveril Point

combe

Acton

Priest's Way

Belle
Vue

Durlston Bay

Eastington

Spyway
Barn

Worth
Matravers

The Wares

Round Down

Durlston Head

Tilly Whim

s

Seacombe

Dancing
Ledge

Blacker's
Hole

Anvil Point

Winspit

el

m's

0   1   2   3   4
Miles

PURBECK
THE INGRAINED ISLAND

PURBECK

THE INGRAINED ISLAND

by

PAUL HYLAND

with photographs by
Bob Groves

LONDON
VICTOR GOLLANCZ LTD
1978

ISBN 0 575 02440 2

Printed in Great Britain by
The Camelot Press Ltd, Southampton

—for Ken, Hetta & Noëlle

"Faire *Purbeck* . . . which no where hath her peere"
MICHAEL DRAYTON

CONTENTS

ILLUSTRATIONS

Following page 32

Following page 96

PART ONE

PURBECK PROGRESS

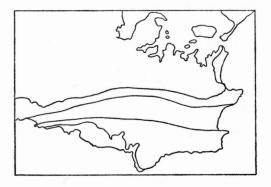

Salt mists creep on the sunlit hills
as if the sea beyond reclaimed
its own pure chalk whose calcined bone
under cropped grass is Purbeck's spine,
ocean's upswelling laid-down dead.

Below are clay-scapes, gravel troughs,
relicts of repetitious seas'
transgressions and retreats; the waste
acidic heath whose flagrant furze
like yeast, works in the sun's oven.

Furrows, like ripples in the rough,
struggle from farmsteads, and revert.
Seawards, ramparts raised on the chalk,
strip-lynchets, stones chart human tides
while mounds like sea-marks compass them.

Those barrows of trussed bones disperse
in mist up on the chilling ridge.
The humming heath lies undisturbed;
men settled on the sun-baked earth
that soon must break over their heads.

I

PERSPECTIVE

WHEN I WAS four, playing alone in the front garden of the house where I was born, a grey van drew up and a stranger got out. He climbed up on our wall and, grinning down at me, knocked a tall post with a sign on it into the bed beside the lilac bush. I didn't look until he'd gone. I don't think I could read it, but I understood. This, my house, my back garden with the sand-pit, chicken-run and apple trees, For Sale. With a few sharp hammer-blows my world was shrunk to nothing. I crashed through the front door, up the passage and into the kitchen where, with surprise and relief, I found my mother quietly making pastry.

My world did not shrink. For though we only moved two hundred yards or so, we moved uphill. My narrow bedroom opened on to a small leaded balcony from which I could see southwards over the birch, pine and rhododendron tops of the steep wood where I later tunnelled back into the grey-sand, white-sand bank causing subsidence to the terrace; over the links where I poached golf-balls; over the colonised heath where smart housing estates elbowed their way between older shanty-bungalows and the mansions of the rich; over the woods that hid the pottery and clay-pits where I admired the brass and bright paint of the shunting-engine in its shed; over the real-estate peninsula of Sandbanks where my uncle lived with his own small and sand mountain in his back garden; over Poole Harbour where he kept the motor-boat from which we landed surreptitiously on forbidden islands, where the Marines still exercised their landing-craft and great sea-planes rode glinting like dragon-flies upon the water; over all that to Purbeck Island and the open sea.

That was always there. The white chalk of Old Harry Rocks stepping eastwards towards the Isle of Wight, and westwards the green Purbeck Hills blocking the flow of the black heath, high downland broken halfway by Corfe Gap, with William's castle powerless to fill it, a decayed tooth; and through the gap, blue uplands of the Purbeck stone. White bits of sails and pleasure-boats moved on Poole Bay or threaded their way through the slight passage where the chain-ferry ran, with coal and grain ships, timber-boats and tankers, into Poole Harbour whose reaches fingered westwards out of sight. Nine years before, that bay and harbour had been choked with craft. My brother and sister had chewed gum and strutted with the Yankees between tanks in front of our old house. Then all one night successive waves of aircraft pounded overhead and in the morning all the ships had sailed for Normandy.

On clear, imaginative days I thought I could see France; but every day I got up and went to bed with Purbeck in my eye, smudged sometimes by the rain or shivering in the heath and water's heat, dimmed by sea-mist or perfect in late sun. Elizabeth's reign was still a year away, but from the moment we moved into that new house I came into my kingdom. Not one square foot of Purbeck has belonged to me; I've never lived there; but was happy from that time to own it; not knowing how hard that was, how hard a country it is. Distance had done its usual job. Later though, when I closed on it, the enchantment grew.

2

THE ISLAND

EVERY SUMMER PURBECK becomes what it has always been: a place for fugitives. No longer pirates playing off the Vice-Admiral of Purbeck against the Mayor of Poole and the Vice-Admiral of Dorset; no longer the smugglers who contrived intricate relationships with the Purbeck gentry; nor recusants and dissenters seeking sanctuary in that "island in the west" that Tichborne spoke of during the Babington Plot trials. Today no armed lads hole up in Purbeck clay-pits to escape the press gang, nor is Piers Gaveston rumoured to be on the run close by his royal lover's prison at Corfe. Today they queue in cars and coaches, with caravans and tents, waiting to cross the ferry from North to South Haven, for the toll-road and the beaches, for Studland village and the town of Swanage. Similar queues congeal at the Northport level-crossing, then press across the north causeway and the bridge over the Piddle into the old walled town of Wareham and out again over South Bridge and the causeway to Stoborough and Corfe Castle. A few come from the west along Holme Lane or, most spectacular of all, when the army range is open, from Lulworth over Whiteway Hill past the Iron Age fortress of Flower's Barrow.

In any numbers, fugitives become invaders. Wareham was razed repeatedly by their incursions, but Purbeck usually succeeded in moulding them to its discipline or repelling them, as with the Saxons, until they had mellowed or been converted to its ways. This, together with its isolation, the venerable restrictive practices exercised in the stone trade, and its long status as a royal forest or warren whose inhabitants could not marry outsiders without a warrant from the Crown, means that Purbeck has maintained a curious continuity and integrity, a closeness and secretiveness unusual in the south. It was the last place on Dorset's coast to open up and adapt in any way to the tourist traffic. Today's invaders are perhaps the most intransigent, for they pass in and out to view and to enjoy the island, hermetically sealed against real contact with it, or settle in its stone cottages, innocent and ignorant of the ancient fabric upon which they impose their new pattern. Most natives do not welcome them, for as their appreciation of the place is superficial, so their impact upon it is profound. The tourist traffic, once a luxury trade, has become an economic necessity for a proportion of the population who have grown more and more dependent on its annual injection of wealth. Some farmers, queueing up for the necessary permission, find tents and caravans more profitable crops than barley; and Corfe Castle readily surrenders to the furriner, its coffers less decrepit than its keep.

During the summer migrations, when Purbeck wears the mask of extraversion, it is hard to see the private face or read the lineaments of its landscape, to understand why it is an island. Those who write about the place seem obliged to apologise for it on that score; of course the Isle of Purbeck is no such thing, "surely but a peninsular, for from Lulworth there is good passage into it without crossing anie water at all". Thomas Gerard, alias Coker, is right. That entry at the extreme south-west was the most ancient land route and, on the green road of the chalk hills, the most reliable one in winter. Holme Lane, running parallel with the Frome, was, within living memory, a muddy track with fords through its tributaries, while the marshes and water-meadows around Wareham might be flooded for half the year, crossed on sleds when frozen to avoid the dubious causeways. An inquisition taken at Corfe Castle in the fourth year of Richard II's reign quotes a document, ancient then, which affirms "that the whole Isle of Purbeck is a warren of our lord the King and pertains to his said castle, and it extends from a path which is between Flouresberi and the wood of Wytewey and thence as far as Luggeford, from that to the bridge of Wareham, and so along the sea, in an easterly direction, to a place called the Castle of Stodland; thence by the sea-coast to the chapel of St Aldhelm, and from thence still by the sea-coast towards the west until it again reaches the aforesaid place of Flouresberi". So, bounded on the south and east by sea, by Poole Harbour and the river Frome to the north, and by the stream called Luckford Lake, embedded in Leland's "black moristical ground", to the west, Purbeck's insularity was guaranteed. And seems so still, when caravans and yachts and pleasure-boats are laid up for the winter. Visit it then, and you find another country.

Swanage's shuttered arcades and promiscuous attractions look pathetic out of season but, paradoxically, the notion of a serene sequestered isle that tourists seek and bring with them to Purbeck is shown up for the myth it is. Activities peculiar to the place's several provinces take proper precedence: farmers, clay-cutters, quarrymen, estate-workers and oil-men all pursue trades and industries whose antecedents date back to the Iron Age at least; ages of exploitation of an island and its men and women, of discovery and decline, success and failure, export and introspection. Peace-time gunfire on the army's ranges echoes past battles and skirmishes, while walls and ancient hedges enclose a solid gentry who, via interminable transactions and devious descent, still possess most of the land. Secretly it was, and is, a busy place.

One winter's day at Worth Matravers I went into the Square and Compass, whose name makes it a stonecutter's pub, but which fills with foreigners in summer-time. My intrusion caused no more than a slight lull. The talk there was of soil and stone, and of a half-bottle of white wine one of them had won in the Christmas raffle.

"I won't drink it."

"Yer kids then."

"The older'un won't. Not drink. He'm too nancified fur that. He'll mark a lemonade boddle off, measure each gullup, last it out. Proper office-boy he be. Was born at ten to nine; said then he'd be an office-clerk."

"I was born at ha'-past seven, jus' in time fur an honest day's work."

"I wasn' born; I were dropped."

In the next bar, or rather the corridor beside the bar, a soberly dressed party of men was getting set, with drinks and well-turned songs, to bury a good neighbour. I left to the sound of their voices solemnising the event with proper gaiety, in preparation for their butty's last journey along a lane deserted but for his own kind.

3

THE PROVINCES

TAKE AN EXPANSE of heath, like Hardy's Egdon; set it on the margins of the second largest natural harbour in the world; add the scenery of the Isle of Wight and a strip of valley from the Weald of Kent; buttress it against the sea with Portland Stone and a skirt of dark clays; pack all that into an area of sixty square miles and you have a makeshift recipe for Purbeck.

When I first crossed the ferry it was to enjoy the most recent geological deposits, the growing dunes of fine white sand that fringe the eastern bays. Learning to keep afloat in the gentle flux of the sea was enough for me then, and shifting sand was terra firma to my feet. I could not comprehend the tides that had laid layer upon layer of rock, nor the forces which caused their upswelling and weathering into the shapes I knew. A child needs to pit himself against one element at a time and my eye was not then for the landscape. My imagination would have been stirred, though, if I had known that a walk from Studland beach, cutting across the east–west grain of the island to the bleak grandeur of Chapman's Pool, traverses 200 million years of rocky history.

Each successive province possesses its own legacy of landscape, bequeathed to it by the rock on which it rests. Take the holiday route out of the walled town of Wareham over the river Frome and you can see, with Coker, that "at the first Entrance into the Island lieth a large Flatte of barren heathie Grounde (yet well replenished with red Deere)". Acid heaths grasping a living from the grits and gravels of the Bagshot Beds, planted with coniferous forest and colonised by the greedy, flamboyant rhododendron. Deposits of workable clay were first dug here in antiquity, and man has won agricultural land at the harbour's edge and along the ribbon of richer ground founded on London Clay and Reading Beds, notable for Romano-British settlements, that runs at the foot of the ridge-way.

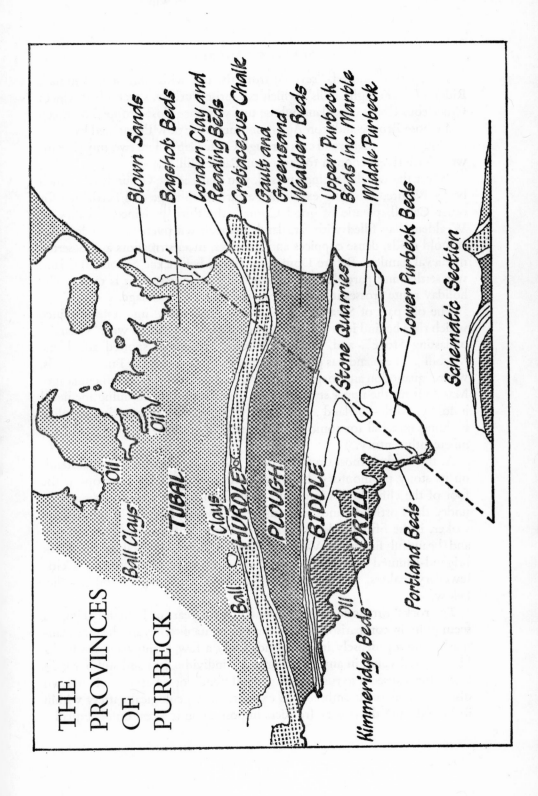

THE PROVINCES OF PURBECK

Ball Clays
Oil
Oil
Oil
Ball
Clays
Oil
Oil

TUBAL
HURDLE
PLOUGH
BIDDLE
ORTLE

Kimmeridge Beds
Portland Beds
Stone Quarries

Blown Sands
Bagshot Beds
London Clay and Reading Beds
Cretaceous Chalk
Gault and Greensand
Wealden Beds
Upper Purbeck Beds inc. Marble
Middle Purbeck
Lower Purbeck Beds

Schematic Section

The heath is, indeed, "severed from the rest with allmost a continuall Ridge of verie highe Hills" which comprise Purbeck's second province: Cretaceous Chalk downland whose turf was once close-cropped by sheep and whose Bronze and Iron Age monuments are now threatened by scrub or plough. The main road cuts through Corfe Gap where two tiny streams were once rivers enough to carve out Castle Hill.

"Over the which haveinge passed, you shall see the Grounde of a much better Nature, affording excellent Pasture for Sheepe and Feedeinge for other Cattell, plentie of good Corne", the third province, a valley of Wealden Clay filled with farmland, mapped with venerable hedgerows and old roads, dense coppices and spinneys, modest manors and deserted medieval hamlets. Before Domesday Book, before the Saxons, this land was settled and parcelled out in much the same way as it is today. The holiday route crosses it obliquely to the resort of Swanage.

The old part of Swanage is built into the fourth, limestone province which rises behind it to an almost treeless plateau, pocked with "Quarries of lasting Stone", and, in Coker's time, "Mines of spotted and bleue Marbill". The island has given its name to these rocks, the Purbeck Beds, where iguanodon and megalosaurus planted their footprints millennia ago. Marble from the upper strata was the foundation of a booming medieval industry, while Portland stone, mostly dug from cliff quarries, supplied building material for some of the great civil engineering projects of the nineteenth century.

At the southernmost tip of Purbeck, where St Aldhelm's Chapel stands on its stony promontory, blue-black Kimmeridge Clay outcrops at the foot of the cliffs, builds into cliffs of its own to the west and disappears under the Portland Sands once more at Brandy Bay. This, ignored by Coker, is the fifth and last province of Purbeck. It encompasses the rich and beautiful Encombe Vale and Golden Bowl, as well as the bleak brigand-haunted coastline whose shaly cliffs were plundered by Celtic jewellery-makers, and where two "donkeys" now tap the oil that lies below.

The rocks' timescale makes a few thousand years of human habitation seem puny in comparison; but just as one strata overlies another, so man-marks outcrop densely in the island. Only a few events have made the history books and, in any case, Purbeck's individualism and stubbornness have often caused it to run against general trends, or reflect them in its own distorting mirror. It embraces an extraordinary geological variety within its bounds, but those very frontiers impose upon it a real unity. Equally,

its geographical singularity has created a continuity of tradition and out-
look from the diversity of interests that have exploited each of its zones.

As a child I thrilled with the challenge of the elements here, the sea, the
wind, the almost unscalable rocks. Later I appreciated the landscape, and
the swift metamorphoses it underwent. I acquired the taste for it, and
wanted more. I walked and talked there, ransacked books and records for
clues, ran with and against its grain, and coaxed it to reveal itself little by
little. It is the result of that unfinished exploration that follows, section by
section, through each of its five provinces.

For it is like a hand that holds a secret. Finger by finger it opens, dis-
closing only itself, a scarred and work-worn hand, an ingrained palm to be
lovingly grasped, and read.

PART TWO

TUBAL

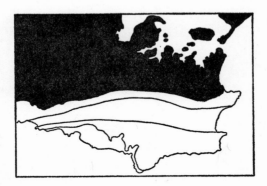

Old hag, the stretch-marked heath, had commerce with
sprawled harbour; watermark, birth-mark, her kith
whose wildfowl kin ride on the wake of yachts.
Her warships, ferries, clay-barges, stone boats,

her passage-houses, ports and wharves are dead;
tracks are ripped up, causeways and piles plumb mud;
her streams drain into saltings, fertile leas
where salters' steam distilled brine's currency.

Where withy-weave was caulked with her white mire
and stone, bronze, iron age pots were born of fire,
today, like hair on hag-skin, pines conceal
steel tongues seeking her juices, her black oil.

Her rusty sphagnum bogs are running sores;
her holy stones are warts; tumuli, tumours;
deeper, close-ranked pine trunks scent dark clay-lanes
where men excise her pressing, secret organs.

Poised above open wounds, great diggers prey
upon her grey-blue, blue-black, iron-bruised clay;
as, coiled at clay-pool, the heron stabs down
among white lilies, jerks flesh from toad bone.

4

GARRISON AND GATEWAY

WAREHAM IS SET on the wrong bank of the Frome but, as Purbeck's main entry and market town, it holds many clues to the island's past. Its old charter was confirmed by Queen Anne in 1703 and the elegant ashlar-fronted Manor House, set back from South Street, dates from the end of her reign. Despite the sleek shop-fronts that have almost supplanted well-fed bow-windows in its main streets, the leisurely country town is apparently firmly founded in the eighteenth century. Ensconced among plush water-meadows, it stands between twin rivers at the point where they approach one another most closely before flowing out into Poole Harbour.

For Wareham's situation is as strategic as it is picturesque. Earthen walls rear up from the banks of the Piddle and still enclose the greater part of the town on the north, east and west, while the waters of the Frome form a natural barrier to the south; defences which pre-date Queen Anne by a thousand years or more. Wareham's gentle atmosphere is deceptive for it is a gateway that was strenuously and repeatedly defended, whose portals were grudgingly opened at the last possible moment to those who successively assumed jurisdiction in Wessex. The threshold of Purbeck bears in its surviving stones the tread of many men whose entry precipitated the turbulent history of the town.

The sinking of foundations, drain-digging and excavation of the Town Walls have yielded Iron Age and Roman finds which, in their irrecoverable context, conceal the commerce, both violent and peaceable, between the forces of imperial occupation and the native Durotrigian tribesmen. What is clear is that Wareham and Purbeck was a dense centre of Romano-British population which resisted Saxon incursions for two-and-a-half centuries after the Romans had withdrawn, long after north Dorset and much of the West Country had succumbed. Bokerley Dyke on Cranborne Chase, Combs Ditch between the Stour and the Winterbourne, and the

Battery Banks whose earthworks extend west of Wareham may represent the course of the Saxon advance that finally, in about 660, took Dorset's last rich stronghold, the Isle of Purbeck.

By this time the Saxons were nominally Christian, according to the Roman tradition, and in Wareham they encountered a venerable centre of the British faith which had long kept in touch with the Gaulish Church from the shores of Poole Harbour. When St Aldhelm, Abbot of Malmesbury and later Bishop of Sherborne, visited the town his missionary zeal was directed, not to the conversion of pagans, but to the unification of the Roman and Celtic traditions. The road climbs into the town from where the north gate stood; above it, upon a stone-clad bank, is the church of St Martin which Aldhelm is said to have founded in 698 while waiting for a fair wind to take him across the Channel. Its earliest fabric dates from about 1020, but this replaced an earlier structure where Beorthric, king of the West Saxons, is supposed to have been buried in 802 after his queen mistakenly poisoned him. Its nave is a small barn, squat yet lofty, while the tower's erratic window-slits stutter between its round-arched entrance and its pointed gable. It is a survivor, tough but delicate, with remains of Norman and later paintings on its rough walls. One of these shows St Martin sharing his cloak with a beggar, and tradition has it that after the royal resting-place had lost its roof in Danish raids shepherds sheltered here all the same, for no rain fell within its walls. After Wareham's great fire of 1762 the little church provided a more mundane refuge, and a fireplace was built into the chancel wall to warm the homeless. Today, its Norman north aisle is a strange sanctuary for the effigy of a twentieth-century knight, dressed in the flowing robes of an Arab, his hand on the pommel of a curved dagger, his head resting on a camel's saddle, carved in Purbeck stone by Eric Kennington: Lawrence of Arabia, crusader without a cross, the lintel of whose Dorset cottage is inscribed with the Greek motto "Nothing matters".

If the learned Aldhelm reformed Wareham's spiritual life, it was Alfred the Great who strengthened its strategic rôle. The hypochondriac king had a great desire for scholarship but was illiterate until middle life; he crept into churches at night to recite the daily offices by heart so that his followers should not discover his piety. Part of his navy was probably built in the Harbour and in his time Wareham's walls were reinforced. The Danish King Guthrum and his host got into Wareham in 876 and made a spurious treaty with Alfred before moonlighting for Exeter. One hundred and twenty Danish ships were wrecked off Swanage the next year and, after Guthrum's defeat at Æthundun, Alfred insisted that he must be baptised to spare the English religious persecution.

Between St Martin's and the north walls, Folly Lane runs to the "Bowling Green" in the north-east corner of the town, where Dugdale's nineteenth-century brick folly stood beside pleasure gardens, where fairs were held, bowls bowled and, some would claim, where an amphitheatre entertained the Roman garrison. Now it is a derelict playground where children on bikes plummet from the walls and circle its rough arena. Now wooded in parts and furnished with seats, the east walls run southwards towards the Frome, broken only where East Street runs out to Bestwall and Swineham Point. From their tops anxious eyes, not least those of nuns from the Priory, kept watch for the marauding host that repeatedly made its way up river. The Priory was a British foundation, reformed by Aldhelm and restored in 915, after Guthrum had razed it, by Ethelfleda, Alfred's daughter. Around the turn of the tenth century it, and the town, suffered at the hands of Sweyn and Canute. The Normans made it a Benedictine cell of Lire Abbey, but at the suppression of alien houses in 1414 it was transferred to the Carthusians of Sheen until the Dissolution of the Monasteries. The oldest part of the present fabric is Elizabethan and the Priory, now a charming house between Lady St Mary's and the Frome, has little to show for its history of mixed fortunes.

Across North Street from St Martin's, Shatters Hill climbs up on to the western half of the north walls. The modern Roman Catholic church there has reclaimed the Saxon king, Edward the Martyr, as its patron saint, Beneath, the mill-house once tapped the Piddle's power and oversaw the sluices that irrigated the water-meadows. In the north-west corner was a cock-pit where baited birds spilt one another's blood, and the west walls, known here as Bloody Bank, flank Westport and the Pound and then run down to the Castle Mound beside the river. Despite Wareham's status as a royal property, 150 of its 292 dwellings were lying waste twenty years after the Conquest. It seems that a building programme of about 1100 set out to repair the damage; the town walls were buttressed with stone and a motte and bailey castle was raised. King Stephen laid siege to it, gained it, and lost it once more to Robert of Gloucester who installed Prince Henry there until his embarkation for France in 1146. The keep soon fell into decay and in 1461 one John Haynes leased the grounds for cultivation. A landscaped garden now exploits the scarps and a house is built over part of the keep's footings. Trinity Lane marks the line of the bailey and an archway, set into the Rectory wall in Pound Lane, is probably all that remains above ground. As to the town walls, although those on the west were steeply scarped this century as a defence against tanks, they are said to be half their original height, for Parliament ordered them to be slighted at the end of the Civil War. The Anglo-Saxon "burh" or fortress was to be transmuted by force into our "borough", redolent of peace and order. It is hard to imagine the internal conflicts of this town that started out Royalist, in opposition to its rival Poole, only to change hands four times while Corfe Castle stubbornly held out for the King.

In the centre, at the meeting of North, South, East and West Streets, the modern Town Hall is the symbol of many of the stresses that the town has suffered. It stands on the site of St Peter's Church, mutilated during the Reformation and turned into a Town Hall and school, before being rebuilt in 1768 by Mr Calcraft of Wareham and Rempstone in Purbeck. The present council chamber contains a plaque, "Let mercy goe wit justice ano 1656", and the Royal Arms of William III, their proximity belying the troubles which separated the Commonwealth and the English Revolution. The Act of Uniformity eased the Puritan rector Thomas Chaplyn out of his living and forced like-minded members of his congregation underground. The Conventicle Acts, with the force of the Dorset militia behind them and a third of all fines imposed going to informers, were potent weapons against such men as Thomas Delacourt who was twice caught using his home as a place of worship. His goods were distrained and put up for sale at the Cross; it is a measure of Wareham's mood that there were no buyers. The rector's widow, Dorothy Chaplyn, returned to her malting business in the town and her house was registered as a Presbyterian Conventicle under the Act of Indulgence, while William Clark, who trudged miles to preach at Stoborough, East Creech, Winfrith and Bere, and founded the Congregational church at Swanage, was licensed as minister. Parson Clark's communion cup, that survived much clandestine use by dissenters, was stolen from Wareham Congregational church during its occupation by the army in the Second World War.

After Monmouth's landing at Lyme, along the Dorset coast, and the abortive rebellion of 1685, some of his followers were hung, drawn and quartered by order of Judge Jeffreys upon the Bloody Bank. The local saying, "He'll rip yer guts out and show 'm to yer aiderwards", though used metaphorically, is still eloquent. At night Thomas Delacourt, with two friends, lifted the heads of Holway, Tyler and Matthews from spikes on the wooden tower in front of the Town Hall. He hid them under his bed and later interred them in the east walls, near the end of Wyatt's Lane.

His treason was not discovered, though he was nearly murdered in the Bull Inn for his radical beliefs and, when William of Orange landed at Torbay, he rode to meet him as sergeant of a company. Some sort of justice was done when he stood guard over Chancellor Jeffreys in the Bloody Tower. Back home in Wareham, Delacourt became a trustee of the Old Meeting House until he died in 1733, with the words, "Come Lord Jesus, come quickly."

Delacourts were trustees until 1834, and must have been saddened by the schism of 1784 which spawned a rival congregation in West Street until the reconciliation of 1849, and that of 1828 when the Unitarian Chapel in South Street was founded. The Old Meeting House of 1667, in Church Lane, was partially destroyed in the great fire and the present building, now United Reformed, dates from that, the last cataclysm that the ancient town was to suffer.

Eighteenth-century Wareham sported comfortable town houses and inns on its main streets, supported by a maze of poor dwellings. Butchers' shambles and charnel houses were crowded in the wider streets near the Cross. Fires of 1704 and 1742 were omens of what was to come when, on 25 July 1762, someone threw glowing turf ashes on to a dunghill by the Bull's Head, now Lloyds Bank, and 133 houses were burnt down. Firemen of the Sun Fire Assurance Office made for those properties marked with the blue disc of Calcraft's Rempstone Estate, and artisans' houses of timber and thatch suffered most, although John Hutchins' rectory was the third building to catch fire. Less than a quarter of his belongings were saved, although his courageous wife managed to salvage the huge collection of manuscripts which was to become the monumental *History & Antiquities of the County of Dorset*. He was concerned about "the bad accommodations the lower part of my people must take up with", and no doubt encouraged them to shelter in the churches of the town. "For my own part I have undergone a severe shock and have a melancholy prospect before me. The Winter of Life, as well as of ye year, is coming on", he wrote, but his new house was soon completed and he lived to finish his history, though not to see it published. Roads were widened, and all subsequent building had to be in brick and tile, though a few thatched buildings still mark the limit of the disaster. The King's Arms in North Street survived, while the nearby Red Lion was rebuilt, and with it half Wareham, around the surviving memorials of its past.

Across the road the new Methodist Church and the modern offices of ECC Ball Clays Ltd signify the continued vigour of the town's spiritual and commercial life. Its prosperity grew out of the Purbeck marble and stone trade, the servicing of Corfe Castle and from more dubious creation of wealth by merchants like Thomas Perkins who found Bestwall, outside the town walls, an ideal station for the smuggling and piratical traffic of the Harbour and of Purbeck. In those good old Elizabethan days for every Wareham man in business there was one of independent means. Humble streets in the north-west quarter of the town are called Cow Lane, Tinkers Lane, Ropers Lane where the Brethren Gospel Hall stands, and Mill Lane which runs up to the north wall above the mill-house. Vegetables, including garlic, were grown in the town's dark soil, and the Thursday market still deals in farm produce. A new shopping precinct off St John's Hill makes money near where it was minted in Athelstan and Edward the Confessor's reigns. The cattle market is now an annual affair whose pens and stalls in East Street are more usually filled with second-hand furniture and boating gear.

Yachts and cruisers lie at the old moorings on the river. The Frome was once called the Var, and Wareham's name may stem from that or from the salmon weir that spanned the river near Castle Mound, for Hutchins says "The hoop net or wear for taking salmon has been fixed in the Wareham Royalty for several centuries". Beside Tanner's Lane, Abbot's Quay served Sherborne Abbey of which Holy Trinity Church, now an art gallery, was a dependency. In spite of its disasters Wareham was a crucial south-coast port for centuries, until the silting of the Frome and the rise of Poole conspired against it. It supplied ships and men for the siege of Calais and Edward III inspected vessels under construction here towards the end of his reign. But the arrest of the *Margarete* of Wareham, carrying Purbeck marble tombs for the Earl of Arundel and his wife and a great stone for the Bishop of Winchester, by the Keepers of the Port of Poole in 1347 signifies the transfer of power in the Harbour. In the eighteenth century merchants strenuously resisted Poole's attempts to collect dues, for Hayter's Quay, where the Old Granary is now a restaurant, was then busy with the export of clay and the import of coal and other goods. In 1848 an Act of Parliament provided for a channel and dock at Bestwall, but nothing came of it.

A salmon weather-vane still rides the winds above Lady St Mary's embattled tower. This church, once attached to the Priory that abuts it, is a glorious commentary upon the history of the town it serves, and would be more complete if, in 1841, the rector's oratorical prowess had not demanded the replacement of the Saxon nave. The tower of *c.* 1500, the

St Martin's, Wareham

Opposite above, Wareham's
South Bridge and Creech
Barrow

Opposite below, Inside St
Martin's church

Above left, Old clay-pit,
Arden

Above right, Oil: Arne
Number 1 Well

Centre, Clay: Ridge mine

Below, Worked clay,
Arden

Heath and Harbour from Dean Hill

Derelict clay tramway

Saltings, Shipstal Point and Poole Power Station

Above, Creech Barrow; *below*, Creech Grange

Studland Cross

One of Rempstone Circle's stones

Chalk stack, Ballard Head

St Nicholas' church, Studland

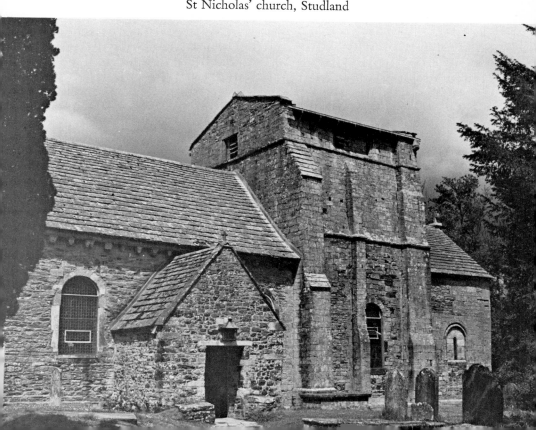

Above, Flower's Barrow; *below*, The ridgeway, westwards

broad-windowed chancel and the tiny vaulted Becket Chapel of *c.* 1325, and St Edward's Chapel of *c.* 1100, said to have been the Saxon king's resting-place before his translation to Shaftesbury, survive to tell their tales, together with an eloquent array of fittings, like the unique hexagonal lead font on its Purbeck marble base whose twelve apostles were defaced by Roundhead soldiers. Here, military man and mariner, mayor and merchant, profiteer from piracy and anti-slaver, medieval knight and eighteenth-century antiquary rest in the town's memory. St Edward's Chapel squats below the level of the church, its vaulted roof supported by shafts of Purbeck marble, and bones of uncertain virtue enshrined in its east wall near a magnificent piscina and aumbry. A round-headed archway leads into the south aisle where a tablet commemorates a soldier who fell at the Somme; "His body was miraculously found by his mother on the battle-field 14 months later". The King and Martyr's remains were discovered too, a thousand years after their removal from this place.

In the north aisle a Norse-style stone coffin from the chapel lies amongst Saxon fragments and cross-shafts preserved there in memory of the church built here about 700. One of the largest Saxon churches in England, it too was a reconstruction, probably inspired by Aldhelm, that served the reformed Priory and a large existing British congregation. The tenacity of the old tradition is evidenced by five Celtic memorial stones of the seventh and eighth centuries whose inscriptions most closely correspond to Old Welsh. Pagan Roman altars there have weathered many centuries of unbroken, if not undisturbed Christian history.

The peaceful market town is no stranger to change, to religious passion, political dissent and economic enterprise, to all those forces which have shaped the Isle of Purbeck, whose gateway it is. Past and present cohabit within its walls, and our brief passage between them has given us a view no less partial than that which presents itself to trippers pressing along North and South Streets into Dorset's last stronghold; but it hints at the sorts of men who preceded us and made their pact with Purbeck. The island offers more than souvenirs: there is a saying that if a man crosses Wareham bridge with one horse, he will need four harnessed to his cart on the return trip.

5

PORTS, SALTERNS, ISLANDS

THE GHOSTS OF the walled town may be exorcised by a leisurely, winding passage down river on the ebb of the tidal Frome towards Poole Harbour. Acres of alluvial water-meadows irrigated by miles of ditched drains surround you, but all you can see is the green cushions of reed-beds, the wide sky and its narrow, sinuous reflection. On this scale, Redcliff's forty-five feet rears up behind the yacht club and the farm that squats in its shelter. Its red sand base is set with mottled clay and its coarse ironstone bluff, capped with the black shapes of trees, hints at tough terrain to the south.

Ridge Wharf is a Yacht Centre patronised by the owners of scores of small craft, but it was once the embarkation point for tens of thousands of tons of clay that each year travelled the tramway to the Pike Brothers' clay-works there. Nearby, Powell's Victorian factory shipped out high-quality cement, made of marl from the Purbeck Hills. Now reeds and tall grasses whistle, warblers pipe and the aeolian harps of steel rigging twang and hum in the breeze. If it is difficult to imagine the recent business bustle of the Frome, how much harder it is to conceive of Alfred's battle-fleet, of Danish raids, of Aldhelm setting sail for Europe and of Iron Age sea-traders, the Veneti, putting into these waters to barter with the Durotriges. Local pottery, a quern-stone and a coin of Septimius Severus found at Ridge give substance to the settlement of Roman times.

Long before that the prehistoric Frome–Solent thrust through these open spaces and out into an estuary beyond the Isle of Wight, laying down gravels and clays from the west which were carved into channels and terraces by its descendants. These persist as the hills, low cliffs, islands and troughs of the basin that was to subside and suffer marine invasions and erosion of its chalk bulwark between the Isle of Wight and the Purbeck Hills until the ragged Harbour and the moorish heathlands of today were born out of their flux. Ten thousand acres of water, with ninety-nine

miles of navigable channels threaded between mud-flats and islands, are
bounded by a coastline of ninety miles or more. This area and the number
of streams running into it mean that tidal effects are damped within the
Harbour, while ebb and flow through the narrow harbour entrance are
strong and have scoured a deep channel. In common with all the coast
from Portsmouth to Lulworth, the Harbour enjoys four high tides, or two
double high waters each lasting about seven hours, each day. While the
Frome has silted and slowed, the main channel to Poole and Hamworthy
is deep enough, and the double high tide long enough for cargo vessels of
about 3,500 tons to make economic use of the port whose merchants
bought its first charter from William Longspée, lord of Canford, in about
1250. Planners expect that 2,000 juggernaut lorries a week will soon roll
through Poole to service the ferry terminal alone, but Hamworthy's
monstrous landmark, its cream-chimneyed power-station, did not always
face grey ruins at Corfe and the Harbour's serene southern shore, for
Purbeck's quays and wharves were long busy with their own trade.

The Frome insinuates itself into the Harbour as Wareham Channel and
makes its way between Swineham Point and Giggers Island, to be joined
by the effluence of the Piddle and nudged towards Poole by the bulky
peninsula of Arne, the northernmost frontier of Purbeck. Its shore was
deserted when I used to land in search of blackberries, prostrating myself
in nettles for my sins, but the name Hyde's Quay is the legacy of Thomas
Hyde who set the pattern for the Purbeck clay industry in 1771 when he
negotiated with John Calcraft to dig it, and with Josiah Wedgwood to
supply it at the rate of 1,400 tons a year. Russel Quay also exported Arne
clay and imported coal or, on occasion, barrels of illicit ballast, while a
Passage House at Gold Point was the terminus of a busy ferry from the
Hutchings at Lake, Hamworthy. Tracks and their shadows still run from
the quays towards Arne village, Slepe and the Purbeck hinterland, like a
dim reflection of the trade network plied upon the Harbour waters in
those days.

The land between Gold Point and Patchin's Point encloses Arne Bay in
its embrace, symbolic of the sanctuary the Royal Society for the Protection
of Birds offers to wildlife there, since it wrested acres of heath and woodland from the clayman's grasp. Freshwater marsh rich with gypsywort,
wild celery and yellow iris gives way to sea rush, sea lavender and glass-
wort salt marsh, and to the hybrid cord grass, Spartina Townsendii, that
has colonised the mud-flats in the last hundred years. The beach at Shipstal
Point is cobbled with solid oyster shells; the Harbour's oyster beds have

been famous since Roman times and Daniel Defoe remarked upon their size and quality, the export trade they generated and the pearls they contained, the largest in all England. The beds are being cultivated in earnest once again, preserved from the hazards of speed-boat and water-ski, in a bid to regain the Poole oyster's proper place in the world.

If the shoreline testifies to the water's harvest, the low cliffs of terrace gravels, with their leached, anaemic upper layers, witness to the poverty of heathland soils. But Arne, from the Anglo-Saxon "aern" or dwelling, has been inhabited from early times and its ground cultivated by continuous application of marl and sweat. The relatively fertile area that in 1750 was divided into thirty-three smallholdings and strip-fields is now combined in the pasture and arable lands of Arne Farm. Though the village is planted inland, its church is dedicated to St Nicholas of Myra, the patron saint of sailors, for Arne was the hub of spokes that led coastwards to the quays and landing-places. Built into the shoulder of a knoll at about the time of John's accession, it is magnificent in its simplicity: a holy barn of sand-stone with ashlar details; a white-painted nave and chancel in one, with fragments of medieval and sixteenth-century wall-paintings, and lancet windows of clear glass that look from one hundred feet above sea-level down to the Harbour's reaches. At night it is lit by candlelight, but there is no elaboration, no recessed darkness to seduce the eye. Its very lack of tower and chancel arch, its openness and warmth give it a solemnity and mystery unmatched by any Gothic architect. Shutters went up and most of Arne's inhabitants were evacuated during the Second World War. Fires lighted on the peninsula drew enemy bombing away from Wareham and Poole. Its people returned to their scarred territory and the church was restored in 1952.

Salterns Copse preserves the memory of the area's major industry and remains of first- and second-century salterns have been found there and near Shipstal Point. The tough brick-clay vessels of the Roman period, in which brine was boiled and evaporated, were replaced by leaden con-tainers, medieval plumba. Arne was a dependency of Shaftesbury Abbey and in the late twelfth century its Rent Roll records that twenty tenants held salt-pans and that a hide of land was devoted to the industry. Salt was more than a commodity: it was wealth, currency in barter, good payment for tithes and debts and root for our word salary. Now, salt mines in Worcestershire and Cheshire have devalued it, and to throw salt over your shoulder to be rid of the devil is a cheap gesture. Wareham enriched itself from the Saxon salt trade, its production was zealously monitored by ecclesiastics, and the trade jealously guarded by its workers. Its virtues were those of healing and preservation, and in John's reign it was exported to Normandy in exchange for wine.

More jealously guarded now is privacy. It is preserved on Arne for the Dartford warbler, the stonechat, linnet, yellowhammer and meadow pipit. But across Wych Channel, landing on Long and Round Islands, linked by saltings, is forbidden. It was on Round Island that Sir Thomas Beecham wrote his biography of Frederick Delius, to the accompaniment of rasping gulls and ducks, mewing curlews and grunting herons.

Between Arne and the Harbour mouth at South Haven, Purbeck's northern shore is cut into fingers and tongues of land or fragmented into islands by stream-mouths, channels or "lakes", inlets and bays. Middlebere Lake is fed by streams off Slepe and Hartland Moors and the seventeenth-century farm is all that remains of a settlement that dates back at least another three hundred years, while a ruin to the north-east marks the relatively recent Middlebere Quay, an eighteenth-century clay-wharf later supplied by tramway. Wytch, across the Corfe River, now better known as the centre of an oil-field, was also a clay port with a Passage House from which the Poole ferry ran. Returning from market in the spring of 1759, this ferry was capsized by boisterous spirits, thirteen souls were lost and the remaining six managed to struggle through the mud to Furzey Island.

In the 1950s much heathland was reclaimed on the Fitzworth peninsula; bombs were frequently unearthed by agricultural machines and detonated safely by army squads. The ground was recalcitrant enough without the danger of explosives and one man told me that the only thing that kept him going, when he was driving fences across newly-won territory, was the notion that in the next post-hole he might strike the treasure that Harry Paye, Poole buccaneer and Vice-Admiral of the Cinque Ports, is reputed to have buried hereabouts in the early fifteenth century. He never found it, but other treasures have been unearthed not far from the brick and thatch of Fitzworth Farm: extensive signs of Iron Age and Roman occupation, sandstone hut footings, pottery and coins of the third and fourth centuries, and salter's waste consisting of props and broken brine-pans. Similar remains have been found on arable land not far from Ower at Cleavel Point, together with a shell-midden and a British pottery-kiln.

Ower Bay is now a very private, secluded place. Deer come and go on the tree-dark shore, battered rowing-boats are beached in mud rich with the flotsam of pottery and old glass, and Ower Quay Cottage's banked garden, now overgrown, looks on to the few remaining piers of a decayed landing-stage. The Domesday Book records thirteen salt-workers there, rendering twenty shillings a year to the Abbot of Milton from three otherwise unproductive hides, and a Saxon church served the port. Lime from Poole and timber from the New Forest were landed in Edward I's reign and dragged across the heath, via hollow-ways and paved fords, to Corfe for the modernisation of the Castle. Stone for the building came from the south but much more, having been dressed at Corfe, was hauled north to Ower, probably the principal port for the massive medieval export trade in Purbeck limestone and marble. Carts and horses waded into the water and the stone was transferred into flat-bottomed barges, with single masts and sweeps at the stern, which took it out the short distance to South Deep, or Sou' Dee' as it is known, to be loaded into cargo vessels. In the twelfth and thirteenth centuries thousands of fonts, tombs and coffin-slabs of Purbeck marble, destined for cathedrals and churches all over England and for Europe too, passed through Ower. A few blocks of stone by the water-side are the port's memorials. It was here that the Quaker poet Bevan Whitney lived and celebrated the "Purbeck Marblers' Road from Corfe" which is still traversed every Shrove Tuesday, as it has been time out of mind, and a pound of pepper paid to the occupants of Ower Farm as toll for the use of the track to the quay. A football used to be kicked from Corfe to Ower as the second portion of the payment offered by the stonecutters.

Pottery and salt was produced on Furzey Island in the Roman period, and a handful of potters work on Green Island today, though not alongside the shale-workers who carved Kimmeridge blackstone in the Iron Age. Later, Milton Abbey owned Green Island, then called St Helen's after the chapel that stood there from the ninth to the sixteenth century, and linked it to their property at Ower with a causeway of stone flags laid upon logs between the island and Cleavel Point. There must have been quite some traffic of craftsmen and pilgrims across South Deep to justify such an ambitious enterprise.

A ferry to Brownsea and Poole continued to run from Ower Quay long after its heyday and a Passage House there, one of a number along the Harbour's edge, offered hospitality to travellers and wildfowlers of the eighteenth and nineteenth centuries. A wildfowlers' houseboat, a one-time sportsmen's arsenal, is still moored in the weed-grown bay. Their punts and the flat-bottomed stone-boats that used to ply here are in a long tradition. In 1964 a dug-out canoe of oak, thirty-three feet in length, was salvaged off Brownsea Island; a humble Bronze-Age vessel related to the nobler sea-going ships of the Veneti, who traded between Brittany and the British ports and levied tolls on other mariners by virtue of their mastery of the sea. Julius Caesar described their flat-bottomed boats with high bows and sterns, durable oaken hulls reinforced with massive cross-timbers and thick iron nails. He admitted that the Romans' only advantage in the hard-won battle with the Venetian fleet was the oar-power of their galleys. Thereafter the Veneti seem to have been accepted as worthy allies by the Durotriges. Perhaps theirs is the credit for the ancient knowledge that shaped Alfred's navy in response to Danish raids nine centuries later.

Some of the old roads and water-crossings are remembered; others have sunk from sight beneath heath and water, while the wharves and industrial sites they served have fallen away until only a farmhouse or cottage or a few rotting piles remain. One port on the Purbeck shore thrived only in the mind of a king. In January 1286, although Poole's first charter was just thirty-six years old and Ower was busy with the marble traffic, such was the volume of trade which the Harbour handled that Edward I ordered Richard de Bosco and Walter de Marico to lay out a new town between Ower and Goathorn. Though Saxton's map of 1575 shows a church at Newton there is no evidence that the planned market-place, harbour, streets and building plots ever materialised. Neither do merchants seem to have taken advantage of the incentives offered, of the twice-weekly market or annual five-day fair that Newton's charter granted them. Edward knew the area well, but perhaps not well enough to understand the restrictive practices of the stone trade or the jealousy of the port of Poole. Newton Bay, a shallow-water wilderness, and the afforested Newton Heath still bear the ambitious name while, nearby, a nineteenth-century Newton brought life to the area for a time; clay was dug there and transported by tramway to the pier at the tip of Goathorn, but its story must wait until later.

Across Sou' Dee', Whiteground and Blood Alley Lakes lies Brownsea Island, presiding over the Harbour entrance. Risk of fire in dry summers means that it is sometimes closed to the public, but its strategic position and its resources ensure that it has always been an incendiary issue. Romano-British pottery sherds indicate the start of a long tradition. Canute carried spoils back here from his raids up the Frome, but later paid compensation to Cerne Abbey for his destruction of St Andrew's Chapel on the island. In the Confessor's reign Bruno was lord of Studland and of Brunci Island. Henry II granted right of wreck at Brunkery to the Abbot of Cerne, but it reverted to the Crown at the Dissolution and Henry VIII built a coastal fort on Brunkesey, the core of the present castle, which he placed under Poole's jurisdiction. Elizabeth granted "the Queen's Majestie's Castell at Brownecksea" to Sir Christopher Hatton, Vice-Admiral of Purbeck, much to the Mayor of Poole's chagrin; for Christopher Anketill, governor of the castle, trespassed upon Poole's illicit trade; fine cloth embellished his residence, good wine was drunk and piratical parrots crowed defiance across the Harbour waters. Legitimate trade suffered too and actions were brought in the Admiralty Court, but it took the Civil War to return Brownsea into Poole's hands.

The largest island in the Harbour, which many people still call Branksea, is now part of Studland parish, part of Purbeck again. Its ochre cliffs of gravels, sands and clays topped with the deep greens of trees, already exploited by Lord Mountjoy's copperas or green vitriol and alum-boiling industries, by pipe-clay pits and brick-works, passed from one private owner to another after the Restoration. In my childhood it was haunted by rumours, and protected against all-comers, except Scouts and soldiers, by Mrs Bonham-Christie, the recluse. On her death in 1961 it was feared that a holiday camp might take it over, but her grandson offered it to the Treasury in lieu of death duties. The family pier's Tudor-style watch-towers now welcome visitors and the castellated village on the eastern shore houses the National Trust shop and information office. Seen through an embattled gatehouse, the castle, rebuilt after a fire of 1896, is the summer preserve of employees of the John Lewis Partnership. Daffodil Field and Peacock Hill both live up to their names; wild and golden pheasants inhabit Beech Valley and Rhododendron Tunnel; and red squirrels chatter in the pine woods where Mad Benson, eminent eighteenth-century lunatic and patron of the arts, is reputed to have practised the black arts. Near Devil's Den Scouts and other youth organisations pitch their tents where Baden-Powell held the first Scout camp in 1907. Shard Point is well named, for it is entirely pebbled with broken pottery and a trackless tramway runs from William Pit, the clay-works and ruined kilns to New Pottery Pier on the west; overgrown bones of workers' cottages stand at Maryland, and near Seymer's Pier and the brick-works on the north shore. Old pyrites mine-shafts fed the copperas works there, but the claims of industry have long since given way to the claims of nature, for the northern half of Brownsea is a reserve run by the Dorset Naturalist Trust. Their headquarters is the Villa between the heronry, the second largest in Britain, and St Andrew's Bay which Colonel Waugh, who invested in clay and built the fussy St Mary's

Church before going bankrupt, attempted to reclaim at great expense. Its hundred acres have reverted to marshland inhabited by terns, avocets and curlews, as surely as Sir Humphrey Stuart's eighteenth-century clover fields have been overtaken by bracken. The island is a bizarre mix of dense growth and open space, of nature and nurture, industry and neglect; wildlife is pampered, and the signs of man's enterprise grow dimmer every year. Man may play, but not make his mark here any more. Lincoln Cliff and Nelson, Elizabeth and Wellington Hills, that overlook the disused pottery tramway, are succeeded inland by hills called Clown, Pantaloon, Harlequin and Columbine, and by Piper's Folly.

A motor-launch takes you from Brownsea to North Haven with its hotel, shops, flats and luxurious houses. In the early years of this century the whole peninsula of Sandbanks, now some of the most vauluable real estate in the country, came on to the market for a thousand pounds. One of my relatives turned the offer down. Across the ferry, wildfowlers and smugglers still put up at the South Haven Inn early in the last century, but it, together with fishermen's cottages and the site of the gibbet, has been succeeded by café and car-park. West of the toll-road from the chain-ferry Brand's Bay is a desolate expanse of water peppered with saltings, invaded in winter by flocks of wildfowl: Brent geese, eider duck, widgeon, black-necked grebes, black-tailed godwit and shelduck that breed on its margins. "A paradise for shooters", wrote Colonel Peter Hawker in his diary for December 1813, but later he found himself surrounded by wildfowlers on every point and mud-bank, in skiffs and punts, "blackguards of all descriptions, firing at all distances". Contraband, landed at Studland and carried across the heath to avoid the searchers at the Harbour entrance, was loaded into flat-bottomed boats at Greenland, Redhorn Quay and Brand's Point, but today the bay is a naturalist's paradise.

While the north shore of Poole Harbour has become progressively built up, Purbeck's ports, salterns and islands, that saw so much competitive trade and investment by the Abbeys of Milton, Shaftesbury and Cerne and by later owners, have declined. Some people fear that the Wytch Farm oil-field threatens the peace and beauty of the heaths, for while a boom was hastily slung across the Harbour mouth when oil from the *Torrey Canyon* threatened to enter on the tide, nothing can now stop the flow of oil from within. But, on the whole, estate-owners have conspired with conservationists to return the southern margins of Poole Harbour to a state of nature unknown for many centuries.

Shell Bay's white sand may throng with summer bathers and cars may

pour down the toll-road to Studland, but a quarter of a mile across the
peninsula a few houseboats are beached on the shore of Bramble Bush
Bay, their rusted anchors maintaining a tenuous hold beneath the dunes
upon the kingdom of oystercatcher, redshank, sanderling and turnstone,
where the occasional pied wagtail plays Canute to the waves. Between
this bay and the freshwater Little Sea across the road are some ancient,
ambiguous man-marks: six stones aligned roughly north–south, seventy-
one earthen circles like heathy ponds, and thirteen sandy mounds. The
dates and functions of these structures are unknown. They are monuments
to all that history which the Harbour shore of Purbeck will not disclose.

6

HEATHCROPPERS, ROYAL CHASE

THE HEATH, BY Romantic definition, is the British wilderness; and the
Purbeck heaths are the largest left in Dorset, stretching from East Lulworth
twelve miles or so eastwards to the margins of Studland Bay, where heathland vegetation claims consolidated dunes as fast as winds and tides can
build them. They are great tracts of furze, heather and ling rooted in a
tough skin only softened by seeping bogs, traversed by rusty streams
sometimes called rivers, and by presumptuous roads. But in many ways
the wildness is skin-deep. Almost everything here is skin-deep.

As you walk across the dark lands, at your feet is the image of tenacity.
Decayed stems and roots mix their black dust with white sand to make a
silver soil in which the living seem to writhe and cling among white-
skinned flints. Bristle-leaved bent grass attempts a ragged turf, and the
tough foliage of small-furze, gorse and heath reaches enough nutrient
from recalcitrant ground for a yellow-purple haze of blossom which heats
and smells of sweet-sour ferment. Baked sand is inhospitable and the rains
conspire to wash what minerals the plants give back below the surface
where an iron hard-pan congeals and sets a barrier impenetrable to roots
searching for the food sealed underneath. It must be drilled to plant a
conifer, and on it the plough founders.

Where clay is skin-deep streams cut their beds, flushing the sand away,
dislodging chunks of Agglestone grit—a half-made rock, conglomerate of
yellow and white quartz set in a matrix of ochre iron—and slicing through
the fine laminae of sandstone. The water itself is red and, in the bogs and
moors, fills up the sponges of sphagnum moss and pickles everything dead
till it settles and compacts into brown peat. White tufts of cotton-grass
signal damp areas and purple moor-grass dies down in winter leaving
stem-bases fat with food and bundles of white leaves like wood-shavings.
The elegant blue marsh gentian flourishes locally, rare yellow-green flowers
of the little bog orchid pitch on clumps of bog moss, and all three species

of sundew supplement a deficient diet by closing their leaves' ruddy tentacles over insects lured there by sweet secretions, which soon turn sourly digestive. Insect protein is a staple of the reptile economy too, and adders, grass-snakes, smooth-snakes, slow-worms and bright spotted sand lizards all resort to the iron-rich waters; while toads and newts breed there successfully.

When I first discovered this heath country it seemed a true wilderness, an escape from the world of men. Here I understood how thin a skin of life grew between the light and the rock, knitting them together into a grudging richness and variety. But it was also the blackness, the romantic bleakness that attracted me, together with a sense of vertigo as if the heath's air, so often fantastically lit, was thinner and less welcoming than that over the water or beyond the hills. These feelings stay with me, but my eye sees more and more the man-marks that testify to attempts to traverse or tame it, exploit or live with it; man-hours and lives spent here; and man's elaborate monuments to his dead.

The western reaches of the wastes are army-occupied. The Ministry of Defence controls over 7,000 acres of Povington, Grange and Holme heaths, and beyond. Tanks firing shake the air and shells exploding jar the earth for miles around. At night their thunder is preceded by green-white flashes that illuminate and bleach the heath again and again, and by eruptions of livid light on target. The name Battle Plain is still appropriate, but refers back to a skirmish of the Civil War. Ruinous Povington preserved until the last century the pattern of demesne farm, small farms and holdings almost exactly as recorded in the Domesday Book. As old again, there, are remnants of Romano-British industry, the turning of bangles and other ornaments from jet-like Kimmeridge shale, while there are traces of Iron Age occupation at Whiteway Farm, near the southernmost sources of Luckford Lake. But across the length and breadth of the heath it is the Bronze Age peoples who have left the most persistent reminder: many nameless tumuli and those, like Water Barrows, Ferny Barrows, Thorn Barrow and Drinking Barrow, used for centuries as landmarks. All but one of the round barrows on Povington Heath, including Povington Barrow itself which held a cremation beneath a flint cairn, have been mutilated, some through use as gunnery targets. The Royal Armoured Corps is now instructed, as an organisation that necessarily respects the dead, not to blast any more Bronze Age ashes to the winds. Almost inadvertently, it is under this latest occupation that the flotsam of the tides of previous invasions are preserved. And not only the dead. Regular batteries of shells disturb wildlife less than gamekeepers and farmers would; the hobby, that can outfly a swift and snatch it from the air, lives here now, and many other birds of prey stoop from above the slopes of Whiteway Hill upon a rich table.

Three Lords Barrow, near East Holme Rifle Range, is the meeting point of three old manors and four modern parishes. King's Barrow, Stoborough, now forms part of the landscape of a modern garden; built of turves and excavated in 1767, it contained a hollowed oak coffin holding bones, though no skull, wrapped in deer skins sewn together, some gold lace and a small drinking cup of oak or shale. These things speak of grandeur, high Wessex culture and international trade. Now, there are some large, and largely tasteless houses on the roads across the heath, but most of the recent inhabitants belonged to a despised race, the heath-croppers, who could expect very little in life and nothing, in death, like their predecessors of thirty-odd centuries ago.

Heathcroppers practised by necessity what is now luxuriously termed self-sufficiency. The only substantial savings they could make were in the currencies of peat, furze, bacon and a little corn and game, flimsy insurances against the next season. Women pushed big-wheeled barrows carrying vegetables, eggs, butter and pork to Wareham market or to the Inn at South Haven, to gain a little cash for things that had to be bought in. Men who drove stone-wagons back and forth across their territory regarded them as the runts, or nesseltripes, of Purbeck's litter. But one heath farmer, determined not to be twitted as a mere 'ethcropper, made his mark at Scotland, a mile north of Corfe Castle. There, the Corfe River's alluvium gave him something to play with, and a little time to build a small farmhouse of solid stone; a type of house that was the rule south of the chalk downs, but unique upon the heath. The name Peter Whefen and the date 16PW65 roughly cut over Scotland Farm's lintel commemorate the fulfilment of a man's ambition in the year of the Plague. The stone trade was in decline at that time but the Castle at Corfe had been slighted less than twenty years before and Peter probably took his chance to filch some of the ancient worked ashlar and drag it across to New Mills Heath. Geese and a chained Old English sheepdog vociferously guard young calves in their hay-bed there, and the farmhouse, dwarfed by its barn, still stands, stone-tiled and beetle-browed, beside the road to Slepe. For the rest, the best were built of carstone, native ironstone rubble; and most were of cob, clay puddled with straw and anything else that came in handy, with straw thatch. Once such poor roofing lets in the rain and weather swells the walls, decay is rapid and ruins are invisible.

To the ecologically-minded smallholder this might seem the justest monument to a life well spent; that there is none, that the heath redeems its own. Others think it tragic that a lifetime wresting tillage from furze and bog, years of marling an acid soil, of carting dung, of dibbling, droshing and wimming, should issue in no more than unrepentant ground, more than ready to revert to wilderness. Now when I walk there and see undulations in the heather where peat was cut and built into turf-pooks for the winter, where dykes were dug to drain the wetlands, where temporary wattles and more permanent fencing staked their claims, and where gorse is thick and wiry, untouched by any vuzz-hook, ideal for the bread oven but not burnt except by accident and therefore unregenerate, I am affected more than by some supposed wildness or by the well-marked Bronze Age dead.

The surviving farms carry out successful dairying and cultivation of oats, wheat, barley and potatoes on river soils, in dips where better topsoil has collected and on fertile land near the Harbour. Good arable and grazing was divided into strips or shotts, but as surely as the heathcroppers were excluded from the heathland by enclosure, together with their rights of commons, turbary and bote, so richer tenants, absentee landlords or speculators more interested in underground exploitation than in cultivation paid the fines on vacant copyholds, and the land fell into fewer and fewer hands. Heathcroppers were forced into cottages provided for them on waste ground or, like some yeomen whose small fortunes were made and broken here, into employment in Wareham or further afield. Whole histories of power politics are mixed in this, but for most of those whose only resource was the earth, the real power in their lives was that of the heath itself.

To the innocent or wilfully romantic eye, the heath looks trackless. But it must now be clear that it is shot through with many paths and cart-tracks, like causeways linking islands in the heath. When these sank back into the swell of furze and bristle-grass the tracks fell into disuse, some-times to be reclaimed by modern hikers. Some, like six roads that inex-plicably met at Broadmoor Farm on Grange Heath, are untrodden. Other routes still have their uses. Thrasher's Lane runs from Wytch Farm on the Harbour's edge to Rollington Farm below the chalk, up a dry valley and over the ridge to Little Woolgarston. Soldier's Road still links the Arne road east of Ridge with the Halfway Inn on the Corfe highway, but many are through routes that have outlived their purpose. There are traces of hollow-way—where heavy stone-carts rumbled through Corfe Gap—which, near Ower, still boast a limestone ballast quite foreign to the heath. Other, especially the clay roads, are still surfaced by ancient custom with hard chalk. The remains of tramways from pit to port still run level across the heath, through cuttings and along embankments, from Furzebrook to Ridge Wharf, from Norden to Middlebere Quay and, longest of all, from Norden across to Newton and along the peninsula of Goathorn. Occasional stretches or fragments of narrow-gauge rail survive, but mostly it is only the lineaments of determination that persevere on the heath's face.

The main-line railway was begun at Wareham on 5 May 1883, driven ten miles through Corfe to Swanage, completed two years later to the day and incorporated into the London & South Western Railway in 1886. For the first time Purbeck was wide open to the foreigner, but to him, as to the present-day tourist in his car, the heath was merely a dull prelude to the curiosities of Corfe and the amenities of Swanage by the sea. Now you can walk into Corfe on weed-grown ballast, under an abandoned tramway bridge, over the road bridge and through a cutting in the chalk where ivy climbs and wallflowers bloom; crates of empty bottles stand on the station platform, for the building is a private club, and a Third Class Smoker with no wheels, salvaged by the Swanage Railway Society, is propped up in a siding with no rails. After less than ninety years the service was suspended, a minor enterprise in Purbeck's industrial history, leaving only a short branch line from Wareham to the Furzebrook clay-works in the very heart of the heath, destined to be the railhead for the Wytch Farm oil-field.

Next door, Furzebrook House, bought by clay entrepreneurs in 1760, is the Purbeck home of the Institute of Terrestrial Ecology and the Nature Conservancy Council. Together with the Dorset Naturalist Trust and the Royal Society for the Protection of Birds, they have vested interests in preserving the wilderness in the face of clay-pits, oil-wells, forestry, farming and tourism. On Brownsea Island the wretchedly ornamental rhododendron is being uprooted to allow native vegetation to regain proper dominance. On Arne Heath, tracts of furze are essential to the survival of the wine-breasted Dartford Warbler, down to ten pairs after the winter of 1962–3 and still in danger of extinction. Ploughed fire-breaks there, and on the Studland Heath reserve around Little Sea, reduce the risk of fire, while areas of heath are mown or deliberately burnt each winter to halt the natural transition to woodland. Woods are coppiced as they used to be,

to encourage bird and insect life in the clearings, and bracken is cut on
abandoned cattle pastures to provoke a less monotonous plant community.
Hartland Moor is similarly managed so that bell heather and Dorset heath
can thrive in a wilderness infiltrated, plotted and monitored by scientists.
Conservation is not passive, but selective; choices must be made and
strenuously implemented, and there is always the danger that our "wild"
places will increasingly become figments of the scientific, rather than the
romantic, imagination.

The old road from Stoborough avoids the boggy areas of Hartland Moor,
crosses Fayle's trackless tramway and runs between banks and ditches
through oak and birch woodland, fringed with pasture shared by a herd of
Friesians and a flock of skylarks, down to the Corfe River. There, shrouded
by willows, Sharford Bridge leads from Arne into Corfe Castle parish.
Many small bridges cross the river and its tributaries from pasture to
pasture, or into gnarled mixed woodland where freshly killed, or not so
fresh, vermin may be found hanging from hawthorn gallows; but none to
match the packhorse bridge of Sharford with its twin spans of rubble and
rough parapets dating back maybe three hundred years. There is nothing
else to indicate that you are on an important route, for if you go in spring
you may cross into a ploughed field piled with marl. From there the road
disappears into Wytch Plantation, where it used to connect up with
Thrasher's Lane.
    The plantation can hardly be compared with the ancient deciduous
wood at Slepe or the Withy Bed at Rempstone; between 1950 and 1954
more than 1,500 acres of Arne, Wytch, Newton and Rempstone heaths
were planted with conifers, a new Purbeck Forest dark and dense enough
to subdue everything but fungi on its floor. Geometrical fire-breaks,
sometimes fringed with larch and Lawson cypress, corral regiments of
Corsican pine trees whose growth is poor on Purbeck soils. Those that are
thinned go for pulping or pit-props, and the Forestry Commission plans
to clear-fell the plantations in the 1980s. Meanwhile the paths that
penetrate them, sometimes old tracks and tramways still used by foresters'
vehicles, are like dim corridors which echo with the calls of jays and
yaffles but are otherwise only too lifeless. Oil-men use these roads too,
for the plantations are buffers between the well-heads and the open heath.
Oil generates far more heat than conifers but should, if the exploitation
of Britain's largest onshore field is properly planned, have a much less
injurious impact on the landscape.

Conservation is not a recent preoccupation. Purbeck was a forest in Saxon times and Norman kings imposed harsh laws aimed at conserving the game in the royal chase for their sport and their tables. Royal fish, grampus, porpoise and sturgeon, and all falcons caught off or in the island were taken by the king, but land-bound creatures came under the most rigorous control. The king's tenants had to be vetted, so islanders could not marry their daughters to outsiders without official permission. They were forbidden to grow hedges or build walls and banks higher than could be jumped by a hind with her calf at heel. Wild boars and wolves must have taken full advantage, in both chase and cultivated plot, of the freedom bestowed upon them by the Crown. On the other hand the inhabitants had to fence their woods to prevent their own cattle trespassing there; and to value the nine chief coverts, and any other covert, as they would their lives. Unlicensed enclosure or building upon the heath was forbidden and trespassers were summarily arrested.

King John reimposed forest laws, though there was some confusion concerning Purbeck's status as forest proper or mere hare warren. Definitions cannot have mattered much to islanders faced with a strict ranger and two warreners who prohibited the use of dogs, ferrets or nets for poaching coneys, hares, foxes or pheasants. Dogs had to be tied up or led, and had the balls cut from their fore-paws to prevent them infringing the king's prerogative. To add insult to injury, these officials and their dogs were entitled, at a day's notice, to be fed with three kinds of meat or fish and boarded by any tenant within the jurisdiction of Corfe Castle. Hunting lodges were built both to police the system and to view the progress of the chase. Camden, in 1575, testified to the abundance of red and fallow deer in Purbeck, but Coker, not long afterwards, maintained that there were no deer left. James I was the last king to hunt here in 1615, certainly, but a survey of 1635 reports that "in this island doth range many goodly deere that are hedged in with a surer pale than wood, which when they are hunted, will adventure into the sea and take salt soils, whereby they stand long and make brave sport". There are no red deer left and fallow deer are uncommon, but fewmets, deer droppings, and fraying stocks, trees and bushes abraded by antlers, betray the presence of deer upon the heath. Roe deer, common both sides of the chalk ridge, may often be seen in ones and twos grazing in the shadow of mixed woods, while the larger Sika deer, introduced into Brownsea Island in 1896, frequently cross fire-breaks or leap into your path in the coniferous plantations where they are regularly culled.

There is no hunting in Purbeck. Otters, pursued for many years in their breeding grounds on the Corfe River by men with poles wielded like lances and their dogs, are now more numerous than fallow deer. Making for Creech Barrow across Stoborough Heath one day, I saw a young stag start out of Stocks Wood only to be frightened by a dun mare, not one of the heathcroppers' ponies that used to graze on the commons but a fine piece of horseflesh being exercised out of a posh paddock. He turned and made straight for me, and being upwind of him I crouched slowly down behind a furze bush in my path. He closed on me till I could feel the delicate thunder of his hooves and, seeing me at last, swerved suddenly, lengthened his stride and leapt off in great bounds, soundless on the heather, to lose himself in a distant patch of scrub. To come within five paces of such elegant energy with no intent to harm it is surely better than to catch up with the hunt when the hounds have already brought it to its knees.

Not that the conservation issue is a simple one. Gamekeepers and other countrymen laugh at the naivety of scientists and RSPB men. They know that managed land, on which birds of prey and carrion, rats, weasels, stoats and foxes are controlled, is much richer in small birds and mammals than unhusbanded reserves. Many of them vehemently reject any abuse of man's hunting skill, but see a *laissez-faire* policy as one of live and let die, as criminal neglect of man's responsibility. The real difference between them and many ecologists is that they see themselves as part of nature, not just as intelligent observers.

One thing that all factions fear is uncontrolled heathland fire. During the drought of 1976 terrible fires were started and Arne and Brownsea Island were eventually closed to the public for fear that irreversible damage might be done to unique habitats there. More than four hundred acres of the Hartland Moor Reserve were destroyed, and of the many fire-fighters at least one estate-worker was overcome by smoke. Even when a heath fire seems to be extinguished there is always the nagging fear that it may flare up again; glowing heather roots creep like live fuses underground for days, needing only a change of wind and some fresh fuel to break into life. Studland Reserve did not suffer, but more by luck than good judgement. Hundreds of bathers trekked, day after day, across bone-dry heath to the beaches, leaving queues of cars parked each side of the scrub-lined ferry road. One cigarette-end could have turned the whole peninsula into an inferno of rare species, with people jumping into the sea to escape. As it was, they just bathed and watched the distant plumes of smoke where fire-fighters worked day and night to save a bit of heather.

Later, at the Institute of Terrestrial Ecology, it was like the aftermath of a funeral. Men and women sat around on the lawn drinking coffee and talking mournfully, for some of them had seen ten years' work cremated on the moor. But there was brave talk of studies in heathland regeneration. It is a marvellous thing to watch. You can break brittle twigs on a blackened heath, enveloped in the stench of resinous smoke, and sap will ooze out of white wood. Then the grasses come, a startling green, and white in winter like harvest out of season. Slowly heather and gorse buds break from the charred wood, and at last the heath regains its drabber more mature complexion.

Whether its wounds are caused by fire, clay-spade or plough the heath soon heals them, recolonises its territory in much the same way that its river-gravels, sands and clays were first colonised. Here is a history of tides: of water, of vegetation, and of men. There are some temporary memorials, but few things stand here for long. Everything, after all, except perhaps the wildness, is skin-deep.

Two stones, though, stand on the Studland side of the wet Godlingston Heath. Some hold that the Agglestone and Puckstone were set up by New Stone Age men who hunted in the Frome–Solent basin, or by the Bronze Age hands that erected Rempstone Circle, or that the devil chucked them in anger and the general direction of Corfe Castle. But it is fairly safe to assume that they are relics of the natural flux that formed the heath's bed. When I first knew the Agglestone, it was balanced on its apex on a conical sand-hill, a five-hundred-ton block of ironstone, roughly anvil-shaped. But subsidence caused its fall in 1970, a terrible declension for the Druids who were thought to worship at it; or a shifting of the Danish warrior's bones which Hutchins supposed it to commemorate. Puckstone was always a straightforward goblin stone, but the iron anvil can be interpreted in many ways—haligstone, holy stone; hagstone, witch stone; hagolstan, hailstone—according to your persuasion. And Purbeck is a place of many persuasions. Not least pragmatic ones; there are some men who will venerate Agglestone grit or ironstone, but others focus beyond the surface layers on lenses of fine clay; something to gladden Staffordshire; the lites and liver beneath the heath's tough hide.

7

CLAY, SCARS AND BEAUTY-SPOTS

EARTH'S KILN EXTRUDED the igneous granites of Dartmoor and Cornwall for air and water to weather; and after the great Chalk Sea retreated, after the lacustrine Reading Beds were laid over ocean's boneyard, to be overlaid in turn by the marine London Clay, then the swollen Frome–Solent River flowed eastwards, carrying the scourings of the granite country to be sifted and bedded down as the Bagshot Series. In the area that was to become Purbeck the water was slow-moving enough for the deposition, amongst the sands and gravels, of lenses of ball-clay fine and pure enough for Josiah Wedgwood. He could not have imagined the the vast sub-tropical delta, with its ferns and palms, that was the birthplace of his major asset, with the fossil plants to prove it. In more temperate times the Alpine earth movement tipped Purbeck's strata and erosion unveiled the chalk hills, the clay valley and the stone coastline, after two incursions of the sea and four eras of glacial flooding, leaving the ball-clays in their present configuration.

The feel of clay forming in the hands is a strenuous pleasure; thrown vessels are the product of a kind of mundane magic, for potters are journeyman-alchemists reversing the natural processes of earth, water, air and fire by their art, in order to make urns, pots, amphorae and teacups according to the commonest or most exalted needs of their civilisation. Between the Purbeck clay reserves and the potteries of Poole, potters still work on Green Island. They dig clay there, make glazes, fire pots and export them to the mainland in small boats, in much the same way as the men of the New Stone Age, who first moulded the white earths, as the Bronze Age men who buried beakers of food or drink with their crouched dead or, later, interred urns of calcined bones in round barrows or cemeteries. Highly ornamented vessels of the period, with incised patterns and applied handles, hand-built and baked in contact with the fire, have survived in Purbeck. Red iron oxide slip and high-shouldered styles were introduced by early Iron Age Celts. The Belgae of the first century B.C. brought the potter's wheel with them, but it was not until Romano-British times that kilns were built with a clay-and-wattle upper chamber where the pottery was fired out of direct contact with the combustion chamber beneath. Such kilns produced harder, more evenly fired, oxidised wares like those found associated with the industrial sites near Stoborough, Shipstal Point, Fitzworth and Cleavel Point. Plentiful sherds of coarse, wheel-thrown pottery suggest that the heath and Harbour margins supplied the local market, at least, with domestic wares at a time when the Purbeck region was perhaps the most densely populated area of Dorset.

But first, before the potter, stands the "man of clay", the finder and getter of the white earths. He came into his own when the seventeenth-century demand for tobacco-pipes, earthenware beer-mugs and teacups signalled the exploitation of clay by Poole and Swanage merchants who were happy to become copyholders in Arne and other parishes for the sake of it. Clay-getters were skilled in locating superficial deposits from the vegetation that thrived upon them, in shifting the sandy overburden, cutting and loading the clay without contaminating it, carting it across the heath by donkey, and building weathering stacks from which it was shipped to Poole. Called pipe-clay through its partnership with tobacco, its alternative name, ball-clay, probably stems from the slim iron spades called tubals with which tubal-clays were dug. Tubals are museum-pieces now, the weathering stacks are gone and prospecting methods are a deal more sophisticated, but the object of the search, sometimes lying deep beneath the heather, remains the same.

Purbeck ball-clays are the most plastic of all the English clays, yet they possess great green strength in the potter's hands. They are fine and white when fired and, with Cornish china clays, were able to satisfy a taste for delicate ceramics whetted by porcelain brought back from China. Not long after Josiah Wedgwood set up in business near Stoke-on-Trent in 1759, Purbeck clay established its reputation as the "bones of all earthenware". The next year the Pike brothers from Devon, who had been prospecting in the island, bought Furzebrook House as a centre for systematic mining operations. Not that they moved into a vacuum; the Hydes of Poole, among others, had already made a fortune from clay, and in 1771 Thomas Hyde was negotiating with John Calcraft of Rempstone in order to fulfil an agreement made with Wedgwood; by that time Messrs Wharton and Stephen had been shipping clay from Rempstone for some years, but when the Pikes signed and sealed an inscribed parchment

contract with Wedgwood in 1791 they were well on the way to a profitable monopoly. They bought and leased land around Furzebrook, where
heath and woods are pocked with two centuries of open-cast workings,
not least the fifty-foot hole known to thousands of tourists as the Blue
Pool. Following the example of Hyde, who had improved his Arne tracks
from pit to quay, the Pikes made a straight road across the heath from the
Blue Pool to Ridge Wharf on the Frome. Barges took the clay to Poole
for shipment to the Mersey ports and abroad, to Bristol, and to Staffordshire by canal. As early as 1769 a canal had been proposed between Poole
and Bristol, and the growth of the clay industry made it an attractive
proposition; both the Land's End passage and the carriage of coal from
Somerset overland to Dorset would be avoided. The scheme lost its
attraction, as far as investors were concerned, and money ran out in the
early 1800s. Eight miles of the colliery branch were constructed, but clay-
shipping continued as before.

One of those who, along with John Calcraft, Nathaniel Bond and other
well-known Purbeck names, supported the canal plan was Thomas
Garland, contracted to cart clay at a rate of at least 6,000 tons per annum
from Norden Farm. There, between Furzebrook and Corfe Castle, a
London potter called Benjamin Fayle became the Pikes' chief rival. In 1806
he engineered a 3' 9"-gauge railway to his quay on the Harbour inlet of
Middlebere Lake. New Line Farm commemorates Fayle's Tramway,
along which a horse could pull five two-ton wagons.

Competition with the newcomer grew fiercer when, in 1866, Pike Bros
opened their 2' 8"-gauge line with a steam locomotive called, in anticipa-
tion, *Primus*. The clay-train offloaded at Ridge Wharf and a steam-tug and
five barges of up to sixty tons threaded their way down the Frome. Pike
Bros extended their sphere westwards; they laid branch lines towards Icen
Barrow and John's Plantation to serve clay-pits that are now beautiful
lakes. Breach Pond's still waters, screened from Old Bond Street by overhanging trees, where wildfowl play ducks and drakes today, was the site
of a pit much larger than the Blue Pool. As the workings spread, so did the
rail-system, until its six miles were served by five engines and 150 ten-ton
trucks. After *Primus* came *Secundus*, *Tertius*, *Quartus*, and so on up to
Septimus in 1930.

Meanwhile, Fayle & Co were looking eastwards. Pits near the medieval
new town that never was at last established a community at Newton.
Clay-workers' cottages and a school were built, and a railway was laid in
1868, for the Poole locomotive *Tiny*, along the east side of the Goathorn

peninsula to the pier and South Deep. Across the heath, Middlebere Lake must have been silting up and New Line, with its tunnels under the Corfe road and beautifully managed gradients, was soon to be abandoned for a newer line whose cuttings and embankments drove through the five miles from Norden to Newton, and so to Goathorn Pier. *Thames* replaced *Tiny*, who could not take the gradients across the heath and was relegated to shunting duties at Eldon Sidings near Corfe. From about 1920 *Thames* drew an extra load, for the school at Newton was closed and the children had to travel in a primitive carriage attached to the clay-train as far as Arfleet; from there they crossed the trestle bridge over the Corfe River and walked the mile to school in Corfe village. Newton school was consecrated by the Bishop of Salisbury, who, with the General Manager of Fayle & Co, Mr Stiff, some other gentlemen and a number of demure ladies, was shunted down to Goathorn. Not quite the church provided for in Edward I's charter, but nonetheless a gesture to halt the nonconformist tide. A roof-tile from Goathorn, preserved in Corfe Museum, is inscribed with a plea for tolerance frequently echoed in Purbeck's history: "Be not a Bigiot against no Denamaniation".

Newton worked clay for eighty years, but the Goathorn Line's most profitable period came in 1924-8 when the rubble Training Bank, that stretches south-east from the Harbour mouth, was made to funnel the tidal scour and maintain the deep-water channel there. Stone was transported to Goathorn Pier and loaded into the tug *Maudie* to be dumped into the sea beyond South Haven. By 1937 Newton was finished. The railway was sold to Major Ryder of Rempstone and, two years later, was ripped up by the army. A few fragments of rail remain and, though the pier at Goathorn's tip has been dismantled to prevent mooring, the bogeys of a clay-truck rust in shallow water beside its piles. Fayle's leisurely gradients still run from Arfleet, site of the medieval Alfledesmulle where corn was ground until the First World War, across Thrasher's and Meadus's Lanes, through cuttings between Bushey and Claywell's pits, through Purbeck Forest's ranks of conifers and on, embanked, to the overgrown footings of Newton and its glinting, stagnant pits where the only industry is that of metallic dragon-flies working the heavy air.

In 1948 the Norden lines were changed to 2' gauge and *Thames* was replaced by *Russell*. It is these rails that run, rusting on their timber stilts, from a corrugated-iron-clad mine-hut looking like a miniature tin chapel whose tower houses old winding-gear; or make up a fragmented line from the pits, resting-place for dilapidated trucks and thoroughfare for rabbits, towards the bridge that climbs over the main line. From up there you can see the workings among the trees and scrub that have overtaken them either side of the embankment. Bits of old rails, bogeys, diamond-shaped truck-frames and sleepers are embedded in clay, and you can follow the tracks down to the sidings by their negative, the impression of rails and sleepers like a shadow in the close growth of moss and grass. Before the last war, most of the clay was handled here and transferred to main-line wagons for export from Purbeck.

While Fayle & Co's Claywell and Newton operations flourished and failed, Pike Bros had been working westwards and the early member of the Pike family who described the business as "an uneventful industry in an uneventful place" might have changed his opinion. 1949 was a land-mark, for in that year work started on what was to become the largest open-cast mine in Dorset at Povington on the army ranges, while any excitement derived from competition was removed when the two firms merged to form Pike Bros, Fayle & Co. *Russell* went to a Welsh museum in 1953, the Pike tracks were replaced in 1954 and diesel engines worked a uniform 2'-gauge rail system until it was finally abandoned altogether in 1970, two years after the combined firm had been bought out by English China Clays. Annual production had increased from less than 15,000 tons in 1802 to 50,000, with Newton at work, in 1859. Before the last war the combined output of the two firms could exceed 100,000 tons a year, rising to twice that today, although the work-force is little more than half of the 350 of a century ago, and only 45 of those actually dig the clay.

There are now eight open pits and eight mines in Purbeck. The con-figuration of the clay lenses is complicated, but they exist in two broad bands: one to the north, from East Holme to Ridge, Claywell and New-ton; and one in the shadow of the Purbeck Hills, from Povington to Creech, Norden and Rempstone. Lenses may overlie one another and pits and mines may work side by side; at Cotness an old shaft, 120 feet deep, was set in the floor of an older 40-foot open working. All the clay is taken by lorry to Furzebrook where it is shredded, dried to a specific moisture content, blended by combining iron-rich and iron-free clays into twenty different grades, milled and bagged. Conveyor belts and sophisticated machinery, including a prototype to automate totally the bagging process, have revolutionised the works; but pit-props are still made in the timber-mill at Furzebrook, carpenters at "Chipstead" there make and repair clay-trucks, while, beside the machine and fitters' shops, the forge, that continued to employ blacksmiths through lean times, produces all the iron-work except bogeys that the mines require. A laboratory checks the physical properties of samples on site, though they are sent to Cornwall for chemical analysis. But ball-clay, unlike almost every other mineral, cannot be modified or purified in processing. The onus of quality control remains with the "man of clay", the clay-getter himself. He is a man of importance in Purbeck and boys with names like Battrick, Marshalsea and Selby still follow their fathers into the industry. Though the overburden may be shifted by earth-moving plant and mine-shafts may be driven underground more easily than in the past, the man with the spade, albeit a pneumatic one, is still paramount because what he digs out the customer receives.

The clay itself is a beautiful sight. At the Norden pit a belt of hazel trees fringes the steep pasture of the chalk hillside that rises to an undulating skyline; but the eye is irresistibly drawn down to the worked clay terraces shot through with yellows, blacks and purples, and to the pure blue-grey depths where the finest clay is cut. At Squirrel Cottage pits, near East Holme, mechanical diggers scoop out trenches to divert surface water, that floods into the hole, from the clay-face. Some overburden is used to screen the operation from the road, and the rest, after back-filling into worked-out areas, is seeded so that reclamation is as quick as possible. Mines are sunk wherever the overburden is more than thirty feet or so; though they are not as efficient as open pits because a thick clay ceiling has to be left to stop water flooding in from above, they account for three-quarters of production. At most mines electrical winding-gear draws traditional wooden trucks up a gradient of perhaps one-in-five or one-in-two from the underground lanes, to be emptied from first-floor height into lorries or skips. However, the relatively shallow mine at Ridge, opened in 1965, has a 108-foot vertical shaft, a hole in the heath unmarked but for pit-head winding-gear and a few vehicles. Miners and empty trucks take the cage down from a world of furze and heather into its fleshy depths. A Davy lamp hangs at the bottom for, though gas is rare, methane may be generated from pit-props in old workings. When a mine is dug, roadways are driven out to the extremities of the lens; at first they are supported by steel horseshoe arches, circular steel, or a tube of concrete blocks; but these give way to five-foot timbers formed into squares, because floors need as much support as walls and ceilings in the plastic clay. Tramways of 22″ gauge, whose curves and junctions are shaped in the Furzebrook forge, run through branching lanes whose air is circulated by pumps on the surface and made fragrant by the close-packed, resinous props of larch and Scots pine. It is humid too, but the roadways are dry, although emergency pumps are primed to cut in if flooding occurs; and on the surface nitches of heather, traditional filters, are kept in readiness. Intermittently there is the sound of wheels on rails approaching and the sight of a runner leant at his laden cart disappearing in the direction of the shaft, but always there is the thud, deadened by timber and clay, of the pneumatic spade in use at the face. Mining is by retreat; props are removed at the roadway's end and the clay either side is cut away; the remaining timbers are engulfed in the slow rearguard action of plastic rock that flows into its spaces. The removal of a six-foot layer usually means about five feet of subsidence at the surface. It was pick-and-shovel work, lit by candle or gas-light, until recently, and though men keep their hand-tools by them, helmet-lamps make the job easier and one old man who had worked clay since he was a boy told me that the pneumatic spade's stutter was music to his ears. Fifteen feet above his head were poorer, yellow- and orange-stained, iron-rich clays, and beneath his feet were friable, siliceous clays; but the transition is gradual, and even in the fine blue clay he was cutting he showed me the dark bands of iron sulphide. But not for him the sophistry of chemical analysis: to look, to sample with a fingernail and to taste it was enough.

Iron-rich clay is ideal for some purposes and it is sold as a binder for animal feed-stuffs, but the search is always on for new deposits that will fire white as snow. Drilling-rigs are now mounted on lorries, but one of the old wooden rigs is still in use in otherwise inaccessible places or for shallow sampling, and an auger is wound down into the ground by hand, through sand and loam, or loom in Purbeck, to the clay layers, and brought up to the surface for analysis. The sight of the wood frame, pegged out on the heath, with a pair of men straining at the ironmongery beneath it, is one that has not changed for generations.

The Purbeck heathland is a Ball-Clay Consultation Area, which means that planning decisions are referred to English China Clays to avoid extraction schemes being unnecessarily impeded. But it does not mean that these schemes automatically go ahead, in fact planning permission granted to Pike Bros, Fayle & Co in 1957, for mining at Froxen Copse on the Arne peninsula, was revoked in 1974, and permission for an alternative scheme put forward by ECC Ball Clays Ltd was withheld. They had planned to extract more than a million tons from the forty-four-acre site over a period of forty years to help meet the demand, sixty per cent of it from abroad, for Purbeck's white earths. For a while it seemed that the market—manufacturers of pottery, porcelain, tiles, abrasives, feed-stuffs, refractory-bricks, crucibles, ceramic insulators and toilets—would have to give way to less tangible demands voiced by conservationists and scientific groups; those of the Dartford warbler, and of the heath itself. But now, the Environment Secretary has overriden local opinion and given ECC the go-ahead they wanted.

Fortunately, clay-mining must be selective. Bulk extraction is impossible because of the nature of the lenses, and a number of small sites is the rule. The largest mine, hidden in a clearing at Aldermoor near Creech, gives up 15,000 tons a year with hardly any waste. Povington's forty acres of open-cast working, on the other hand, is a huge scar on the face of the heath. But the sandy back-filling is being re-colonised, sand-martins nest in the pit, and one can believe, looking at tracts of heathland and woods where only the ground's undulations betray the clay-getter's hand, that regeneration will finally be complete. A few yards from Norden's vivid clay-scape, there is a pool overhung by trees on one side, by reeds on two, and banked by raw clay on the fourth; a small remnant of a worked-out hole, it is thick with pondweed and lilies; moorhens and ducks nest there, and I have seen it graced by a heron who would not drop in for nothing.

Near East Creech is a sight that illustrates what can happen to a pit long after the clay-men have finished with it: screened, it is true, by conifers, brambles and a profusion of sloes, a crater yawns, oozing with stagnant juices and piled with the carcasses of cars and furniture, an evil moonscape littered with abandoned craft. But a quarter of a mile away, as the crow flies, the Blue Pool seems to repudiate all charges of vandalism levelled against the "men of clay". They have created a scene of beauty: a romantic Black Forest lake that, although overshadowed by pines that step up its steep banks, creates by a trick of refraction and reflection from its white clay bed a range of luminous, changing blues and greens. Visitors pay to look at it. They park their cars and buses there. They consume afternoon teas, purchase trinkets and visit toilets. The Blue Pool is a tourist attraction for which the brothers Pike cannot be held responsible.

There are no slag-heaps in the Purbeck heaths, no soot in the air, only white clay-dust on the vegetation and pounding lorries with their settling, fleshy loads. Certainly there are scars; but scars that can become eyesores or beauty-spots, or simply heal and return to us the ordinary heath. There is a choice.

8

HILL-HILL-HILL AND GRANGE

EARLY MORNING IS the time to climb Creech Barrow, when the bracken on its western slopes is still in shadow and the lowing of cattle being led in for milking at East Creech would hardly reach you through the dewy air if it wasn't punctuated by the yap-yap-yap of the dog that will sit in the road and defy all comers there. The name Creech has its root in the British word "cruc", a hill. The Saxons preserved it, although they had their own term, "beourg", for hill or barrow; and we have preserved both in Creech Barrow. Some people call it Creech Barrow Hill which is, being interpreted, Hill-Hill-Hill. Stepping up there one morning I was properly startled when I flushed a hen-pheasant from right between my feet; the Creech Grange keeper would not have thanked me, for she staggered out of my path, got up in a flurry and coasted downhill westwards, till she ducked into the birch and scrub that covers old clay-workings. Beyond her, on the East Creech pond, white ducks preened themselves, and beyond them the heath opened up, dark and yet luminous against the sun.

A few yards from the top of the Barrow dense bracken is suddenly and decisively succeeded by grassland. When the bracken is dying back, the green-capped summit stands out from a distance, demonstrating that one of the highest points in Purbeck, at well over six hundred feet, is something of a geological puzzle, a freak of nature built of the youngest rocks in the area, deposited long after the upfolding and early erosion of the chalk ridge. It is firmly founded in Agglestone grit, with outcroppings of ball-clay, once served by tramways, on its eastern and north-eastern flanks. Above these are sands, that were worked in a pit now hidden by Cotness Wood, and buff clay that fed Mr Bond's brickyard there until 1908. Younger sands and flints, continuing the acid soil on which the bracken thrives, climb to within ten feet of the summit whose grassy scalp consists of limestone; a lake deposit, probably related to that of Bembridge in the

Isle of Wight. Only ragwort flourished in its alkaline soil during the summer drought of 1976; the hardy bracken of the slopes stayed green while the parched hill-top rusted in the sun.

The mysterious outcrop was a foundation for other stones. Substantial limestone footings of a building can be found, set at the centre of a system of banks and ditches whose remnants are best seen in winter. They are in the form of a cross whose arms, bent downhill, are linked by the sides of a hundred-yard square. The north-west corner is joined, by a later earth-work, to the parish boundary bank that runs from the chalk ridge, cuts through a tumulus just west of the Barrow's summit, proceeds downhill to Creech village and across the heath to Three Lords Barrow. Such a boundary, linking man-made landmarks, makes sense to us; but what description, however pedantic, can elucidate the cross-in-the-square here? Did the banks pen animals, or protect from men or wolves? Or are they the earthen expression of a metaphysic lost to us for ever? Geological dilemmas fade in the face of mysteries which, because human, we feel we ought to understand.

There are clues about the building, though. Tradition assigns it to King John, as one of three royal hunting-lodges in Purbeck Chase. In 1583, Sir Christopher Hatton laid allegations before the Star Chamber of damage to the building; by that time it had become a symbol of frustration, enmeshed in a web of piracy and poaching. Humus within its walls contained pottery of the sixteenth or seventeenth century, and a medieval green-glazed sherd was found nearby, but there is no way of telling whether John, on one of his many business-with-pleasure trips to south-east Dorset, ever climbed this hill to rest or to spy out prey. What is certain is that he could have been seen, by the warrener posted here, urging on his men and dogs from a well-lathered mount.

It is a look-out from which to gloat over a kingdom. The morning sun makes molten metal of Swanage Bay and begins to light the fractured spine of chalk that sweeps from the east, Corfe Castle hidden in its cleft, just south of where you stand and westwards to the steep beech wood of Ridgeway Hill, to Flower's Barrow and, when the air is clear, to Portland's stony hulk brooding in the Channel. Inland, the hills of Devon and Dorset are the world's rim, while, in the basin to the north, Frome and Piddle flow either side of Wareham whose glinting glass now overflows the banks of its walls. The rivers lose themselves in the Harbour's reaches, where Arne's mass, the flats of Middlebere and Fitzworth and the wooded islands absorb rather than give back the light.

Old and new clay-scars are gashes in the heath, but an invisible working undermines the hill beneath your feet. Huts, beside the road that runs over the saddle between the Barrow and the ridge, might be taken for saw-mills until you realise that there are no trees near enough to feed them, that the timbers piled beside them are pit-props, and that the sounds that start as the working day begins are not those of saws, but of a generator and a compressor that pumps fresh air 350 feet down into the mine. The huts conceal a rickety-looking timber platform with rails and a turn-table where about seventy tons of clay each week are brought up into the light.

Lying to the east and west, in the shadow of the chalk, is a belt of country quite distinct from both the heath and the hills, where the Bagshot Beds give way to narrow bands of London and Reading Beds. The London Clay formerly grew good crops of wheat, but working it increases its tenacity so that it is mostly given over to permanent pasture. The Reading Beds, joining and mixing with the chalk, make excellent arable land whose virtues have been exploited from early times. An East Creech farmer's plough foundered on a stone Tuscan column in 1869 and, subsequently, building stones, wall-plaster, broken pottery, a pot full of shale lathe-cores, and a tesselated pavement ten feet square were found associated with the foundations of a large building. Loose tesserae of white limestone and red tile could be picked up until recently, and probable remains of a hypocaust system belonging to a second Roman house were discovered nearby. Perhaps the villa belonged to a Romano–British Kimmeridge shale merchant, but whoever he was he almost certainly cultivated the land that lay between his home and the downs. East Creech, with its seventeenth- and eighteenth-century cottages, is probably older than Church Knowle over the hill. The Domesday Survey's Criz was a large manor granted to Roger de Belmont, and later inhabited by a family, perhaps his, called le French, le Frank, Franke or Frank. A land dispute was put to the old men of the county in 1401, when Robert Stokes of Barnston maintained that he was entitled to common at East Creech; they decided that the liberty and freedom of William Franke had been infringed because it had not been so within their or their father's memory.

At Creech Grange this strip of land is at its most beautiful, and "grange" was a granary before it came to mean a country house with a farm. From Creech Barrow these are almost hidden from sight, but the Chapel of St John the Evangelist, with its tower and bell-turret, stands up out of the trees on its knoll, brilliantly white in the morning sun. The Bonds of Grange are said not to survive long out of sight of the Barrow, and a road runs directly from its foot to the house. Where the Grange road from Stoborough crosses it, a pair of open wrought-iron gates mark the entrance to the private drive. An archway of trees casts shadows and veils the much-gabled, grey east front, but from the road that climbs through Great Wood, the broad Palladian south front is suddenly exposed to view, with lawns, well-disposed trees, roofs of stables and farm, signs of a mature estate bitten out of sands and grits across the ribbon of richer fields that feed it.

Domesday Book records the grant of the manor, together with that of Tyneham, also Bond property until the Second World War, to Robert, Earl of Mortain and half-brother to the Conqueror. Grange passed to the Abbot of Bindon, whose Cistercian foundation was shifted from Bindon Hill to Wool in 1172. After the Dissolution of the Monasteries, Sir Oliver Lawrence built a house here, from which a later Lady Lawrence had cause to flee into the woods in 1643, when it was fired by the Parliamentarian Sir Walter Erle, leaving only the walls standing. Sir Walter's own house at Charborough Park was razed to the ground, and he carried old antagonisms into the Commonwealth by filching timbers for it from Corfe Castle. The same violent tempest that presaged Cromwell's death took Denis Bond first, a bond, his Royalist enemies said, on account for his master's soul. His family were to purchase Creech Grange, but not before Captain John Lawrence had brought a little notoriety to the place, in the heat of the Popish invasion fears of 1778, by alerting Wareham and London after seeing a ghostly army marching from Flower's Barrow.

After the Lawrences had sold up, Nathaniel Bond and his descendants extended and remodelled the house in several stages, until, in 1847, the Revd Nathaniel Bond completed it in its present form. The west front is rendered in stucco, the south and east are of finished ashlar, while the hinder portions of the house are of humbler, and much more attractive, Purbeck rubble. When John Bond of Tyneham inherited Grange, he planted the heath with silver and Scots firs to make Little Wood. Nearer the house, ilexes and yews were trained and cedars spread genteel contentment. Springs were tapped to fill the Long Canal and lower ponds. Facing the house, across formal water, is a laurel-crowned, marble Roman on a Portland stone pedestal. He dates from about 1700 and shares no kinship with the red-and-black pottery of the second or third centuries dug up in the kitchen garden; nor with the quern-stones, remnants of shale-working, and Roman pillars found in the grounds.

The Chapel of St John the Evangelist is the setting for a Romanesque chancel arch of about 1170, richly carved with chevrons and bead and nailhead ornament, but this too is an anachronism. It was removed from the Cluniac Priory at East Holme, on whose site another Nathaniel Bond built Holme Priory House. The chapel at Grange was built by Denis Bond in 1746 and used as a carpenter's shop for a century, until the Revd Nathaniel judged that its material service to the estate was no longer required. In 1849 he built the nave, tower and north transept, and the west doorway of that date has a chevron-enriched archway of twelfth-century style. Steeple church, over the hill, gained a chapel-of-ease when St John's was at last consecrated in 1859.

House, farm and chapel underwent many more alterations and embellishments than I have hinted at, but because they are documented we are at least aware of them. They should, however, make us wary of concluding too much from appearances. From the earliest earthworks onwards we must assume that man's penchant for imitation, for fashion and nostalgia will play tricks on us. It is sobering to look back towards Creech Barrow, dominating the chalk ridge and the hazy heath; the Hill which, though disembowelled of its clay, squats firmly enough on its unplumbed, and perhaps unplumbable, history.

9

CIRCLE, CHURCH, CLIFFS

THERE IS A cottage in East Creech called Teneriffe, which says something about greener grass, or warmer waters. The sand and sea of Studland Bay comprise, to my Purbeck-prejudiced eye, the finest beach in Britain; anyway it will have to do. But first, the road out of Corfe Castle skirts the ribbon of London Clay and Reading Beds that runs beneath the hills. At Brenscombe Farm two mosaics have provided more evidence of relatively luxurious villa life, while at Rempstone a rotary quern for grinding grain, a shale bowl and shale waste gave fragmentary glimpses of the native economy under Rome.

Rempstone Hall is set in its own lush landscape, facing rolling fields under the downs and backed by mixed woodland, where a lake feeds the gwyle that snakes back into Foxground. Another barrow to add to the heath's tally has recently been uncovered in Nelson Plantation; burial mounds are grouped on the hill above, but the notion that the Beaker Folk were a downland people shunning the dense forests and wetlands below is now thoroughly discredited. Indeed, at the edge of the Withy Bed, across the road from Nelson Plantation, there is a lump of rough brown heathstone jutting out of the leaf-mould. Though it is hard gritstone from the Bagshot Beds, it is not a natural outcrop; beyond it in the wood, through vigorous young growth of willow, hazel, fern and bramble, there are more stones, dappled with yellow-green light and blotched or streaked with grey and orange lichens. Five of them are standing, seven are fallen, and some have been moved. The wet, dark ground is treacherous with ditches and pools beneath the undergrowth, from eighteenth-century clay-workings which may have been the cause of their disturbance. However, they still form the greater part of a circle twenty-five yards across. In harvest fields to the west a combine-harvester may drone and drive its swathe through up-standing corn where, in 1957, the wake of ploughing washed up a flotsam of more stones; two straight

CP

rows of them lined up like a processional way leading to a point just north of the circle. They were removed in the interests of agriculture, but it is clear that here are the remains of a major monument of the early Bronze Age, so well hidden that most people hurry past on their way to Studland, quite unaware of its existence. The youth of the Withy Bed, and old photographs, prove that the site was not overgrown early this century, but it is difficult to imagine it otherwise. The claustrophobic growth, with one stone invisible from the next, and the secretive light seem essential qualities of the place.

If the stone circle was a place of worship, there was another behind Rempstone Hall at Foxground. A cottage was converted to Wesleyanism by the removal of its upper floor, and tenants who rendered bi-annual rents, about one pound in the 1870s, to the Caesars of Rempstone, rendered spiritual worship to God in their own chapel until it was razed by fire in 1920. Alternative forms of Sunday worship are conducted a mile and a half along the road at Dean Hill, an outcrop of Redend sandstone furnished with a pull-in. Rows of cars point north towards the harbour, their occupants doing comfortable obeisance to the open spaces, the dark stretches of Godlingston, Newton and Studland Heaths. If it is not a religious experience, perhaps the sight of Agglestone and the burial mounds below tinges it with *timor mortis*. The more active ritually pursue a small white ball from green to green, via hole and bunker, on the golf-course that spans the road.

Woodhouse Hill, which drops down towards Studland, is another sandstone outcrop. Ahead, valley slopes dense with trees frame blue sea in Mediterranean style; Romans probably felt at home here, but the inhabitants of the settlement whose relics lie on the left of the road were British. Two groups of buildings, inhabited from before the Roman invasion until the fourth century A.D., were excavated in the 1950s. The shadows of circular Iron Age huts were given substance by signs of copper-working within them, and a squarish building, superimposed upon them, contained a samian plate stamped with the name Primulus, a first-century Gaulish potter, a dolphin-style brooch and a coin of Vespasian of A.D. 73. Shapes in the ground left by our ancestors are as shadows are to the childish imagination: crude and primitive. The flesh that cast them turns out to be recognisable and refined. Next door, houses with sandstone and flint footings and floors of earth and clay had sheltered weavers and iron-workers, and one was probably divided into a living-room with a hearth, a workshop and a byre with headstalls for oxen. The second group of buildings, to the south, showed much the same features and a rubbish pit there yielded shale lathe-cores, evidence of spelt wheat and animal bones, and iron spikes and nails. Mosaics, pillars and statuary are more spectacular, but here at Woodhouse Hill is a rare, if fragmentary, portrait of a plebeian settlement that lived off its cottage industries, its smallholdings and, probably, the Celtic fields that survive on Ballard Down.

The red-brick village of Studland, predominantly of the twentieth century, straggles away from the cross-roads where shops service bathers and hikers. Though small and apparently insignificant, Studland has always had ways of making a living from the sea, and not always so respectably as now. The older, mainly eighteenth-century village is scattered too, but finds an eccentric focus in the village cross. Down a steeply-banked road at the junction of what were farm-tracks before holiday traffic came, it stands, a shining piece of freshly-worked Purbeck-Portland stone, mounted upon an ancient, circular block of heathstone which, until 1976, had nothing but an empty socket to show for its Saxon cross. Bereft as it was, it was even then unique in Purbeck, although the stocks that stood alongside it until 1850 were not.

A delightful approach road runs from the cross to the graveyard where the church stands, idyllic and serious among yew trees. The farmyard with its great barn lies through a gateway on the right, opposite Studland Manor farmhouse, whose rubble and brick is half-hidden by fragrant shrubs, and the Purbeck stone church hall of 1952. The church's sandstone is just pre-Conquest, but it was erected on the foundations of an earlier place of worship that may have been built under the aegis of the energetic Aldhelm. Ancient work is knitted into the north wall, representing part of what was left when the Danes had finished with it. Perhaps it was obvious, even in construction, that the foundations would hardly bear the later structure, for the builders left the tower unfinished. Resourcefully, they, or the Normans who remodelled the building in the eleventh and twelfth centuries, capped the truncated bell-storey with a saddle roof which, makeshift or not, only adds to the muscular stolidity of the whole. Solidity is a different matter: thirteenth- and fourteenth-century buttresses shore up the tower, and from 1880 until now exemplary efforts have been made to preserve the fabric, involving underpinning and the diversion of water from the old footings. Thanks to all that, the structure is safe, and fantastical corbel heads still squat wickedly under the eaves. A squint through the hagioscope into the sanctuary gives a foretaste of what is in store.

Solemnity and joyfulness, emotions at the core of worship, seem to mix in the very masonry. Crude mass and whimsical detail combine to give a sense of justness. Round-headed arches under the tower are each of two orders springing from shafts with decorated capitals; the impression of strength is undiminished by the iron bars that brace them, even though the chancel arch is badly fractured. Limewash concealed wall-paintings on plaster which, sadly, was broken off the rubble walls in 1909, leaving part of Psalm 84 over the chancel arch and some medieval red-and-black decoration on the north wall. Norman windows there, elegant Early English ones behind the altar and enlarged ones on the west and south hardly light the church; rather, they make its weighty darkness luminous: a setting for rich furnishings, for the Purbeck marble table tomb in the chancel and the plain twelfth-century font. At Easter, clumps of primroses set in moss all around the nave generate their own light; and, in a recess opposite the south door, palm frond and jagged thorn, eucalyptus and veronica, bay and hyssop frame the figures, sculpted in clay and fired by the patron of the living, of disciples and angels who stand between the Place of the Skull and the empty stone tomb.

In 1952, the sexton's spade struck a stone tomb outside in the graveyard. This was nothing new, for restoration work of 1881 had uncovered similar graves, pronounced to be Saxon Christian, as well as pagan flint-lined graves and a pair of circular quern-stones. This latest grave was examined with care, however, and within its weathered Purbeck marble sides and lid, upon a limestone floor, was a cockle shell and a shale spindle-whorl lying beside the pelvis of a headless female skeleton, whose skull, with its loose jawbone, was resting by the left foot. It has been suggested that, given hands busy with spinning and a disarticulated jaw, the lady would have little chance of mischief-making *post mortem*; or that such dis-memberment ensured that food destined for the gods was not diverted down the gullet of the deceased. Our suggestions almost invariably sound flippant; for, although our ancestors' dead imprints are so frequent in our soils, we can hardly retrace our steps and stand with them in the same faith and fear by which they governed their lives. Whatever happened here, with its liturgy of ritual beheading, was solemnly interred within a marble cist to be preserved for its own sake, and not for our uncomprehending eyes.

There are other graves here; of Francis Fane MP who never spoke again in the Commons after the village idiot prophesied his death, and of Sergeant William Lawrence who had plenty to tell. He was apprenticed to a Studland builder in 1804, ran away more than once from this hard taskmaster, joined the army, fought in the Peninsular War and was wounded at Badajoz. After the battle of Waterloo he was stationed at St Germain-en-Laye where his new wife, Clotilde, bore him a daughter who had to be left in her brother's care when they were ordered back to England. Perhaps the guardian had disapproved of the match, and of its issue, from the start, or simply decided to profit from it; he kept the maintenance money they sent him and left the girl in an orphanage. When the couple were settled they sent for her, but she was never traced. Following William's discharge, they ran a hostelry in Studland where the regulars must often have been regaled with colourful reminiscences of distant glories. After Clotilde died in 1853 the hero of Badajoz had nothing left of his life but memories, and dictated his autobiography to a friend before his own death in 1869.

Not that Studland was a stranger to the outside world. Tales of less honourable bravado had echoed, during Elizabeth's reign, in the disreputable houses of Joan Chaddocks and Roger and William Munday at the top of Water Lane. These three establishments were devoted to the service of gaudy customers whose trades were piracy and smuggling. The church is dedicated to St Nicholas, patron saint of honest mariners, but the manor barn beside it was a store for contraband. Francis Hawley, deputy Vice-Admiral of Purbeck under Hatton, owned a property at Woodhouse from which George Fox, his deputy, supervised rather than curtailed the illicit trades. Hawley and Purbeck came into their own when the family monopoly of Sir Richard Rogers was broken after an enquiry into the business at Lulworth. By virtue of his position, Sir Richard was forced to dismantle the apparatus that unofficially enriched him, and the network of trade that embraced every level of society began to crumble.

In the meantime, Studland Bay was ideally suited to support the pirates, mostly outsiders, and the Purbeck families such as Uvedale and Clavell who made or increased their wealth by means of them. Until well into the last century barrels of herrings, kegs of spirits and other goods were stored under piles of seaweed collected for fertiliser, then carried overland to Greenland and Goathorn and loaded into flat-bottomed boats, thus avoiding the well scrutinised Harbour entrance. The customs officers, Searchers and Deputy-Searchers, who made an excellent living out of bribes, were not the only ones to be avoided. The Mayor of Poole, robbed of a rich harvest on Brownsea when the Queen granted the island to Hatton, still reaped the rewards of his two-faced control of the port's traffic. Lord Mountjoy, with legitimate mineral interests on Brownsea, vied with

Hatton's deputies for invisible earnings. If Purbeck, Poole or Brownsea became too hot a man could always resort a little further along the coast, within the jurisdiction of the Vice-Admiral of Dorset. Little wonder that pirates exploited every possible configuration of intrigue and hypocrisy hereabouts; and always with Studland Bay offering safe anchorage, entertainment, easy victualling by Poole boats, and quick escape in times of emergency, leaving Purbeck men to carry the can and stab one another in the back. Blood certainly was spilt on the boards of the Water Lane hell-houses, and on the silver sands, in the days when cut-throat competition was more than a figure of speech. John Piers and his men were captured and tried by rival pirates and controllers of the trade. They were drawn from their dungeon in Corfe Castle along the ridgeway, hung from gibbets on Studland beach before a large crowd, and left, as the tide came in, to tread water with leaden feet. Clinton Atkinson, who was to suffer the same fate at Wapping, cut Piers down and gave him a decent burial at sea.

The beach seems an altogether more innocent place today. The bloodiest object there is a gory anti-rabies notice whose dripping fangs threaten those who dare to land pets from boats. Beach-huts provide a haven for bathers, and the coastguard's main concern is with the hundreds of small craft that cruise for pleasure. The Bankes Arms, in the village, fills with week-end sailors, though its beer-garden sports a merchantman's anchor of about 1850, as a reminder of more serious times. The Manor House Hotel, with its spiky roofs, turret and round towers, doubtfully commemorates the site of Studland Castle. On the beach below, each tide dispatches bucket-and-spade castles made from the fine white sand. Waves from the Channel do not maintain sufficient momentum to deposit stones or shingle on the east-facing coast; but marram grass extends its rhizomes wherever new sand builds up; as its old leaves are submerged by the dry, shifting tide, new ones develop at the new surface and the dunes are continuously consolidated. They are then colonised by sea lyme and sand-couch grasses, by sea bindweed, saltwort and sheep's bit, and, beside the nature reserve between the village and Shell Bay, by sunbathing naturists. Over the last four centuries a series of ridges, now colonised by heathers and separated by peaty pools, have been built out of the sea, so that the South Haven peninsula has steadily grown to its present width. Engulfed in the sandy heath is a stretch of water, one mile long, called Little Sea, whose western shore was once coastline. Just south of it, by the toll-gates, is an area called Salterne; one-quarter of the value of Robert of Mortain's £8 manor of Stollant was derived, according to the Domesday Book, from its thirty-two salt-pans, in the tradition of Romano–British salt-boiling whose remains have been found across the heath near Thorny Barrow. Man-marks are usually so young compared to the history of the earth on which they stand, but Little Sea and the ground to the east is a fraction of the age of Rempstone circle, and when John Piers was hanged it did not exist. A map of 1721 shows it as a tidal inlet in a dune ridge; by the end of the century another ridge had transformed it into a lagoon; in 1849 the highest spring tides still invaded it, but today it is a lake rich in freshwater life. Sticklebacks, newts and toads feed cormorants and herons; otters are often seen in the waters, and shrews and harvest mice inhabit the furzy dunes, attracting merlins, sparrowhawks, peregrines, hen harriers and other more common birds of prey to Studland. Warblers breed in the reed-beds where meadow-pipit, stonechat and linnet can also be seen, while redpolls nest in nearby silver birches. Sallow graces Little Sea's margins, making a refuge for the water rail, and yellow flags, bog bean and reed mace are rife at the water's edge. Some Arthurian souls maintain that it was here that Sir Bedivere flung Excalibur into the lake's depths, unwittingly crediting him with remarkable powers of foresight. The only weapons to be raised above its surface were fowling-pieces from flat-bottomed punts; and, more recently, powerful binoculars aimed at mallard, pochard, wigeon, teal and the rest. So sand, Studland's major present-day assest, has grown into a rich reserve and has shaped the wild and beautiful beach that attracts twentieth-century hordes.

The peaceable landscape was suddenly transformed during the war. Summer invasions would not now be possible if the debris of that one had not been cleared, over a period of nineteen months, by a large Royal Navy party. Little Sea and the coast were cleared by frogmen, and heather was burnt off the peninsula, detonating many explosives. Searches with mine-detectors recovered 84,000 missiles and 200 unexploded bombs. The savagery was largely self-inflicted. In 1940 an anti-invasion oil-flame barrage was tested off the beach, creating a livid, fiery sea and clouds of oily smoke that killed cliff-top trees and briefly shut out the sun. Studland Heath was taken over as a battle range in 1942, and in the following year the roads to Corfe and the ferry out of Studland village were closed. Almost 350 people were evacuated and those that remained had to carry identity discs for a time. Their houses shook with heavy naval fire and, once, with an air bombardment that prepared the way for troops discharged from new-fangled landing craft with guns and tanks, until the village was crammed with hungry soldiers glad to be on dry, British land. The King, Churchill, Eisenhower and Montgomery also visited Studland to inspect secret weapons like the Valentine amphibious tank. Canadian Engineers built a huge observation post, Fort Henry, on the cliffs and, for a time, a friendly army transformed the village and its bay out of all recognition, until, on the night of 4 June 1944, the invasion was transferred to Normandy.

It is said that, from the sea, at night, one Studland cottage used to appear to be continually in flames, though on land nothing more than smoke drifted from its chimney, until the Rector exorcised the spirit of a smuggler who had been murdered there in possession of a bale of silk. So, when the summer sea is full of bathers, it seems that Studland's violent past has been erased; but perhaps that cannot be done so easily. Between the village and the beach stands the old buttress of Redend Point; yellow sandstone streaked with crimson, fantastically carved by wind and water, and bearing initials and dates which belie its soft complexion. It represents the base of the Bagshot Beds here, while the London Clay and upper Reading Beds form a poor sort of cliff, land-slipped and overgrown. Mottled clays and multi-coloured sands are bedded upon dark ochre iron-stone with black flints which abut directly on to the deeply-scarred, anciently-weathered chalk. South-eastwards, the sands give way to a rocky shore, covered at high tide; white cliffs stand up out of the water; the transition is sudden and complete. Sheer, naked chalk marks the frontier of another country.

PART THREE

HURDLE

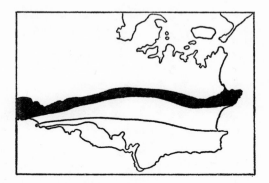

Causeway from sea to sea dividing corn from heather,
sheepwalk once; now herbage clots with bracken,
curdles round flinty skulls, claw-hold for windhover;
and ploughshares strike up sparks, bite to the bone.

Tracks trickle down dry valleys to their source
where water, gone to ground, springs out like nerves;
man's monuments are sapped, precarious,
slight punctuation on the ridgeway's curves.

Corfe Castle's gap-toothed stones seem disinterred
and midwived mounds bear bones with backs to death,
bound foetus-shapes waiting for flesh and blood;
so Purbeck's fractured spine backs on to heath.

It starts from splintered stack and faulted cliff
and stops where men dug in against the foe,
banks and last ditches now defended with
a wall of air founded on waves below.

High seas gnaw softly at the chalk beneath
tall ramparts where a torn crow tempts the wind,
unpinioned, lifts off into the gale's teeth
and leisurely flails backwards, deep inland.

10

BATTERIES AND PINNACLES

EVEN THE AIR seems to change as you leave Studland village for the cliff path that passes Warren Wood and skirts the tilting chalk farmland that juts into the sea. A narrow strip of cliff-top soil sports a makeshift potato crop and, below, the wide arc of Studland Bay sweeps north, peppered with the bright flotsam of yachts. To the south, corn-fields rise gently and spread to the horizon. A dark clump masks King Barrow and Studland Wood builds a dense green wall against the sky. The path enters its thicket of hazel, elder and butcher's broom where the soft scents of the chalk flora are instantly swamped by the pervasive, magical stench of stinking iris and wild garlic. Water glints between the trees, but it is only as you emerge from the darkness of the wood that, abruptly, you understand where you are. The springy turf of Handfast Point clothes the ragged stump of Purbeck that protrudes into the sea; there, magnificent chalk stacks stutter to a tentative stop, proclaiming their kinship with the Needles of the Isle of Wight, shining distantly across a sea which long since demolished the ramparts in between.

The gap between the Foreland and the biggest stack, finally breached in 1921, is called St Lucas Leap; only a saint could jump it now and, if he did, a flurry of screaming gulls would not thank him for so peremptory an invasion of their colony. Spare grass caps its hard chalk, but, resistant as it is, the sea ineluctably gnaws at its foundations; slowly the needles' eyes that pierce it widen, and will eventually split it into smaller stacks like that of slim, upstanding Old Harry, finally reducing them to seaweed-festooned footings, like those of Old Harry's Wife, fallen in 1896, that squat in the sea between them. Old Harry is a synonym for the devil, and the cliff-top is named Old Nick's Ground; but on sunny days when leisurely gulls wheel below and cormorants skim and plunge into smooth, clear water, it is hard to appreciate such black designations. Swap holiday weather for wintry storms, when heavy seas hack at the rocks, when birds rise tattered into the wind or cling to exposed perches, when you must fight to keep your footing on the cliff, and all your sympathy will be with St Lucas, poised somewhere between the devil, his ground, and the deep, angry sea.

In such weather, straining ears are said to pick out a ghostly tocsin tolling from the sea bed where a ship carrying bells for the Church of St James at Poole is supposed to have foundered as a consequence of its crew's blasphemy. The U.S. frigate *Constitution*, heedless of this warning, ran aground here in January 1879, with a cargo of French goods *en route* for the Paris Exhibition in America, and was fortunate to get off. A more deadly reception was prepared for enemy ships; Coker describes a block-house "for the more grace called Studland Castle" that was furnished with ordnance in time of war. Together with batteries at Peveril, across Swanage Bay, at Redend Point and at South Haven, it guarded Purbeck's east coast and the approaches to Poole Harbour. In the 1940s, the cliff near Old Harry became a practice-range for rocket-firing aircraft.

Man-marks on the Point pre-date all this. Remains of lynchets, destroyed inland by medieval and later ploughing, edge Celtic fields that have mostly fallen into the sea. Pinnacles of chalk to the south, one like a twisted steeple where peregrine falcons used to nest, are like the pillars of a ruin that now support nothing but air, and boundary banks run straight off the edge of the cliff. Beneath is a huge cave, rising to forty feet above its pebble floor, called Parson's Barn, where smugglers' "tithes" might be stored. In 1747, a cargo of tea was seized there by Customs officers and laid up in Poole Customs House; but a gang of smugglers broke in and retrieved £500 worth of their contraband, killing two officers in the process; six of them were hanged for their pains. Perhaps it was the parson's idea to scare the credulous from a sensitive area with devilish names, so that fires and flickering lights that signalled from Ballard Down might be dimissed as will-o'-the-wisps. If so, the ravens that nest above the store-house must only have aided him in his purpose. The parsons of Swanage and Studland are known to have received bibles and prayer-books, among other things, from the piratical prizes of Elizabethan times.

The chalk is at its widest here, and the path rises slowly up from the Foreland to Ballard Point, with apparently uniform cliffs falling sheer away. The light they throw back is blindingly white, but seen against the sun their texture shows up in relief, that of rugged, bedded building-blocks that lie almost horizontally until, just north of Ballard Point, they climb up steeply, following the line of a gigantic fracture. Rough pasture, where bullocks and dairy-followers graze, undulates gently enough on the surface, but hides the evidence of a violent convulsion of the chalk that can be clearly studied from the sea. Beyond the break, the beds are quite vertical for a short distance, until they begin to lean over towards the south. The chalk and flints to either side of this, the Great Purbeck Thrust Fault, are pulverised and polished into slickenslides that hint at the forces which must have been brought to bear on Purbeck's spine, causing a break perhaps a quarter of a mile deep by who knows how long. Geologists argue about the extent and mechanics of this distinguished fault of the *Belemnitella mucronata* zone of the Upper Chalk, but the Cretaceous sea bed's wounds have long since healed, and the only visible disturbance towards the foot of Ballard Down are two long medieval strip-lynchets beside "Long Lands".

The north side of Swanage Bay is walled by three hundred feet of Middle and Lower Chalk, whose uptilted beds step and slip down towards the water. In the bay's lower cliff, Greensand and Gault are quickly succeeded by the red and grey clays of the Wealden Series, and by the sandy beach and red-brick sprawl of New Swanage. Peveril Point, beyond the town, juts its Purbeck stone into the sea, while the mass of Durlston Head in the distance is founded on the Portland Beds. Our path, though, leads us inland where the chalk concentrates and gathers itself into a ridge, like a wedge driven inland; it climbs a little, levels off for the old rifle range, and runs towards a group of barrows, two of which contained contracted skeletons in chalk-cut graves with later burials above, while the third was probably a banked pond at the extreme north-east corner of Swanage parish. The boundary with Studland runs up from Ballard Cliff and turns, following the line of boundary stones beside the path, along the spine of the hill; but it divides far more than parishes, it separates the dark expanses of the heath from the dense patchwork of the narrow valley to the south. The chalk ridge which it surmounts is a kind of no-man's-land, or a wall built between the lowland provinces, twelve miles long from east to west, from sea to sea.

Today, when so few roads breach or climb them, the hills are more of a barrier than they ever were. They were a causeway, reliable when tracks below were impassable, a green road with many branches running down to settlements both north and south. Traffic from Corfe for Rempstone or Studland customarily came along the ridgeway even in the early 1800s, and, as always, smugglers carried their contraband westwards along Ballard Down before dropping down to Jenny Gould's cottage, whose cellar was a halfway-house on the trip to Redhorn, Greenland or Ower. At about 450 feet, our path is crossed diagonally by an old track up from Studland and down to Whitecliff Farm, Domesday's Witeclive, now nearly engulfed by New Swanage. At the junction there is a stone "rest and be thankful" seat, where you can do just that.

The seat was placed there, at a time when the ridgeway route was beginning to be used less for business than pleasure, by the goodwill, if not the hands, of David Jardine. He was a Bow Street magistrate who frequently resorted to Swanage to recover from the rigours of city law-enforcement. Not that Purbeck was a sweet haven of contented country-folk. Indeed, in 1851, Mr Jardine recommended to John Mowlem, Swanage's stone magnate and magistrate, a certain John Cripps as the town's first policeman. His reception was not a kind one: on Christmas Eve of that year he was barely saved from lynching at the hands of a mob of quarrymen and sailors with whose festivities he had interfered.

If small changes of habit or jurisdiction provoke protest, enjoyment of the view from the magisterial seat may be tempered by reflection upon the large flux of human affairs and passions which even the slight marks upon the downland symbolise. What Stone Age men began to walk these hills, beating a path, a green road so hard-packed that gorse and fern could hardly root in it if it were left untrodden for generations? What kind of scenery was there northwards in Palaeolithic times, when the great Frome-Solent flowed, when land fell under the northern snowfields, and rose so that rivers cut deep beds where human and mammoth remains may still be found? Did man survey the hunt from these hills then, looking out for bison and hyena, woolly rhino and sabre-toothed tiger? Antler fragments in chalk-workings suggest that Neolithic man was here, and the barrows that outcrop still along the hills' skyline were built in the Bronze Age. What impact did each successive wave of settlers make, what tribal wars, what treaties? Early Iron Age Celts and trading Veneti, Durotriges and Belgae, Romans and Saxons, Danes and Normans all contributed something to Purbeck, though their grasp upon it was often tentative, and those that stayed often changed what they found less than they themselves were changed.

Mr Jardine sat beside a centuries-old high-road along the downs, unfenced sheep-walks, pasture punctuated only by tumuli and boundary stones. To the north, squarish Celtic fields of half an acre or less, with lynchets up to eight feet high, still cover twelve acres or so, establishing the pattern of agriculture long before Saxon shotts and medieval fields ate into them. Larger fields have long since superseded these, and part of the tithing has been built over by the Glebeland Estate. Time out of mind, the top of the chalk ridge has been reserved for grazing, but today Mr Jardine's seat is in the corner of a fenced field where the plough has sliced through the thin rendzina soil and dragged up raw chalk and flints which, in recent years, have nurtured a wheat crop outnumbered and outgrown by every kind of weed.

Rough pasture and gorse scrub take over as the path continues to climb westwards along the parish boundary, but the ground is far from undisturbed. A group of five bowl barrows, at well over five hundred feet, were mutilated by war-time building and later ploughing, but the ridgeway on the green roof of the world seems wild enough when the Godlingston Gap opens up beneath, where the road, said to be haunted by a demon rider, runs; the only present-day route to cut through the chalk between the coast and Corfe. The erosive forces that gouged the gap are no longer at work, but chalk beds are visible in the quarry-cliffs of Round Down below; there are no chalk-stacks inland, but a pinnacle of Cornish granite is dramatically sited on the saddle of the ridge above a reservoir. The two are not unconnected. George Burt, stone magnate, who already supplied Swanage with water, ordered test borings to be made in the chalk and greensand in the search for fresh sources; as a result a well was sunk and the reservoir constructed. To celebrate his benefaction he erected the conspicuous, incongruous obelisk on a plinth of local stone in 1892. He was not the first to choose its position, for he planted it fairly and squarely on top of a Bronze Age barrow. This had been excavated earlier; Iron Age or Romano-British debris and two cremations with urn sherds topped the mound; underneath, a deep grave held antler fragments, a fine red cup, and the bones of a tall man whose distorted lumbar vertebrae betrayed the tight trussing which he had undergone before burial. The wells did not live up to Burt's expectations and the obelisk collapsed, but he repaired it anyway, and it stood until about 1940 when it fell, or was pushed, once more. It is upstanding today, one section short, thanks to the Royal Engineers who pieced it together again in 1973. Would that prehistoric monuments were treated with as much care. Burt's memorial must have looked much more impressive in the 1880s, standing at its full height across the road from St Mary Woolnoth in the City of London where he found it.

II

DRY VALLEYS, DORSET DOWN

BELOW THE ULWELL BARROW and its obelisk, a road-widening
scheme near the waterworks revealed traces of the first inhabitants of
Purbeck known to have had a hand in shaping the landscape. Pits of the
Middle Stone Age contained flint tools, animal bones and the shells of
limpets, cockles and periwinkles testifying to their nomadic hunting and
fishing life. With stone axes and fire they could make clearings for themselves in the wooded valley, but they probably left the hills in their
primeval afforested state. We are so used to the cropped contours of the
downs that it is hard to imagine them thickly quilted with trees. Before
the third millennium B.C. New Stone Age immigrants from the Iberian
peninsula, eastern France and Switzerland introduced a mixed farming
economy which was to have a much more dramatic impact. They hunted,
certainly, but they cultivated plots and small fields with antler picks, flint
hoes and possibly ploughs. Most significantly, for the hills, they kept
domesticated short-horned oxen, goats and sheep. Once cleared, the
upland pastures were maintained and modified by these grazing flocks
and herds until the chalk grassland, which we tend to take for granted as
entirely natural, came into its full glory. Once destroyed by ploughing,
mature downland vegetation may take a century to re-establish itself; if
left ungrazed, it will revert to scrub and woodland within the same period.

Scores of herbs, including rare orchids, ploughman's spikenard, bird's-
foot trefoil, squinancy wort and the horseshoe vetch that feeds the chalk-
hill and Adonis blue butterflies, richly adorn a turf of perhaps two score
grasses. The constellation of species is determined by slope, aspect, alka-
linity and the amount of grazing. These factors, together with the hardness
and dryness of the chalk underlying the grey rendzina soils, or the angular
flint gravel under brown earths, have encouraged a remarkable diversity
of hardy plants that batten on every available niche in a habitat under
constant pressure.

The pressures of increasing population in the Iron Age and Romano-British period demanded more and more cleared land. Indeed, the plough made inroads on the downland at this time, and people made farmsteads as well as forts on higher ground. By the fourth century, better ploughs made heavier lowland soils workable and continued woodland clearances lowered the water-table in the chalk, so that wells could no longer be dug deep enough to supply hill settlements. These radical changes in the landscape set the scene for the pattern of Saxon life, and were not caused by it; it was the Romano-British pattern that came to maturity in the Middle Ages.

West of Godlingston Gap a dry valley like a notch in Forked Down End climbs up beside Godlingston Hill. Modern earthworks there are already becoming overgrown, and two ancient barrows at the top, known as Giant's Grave and Giant's Trencher, are obscured by a rich flora of ragwort, bracken, gorse, blackberry, elder, hawthorn and honeysuckle. The air is heavy with scent and birdsong, proving that neglect can be very attractive. The hill-top, though, is well-cropped pasture; but, one scorching summer day when I walked there, its only occupants appeared to be a cow and her calf in the shade of a small police communications station which shares the down with a burial mound, a triangulation point at just over 650 feet, and white concrete, flaking off brick, that marks the entrances of two underground bunkers. Everything was quiet, but when I peered into the dark of these there was an exhalation of foul air, a hurried shifting and anxious bleating; as my eyes got used to the dark I could see sheep and more sheep, packed solid, fleece to thick fleece, lying or standing on a floor of black mud and droppings, chewing and gazing up at me with injured inanity. I left them to the privacy of their stench, and though I envied them the damp shadiness of their shelters, I don't think they begrudged me the freedom of their parched, unappetising pasture.

The Domesday Book shows that eleventh-century manors, which have a remarkable survival rate in Purbeck, both north and south of the chalk, possessed many hundreds of sheep each. Arable land expanded in medieval times, and the remains of strip-lynchets nudge into the ridge beside the gully that runs down to Knitson Farm. As lines of springs feed wells, and sometimes reservoirs, along the flanks of the hills, so numerous ancient and modern chalk-pits have been dug for the marling of clay soils. The tide of cultivation receded once more after the Pestilence or Great Mortality, later known as the Black Death. A monk of Malmesbury wrote, "In the year of our Lord, 1348, about the feast of the Translation of St Thomas, the cruel pestilence, terrible to all future ages, came from parts over the sea to the south coast of England, and into a port called Melcombe, in Dorsetshire. This sweeping over the southern districts, destroying numberless people in Devon, Dorset and Somerset." Imagine the scene in the Purbeck clay valley below, so close to the advent of the plague: fields left untended, clergy in barefoot procession chanting the Greater Litany, burial grounds filled and overflowing, and the carcasses of cattle and sheep rotting in hundreds on field and down. Because labour was so scarce its value doubled rapidly and arable land was turned over to ewe-leazes; so much so that when, after a century, the population recovered itself, shortage of work on the land caused a migration to the towns. The shepherd became a key figure, and his flocks built a foundation in woolsacks for the landed prosperity of Tudor times. Abbey lands supported many thousands of sheep and, after the Dissolution of the Monasteries, passed into the hands of wealthy men and rising yeoman farmers. Henry VIII noted with distaste the tendency of his newly-landed subjects to gather farms, cattle and especially sheep into fewer and fewer hands, while his vagrancy laws attempted to control the multitudes of vagabonds and beggars on urban streets. Prosperity, as always, had its obverse.

The Dorset Horn breed of sheep was already "very scarce to be met with" when Claridge described it in 1793. The ewes are all white, short-legged, broad in shoulder and loin, long-nosed, with curved horns, while the ram is even deeper in the carcass and his horns are heavily coiled. Their ability to lamb twice a year was valued highly, and ewes and their offspring were often sold at sheep-fairs as early as September. But they were crossed, over many years, with larger breeds, and slowly ousted, despite their vigour, by the Dorset Down breed which needs less pasture per head.

Leazes on the hills were stinted in proportion to the tenants' arable holdings in the valley. Though sheep tided many farmers over the vicissitudes of the Napoleonic Wars and the agricultural depression and ferment that followed, their numbers dropped by about two-thirds during the course of the nineteenth century, and much land was left both fallow and ungrazed. The laying of the railway from Wareham to Swanage gave access to ready markets for dairy produce, and cattle became more and more important in Purbeck. New manures, new methods of fencing, steam tractors and other implements threatened land, where sheep had reigned supreme for centuries, with the plough in the early 1900s. Demand for food production in the 1914–18 War was followed by depression until the compulsory cultivation orders of the Second World War. At the same time, sheep returned to the hills above Church Knowle, but the ploughing grants awarded by the Ministry of Agriculture until 1972 encouraged destruction of downland monuments and flora. Some areas of the hill-tops whiten with corn in the summer, and substantial tracts have been ploughed up and re-seeded; such improved grassland is more productive in the short term, but the range of species is impoverished. Ploughing has damaged the downland vegetation, but the chalk ridge's most likely fate is reversion to scrub; it is a rich, cultured resource that must not be lightly tampered with or neglected. Both vices are rife on the Purbeck Hills.

People still remember the days when the downs were dotted with grazing sheep among numerous small enclosures made of hurdles. At the beginning of the last century the shepherd still ruled the farm; he belonged to an élite, his position was envied, and his skills were jealously guarded and painstakingly passed on. For all that, his wealth, apart from the gift of a great-coat once a year, Sunday breakfasts and wages of six or so shillings a week, was not his own. He was strictly accountable for it, and the fleece of every dead sheep had to be handed over to his master between polls. It was his responsibility, and his pride, to choose, train and feed his dog, the essential tool of his custodianship. His flocks were folded at night on the downs themselves or in the valley below. Hurdles, often pitched by the shepherd's boy, provided ideal, portable shelter, sometimes thatched with straw for greater protection in the lambing season. The frequency of coppices and withy beds on both sides of the hills witnesses to the scale of the wood-weaving trade which supplied this and many other needs; while the halving of the price of hurdles between 1750 and 1850 indicates the falling-off of demand, as well as increasing competition between men who turned to such work for lack of employment on the land. Writh, or wattle, hurdles were made from hazel cut from six- or seven-year-old coppices; nine vertical spars were planted in a slightly-curved former, or flake, and horizontal strands were closely woven into a dense hedge-work structure. Older hazel or ash was cloven to make open-work bar, or gate, hurdles which allowed lambs to pass underneath while the ewes remained in close confinement. Hurdles are still employed in Purbeck, though in very small numbers, and at lambing-time they are more than likely to be roofed with corrugated iron and plastic fertiliser bags.

The shepherd was the last inhabitant of these hills, but his reign has ended now. His was the only major trade in the island which did not disturb the ground by ploughing, digging or mining. His creatures' close-cropping teeth created and preserved a vivid carpet for the open spaces, grazing the sites of ancient fields, settlements and burial places for many centuries without molesting them, but rather preserving their outlines clean against the sky. Ballard Down, Godlingston Hill and Nine Barrow Down, and Stonehill Down to the west have all been designated Sites of Special Scientific Interest but, even if that were enough to prevent ploughing on their slopes, nothing can replace the sheep as the active agent of conservation. Exploitation of this downland resource is precisely what preserves it, and if agricultural fashion or economics militate against sheep there seems nothing that a lobby of naturalists, or even rabbits, however active, can do about it. Only direct encouragement of grazing here, by means of something like the hill sheep subsidy, which does not apply in most downland areas, might prevent the unfenced, rounded grasslands being overtaken by a ragged flora and lost to us for ever.

Under their Enterprise Neptune scheme, the National Trust have purchased 220 acres around Whitecliff Farm and on Ballard Down. The Forestry Commission have taken charge of a scheme to replace elms, stricken by Dutch Elm disease, with mixed hardwoods in the valley there, while the Nature Conservancy Council, the Countryside Commission and the County Council are all working together, with the National Trust, to restore the downland turf. The raw, ploughed chalk is to be re-seeded with "traditional downland mixture", and children from the Field Study Centre at Leeson House are to distribute kidney vetch seed by hand. When the turf is finally re-established, Whitecliff Farm's sheep will be grazed once more up there, between Studland and Swanage, heath and valley, upon the green roof of the world in sight of the sea. Paths will not lose themselves in scrub or struggling corn-stalks, and Mr Jardine's seat will be one more white shape upon the sheep-walk.

12

BARROWS AND LONG VIEWS

EVEN ON STILL days the thorn trees on the crown of Nine Barrow Down lean and fly their tatters, black against the sky, in the direction of the prevailing winds. Deciduous and mixed woodland breaks along the northern foot of the hills like the dark surf of the surging heathlands. Hidden down there is the Rempstone stone circle, and above it on Ailwood Down lies a still older memorial, a Neolithic long barrow whose hundred-foot outline, just below the summit, was designed to be seen from valley settlements to the south. If Stone Age men looked up to their dead, later peoples seem to have recognised the sanctity of the site, for a line of fourteen Bronze Age round barrows, or their remains, many with surrounding ditches, punctuate the gorsey ground above it, and one eats into its eastern flank. Two more lay below it, across the path, but these have been swamped by the wash of ploughing and almost submerged in an extensive slope of "improved" grassland. Even so, the name Nine Barrow Down is a Purbeck understatement.

The highest point on the Purbeck ridge may well have been a beacon site which sent messages about the progress of the Armada as it sailed eastwards from Portland and fought a short bloody engagement off Purbeck. Then, on an order of a Justice, a man would have clambered up the ladder that leant against a cone built on the hill, and fired the brush-wood that surmounted it to mobilise the militia. Nearly four hundred years later, a beacon flared up on Nine Barrow Down, throwing merry-makers into strange relief against a flickering sky high above Purbeck's lowland provinces, on the night of Elizabeth II's Silver Jubilee.

It was probably the long barrow a short way westwards, "a giant's grave in this antique land", from which Hardy's Ethelberta Petherwin, astride a donkey, surveyed the weather battling above the ridge, the valley's storm-clouds and the heath's sunlight vying for mastery. From the ancient mound the path drops gently away, and the undulating spine of chalk can be seen, receding into shades of blue, almost to its western limit where the sea breaks against it. The craggy ruins of the castle, Ethelberta's destination, mark Corfe Gap and spawn the honey-grey stone village that spills southwards from it. To the right, Rempstone Hall can be glimpsed down a scrub-ridden dry valley, while at your feet the green road becomes a white, stony track running between dense gorse and bracken, until it crosses the old route up and over, in a crease in the downs, from Rempstone to Tabbitt's Hill. More improved pasture has ironed out the south slope of Rollington Hill, but a stretch of old hollow-way still runs between gorse-covered banks that often echo to the sound of horses' hooves; no longer the reddle-man's lonely donkey, the lumbering farm-cart, or the tumbril bearing pirate convicts from Corfe Castle's bowels to their sea-side gibbets, but a riding-school party in procession, attempting a ragged canter.

Long views are not always possible up here. Sometimes a wind off the sea drapes the cliffs and stone uplands with a white mist, shrouds the valley and engulfs the hills. At one moment the noon-day sun may be shining both sides of the hedges, and the next the driving, luminous stuff blots the island out. It is all wind and whiteness and filtered heat, quieting the birds and causing you to stare like a lime-burner after the green road which falls away either side into nothingness. Landmarks mean nothing unless you trip over them; bush and beast are all the same until the one shifts itself out of sight. All the time now the path descends towards Challow Farm and Corfe village, but it is best to abandon it at the next "cross-roads", though not if the mist still blows, as it may do, on and on over everything.

When you can see where you are going, at the point where a track climbs up from the direction of Little Woolgarston to about 350 feet, descends through the broad, dry valley that gives on to Rollington Farm and continues along Thrasher's Lane, you can make across rough pasture for the summit of Challow Hill. One day, as the morning mist was clearing, I stumbled upon a cow grooming a sodden, new-born calf whose legs could hardly stagger amongst the yellow ragwort. I kept clear of her, for she would be more temperamental than any bull; but what a place for any creature to be born, on the sea-bed spine of Purbeck, the grown-up skyline overgrown with the graves of the prehistoric dead.

On the brow of East Hill stands a round barrow, forty feet in diameter, surmounted by an apology for a cairn, turf-covered for many years but much levelled by ploughing in the past. Fields up here probably fed the settlement down in Corfe Gap in Iron Age or Romano-British times; pottery of the Roman period has been found in these soils, and it is likely that the Durotriges first dragged their ploughs across the dome of the hill. More than thirty acres are covered by the remains of Celtic field-banks, bounded on the east by a lynchet line across the hill above Rollington Farm, and two complete fields survive above Rollington Wood.

From the barrow's vantage-point, West Hill's bulk is the backdrop for the castle's decayed keep which rears up in the gap, taking strategic advantage of the mound of chalk that almost plugs it. The broken masonry is drab buff and grey in dull weather, but is transmuted to silver and gold when the sun shines full upon it, though never as bright as in the days when the whole keep was lime-washed as white as the rock in which it is founded. A narrow chalk causeway climbs from the outer bailey, across a bridge over the great ditch, between the Scylla and Charybdis of the Martyr's Gate, and out of sight into the west bailey. It reappears in the topmost inner ward where, this side of the King's Tower, the garden-site, the courtyards surrounded by the remains of royal chambers, the kitchen range and the Queen's Tower are still guarded by massive fragments of ward wall.

One hundred yards northwards, the half-overgrown face of a large chalk quarry contrasts vividly with the pocked limestone above. Just as each settlement that flanks the ridge has gouged its own pit, for marl or mortar, in the fabric of the hills, so each is liberally supplied with water from the same inexhaustible source. However dry and parched the downs may become when the water-table drops, the rock reservoir still maintains a sufficient head of water to feed the lines of wells and springs beneath. Another line, which rises at the junction of Purbeck limestone and Wealden clay feeds the southern side of the the valley, so that streams flow into its river beds from north and south. It would seem natural that these should run into the sea at either end of the valley; brooks do empty into Swanage Bay to the east and Worbarrow Bay to the west, but the main drainage is actually in reverse, towards the centre of the valley. Two streams, the Wicken and the Byle, from west and east respectively, both turn north and almost merge, but pass either side of the castle mound and join immediately to the north of it, to flow across the heath as the Corfe River and drain into Poole Harbour as Wych Lake. It is impossible to believe that the slight water-courses of today were the architects of such a massive bulwark; but if we imagine the time when the valley was not eroded we can make sense of the dry valleys that once drained the vanished highlands. They were left high and dry, in both the limestone cliffs and the chalk ridge, as the valley floor subsided and the brooks captured one another and flowed east–west, finding their dual exit, fortuitously, at Corfe Gap which, as time went on, was cut deeper and deeper by their torrents. The view from the castle battlements down to the trickles below is a very long view indeed.

The inhabitants of Corfe variously exploited the water. A well in the inner ward and one in the outer bailey plumbed the mound's depths for the castle's supply. The Wicken was tapped, about five hundred yards upstream, by stone sluices which fed a system of ponds, controlled by wooden sluices, used for fish-breeding just north of the Vineyard. The area was called Mill Close, and, nestling at the foot of West Hill, over-shadowed by trees, are the remains of the eighteenth-century West Mill and its sluice-gates, of which photographs are extant, and whose prede-cessor was marked on Ralph Treswell's map of 1585. East Mill, between East Street and the outer bailey's escarpment, is of the same pedigree, though it was converted to turbine-drive early this century. It has been dismantled inside and blocked off from the adjoining miller's house and the nineteenth-century bakehouse with its projecting oven-stack, so that the water rushes beneath it unchecked, under road and railway and on past the waterworks at the north-west foot of East Hill. Borings there hit on a spring in vertical chalk near the junction with the Reading Beds from which hundreds of thousands of gallons could be tapped per day. This, though five miles from Swanage, superseded Mr Burt's wells as the supply for that town, and a pumping-station, like a nonconformist chapel, was built not far from Corfe railway bridge to feed the Ulwell reservoir.

The railway embankment thrusts sinuously through the gap to the east of the castle, on its way to Swanage. Now bereft of track, it once brought tides of visitors to storm Corfe's defences. Today, before they even reach the Gap, a large gravel-covered car-park in the old chalk-quarry offers itself to those who want to plunder for refreshments and souvenirs, or admire the menagerie of birds, rabbits, goats and other animals corralled in the castle's shadow. The road divides for Church Knowle or Swanage, and it is summer traffic that flows incessantly, or queues, around the ramparts' base. Corfe was once called Corvesgate, from the Anglo-Saxon "ceorfan", to carve or cut. The noble cleft in the chalk range, always the main through route and long valued for its defensive rôle, is nowadays more likely to be stigmatised as bottleneck.

13

VIOLENCE AND POLICY

FROM BELOW, LOOKING up almost unscalable slopes, Corfe Castle's bastions lower and sway against shifting cloud; the privileged view of the interior is denied us and the castle rises to its proper eminence. Castle Hill is so exactly fitted by its fortifications that some have thought, mistakenly, that it is a man-made mound. Builders of the tenth to thirteenth centuries were adept at making virtues of necessities, and only superficially embellished natural features by flattening some areas, digging ditches and steepening scarps. The summit, crowned by the inner ward and keep, and the triangular west bailey are on the Upper Chalk; the terraces of the outer bailey are dug into Middle Chalk, the sloping area of the original first ward is Lower Chalk, while the outer gatehouse is founded on the Upper Greensand.

Purbeck was perhaps the most populous area of British Dorset, and no people concerned with its jurisdiction and defence could have afforded to ignore Castle Hill's strategic value. It is possible that some of the earthworks that underlie a whole history of building on the site may pre-date the stones, but there can be no firm proof of this, though second-century samian ware, coarse ware and fragments of Roman flue-tile have been found on the highest parts of the hill. The oldest portion of the fabric is a wall of herring-bone work, standing immediately within the south wall of the west bailey. Thin, flat-bedded Purbeck stone laid diagonally in zigzag courses makes a wall like stitchery, pierced by windows of ashlar that were blocked by the later defences. In 1883, Thomas Bond presented an impassioned case, based on his excavations, for these remains being those of an early Saxon church. There is good cause to believe that Aldhelm erected a church at or near Corfe, but that its stones survive is more doubtful.

The building, measuring 72 by 17 feet, was certainly the Aula, or Hall, to the Turris on the hill-top in 1080, and some people think that it was

part of the palace that Edgar (959–975) is said to have built here. It is
possible that the king and his second wife Queen Elfrida feasted within its
walls. What remains is the undercroft, with a drain and soakaway at the
west end to serve the buttery, probably installed when the building was
enlarged in 1240. I feel, in my bones, that the pocked and weather-
beaten walling is pre-Norman, but bones are singularly unreliable
chronometers. Excavation of buried foundations revealed that they had
been set on even earlier rubble, and post-holes and pottery of late Saxon
type demonstrate that a building of some sort stood on the site before the
Conquest.

Post-mortem examination of bones provides objective evidence, and
in 1931 shed clear scientific light on the most infamous act associated with
the place. Digs, of themselves, seldom tell tales; excavation disinters a
hardly-clothed skeleton of events, while colourful tale-telling was the
business of bards and monkish historians who often resurrected a
monstrous body, encumbered with a surfeit of flesh. But sometimes the
two can be profitably married, as in the case of Edward, King and Martyr.

When Edgar died he left two sons: Edward, aged fifteen, fruit of his
first marriage, and Ethelred, about seven years old, son of Elfrida.
Edward's legitimacy was in doubt, and his father, although occupying
the throne, had not yet been crowned when he was born; but Edgar had
designated him heir before his death. He was a stormy character, like his
father, and he inspired terror in the royal household. Ethelred was
certainly the son of a crowned king, and his supporters knew him to
be gentler and more malleable than his brother. Malleability was a kingly
attribute highly prized by nobles, particularly those led by the Earl of
Mercia, who opposed the reforms of church and state that Edgar had
carried out and which Edward was likely to continue. However, the
reforming bishop Dunstan, assisted by Oswald, crowned Edward king
of Wessex and all England.

Stories of how he met his death vary in detail; Geoffrei Gaymar of
France pictures him chasing his recalcitrant dwarf Wolstanet, who had
refused to perform and insulted his master, through the forest until he
arrived at Elfrida's house, but he was writing in the twelfth century;
while the *Vita Sancti Oswaldi* was compiled about the year 1000 and, with
William of Malmesbury's *Gesta Regum* and the *Anglo-Saxon Chronicle*,
presents a reasonably consistent account. On 18 March 978 Edward was
hunting, his companions were chasing the dogs in all directions, and he,
tired and in need of refreshment, decided to go and see Ethelred, the

brother he loved, at Corfe passage. He never saw him. He was greeted by Elfrida's chief men and was offered a cup of wine, perhaps by the queen herself; he was drawn to the right as if for a kiss of welcome, when his left arm was twisted and wounded; Elfrida or one of the conspirators pierced him with a dagger; his right arm was seized and broken. All this happened in an instant, the king's horse plunged forward and he was bent violently back over the high cantle of his saddle, his left foot trapped in the stirrup, so that when he fell he was dragged for some distance, until his dead or dying body finally fell free. What happened next is not so certain. The corpse seems to have been hidden in the house of a blind woman who, at midnight, is said to have seen the house fill with blinding light. The next expedient was to bury the king in a well, or in a marshy place, but a pillar of fire revealed the spot and an efficacious spring issued there. St Edward's fountain, near St Edward's Bridge at the foot of Castle Hill, was long used for bathing weak eyes, and may be still. The royal corpse was disinterred and re-buried at Wareham without honours.

Ethelred, nicknamed Unraed, or ill-advised, was crowned at Kingston. Perhaps chastened by later events, or in an act of sublime hypocrisy, the Earl of Mercia had the uncorrupted body of the murdered king translated to the abbey at Shaftesbury with much ceremony. Elfrida is said to have attempted to join the procession from her house below Woodbury Hill at Bere Regis, but her mount adamantly refused to move an inch. On 2 January 1931, while excavating the site of Shaftesbury's abbey church, J. Wilson Claridge discovered a casket containing bones which he suspected might be the long-lost relics of Edward the Martyr. Thomas Stowell, surgeon and authority on Jack the Ripper, was called in to perform a post-mortem. The skull was long, Saxon rather than Celtic; the development of the bones was that of a young male between the ages of seventeen and the early twenties; greenstick fractures indicated the earlier part of this age range; and all the injuries were consistent, to the last detail, with the sequence of events so vividly portrayed by the monk of Ramsey. Thomas Stowell was convinced that he was handling King Edward's bones.

William I did a deal with the Abbess of Shaftesbury for land at Corfe and built his castle there. Great rubble-hearted chunks of the inner ward wall, which crowns Castle Hill, date from about 1080. In 1086, Durand the carpenter held the manor of Moulham in Swanage, by virtue of the contracting work he performed in the service of the king. The keep, now a ruinous refuge for jackdaws and rooks, was a stronghold by the time Henry I chose it for the incarceration of his brother, the Duke of Normandy, in 1106. A bailey wall was built where the great ditch is now, to defend the weakest side of the hill. A gatehouse fronted the outer bailey's wooden palisades and, by the time of the Anarchy in Stephen's reign, it was said to be one of the most secure castles in all England. Little wonder then that Robert of Gloucester, half-brother of Matilda, occupied it, and Wareham castle, in the revolt against the usurper-king. The Rings, an earthwork beside the Church Knowle road, are probably the remnants of the ring-and-bailey siege castle that Stephen threw up. Much of the bailey has been ploughed, and the ring is overgrown with bracken and bramble. Its other name, Cromwell's Battery, dates from its employment in a later civil war.

Griffin, Prince of Wales' invasions of England culminated, in 1198, in his imprisonment at Corfe, and the next year John came to the throne and soon set about improving the living, and dying, conditions in the castle. Buildings known as the Gloriette, beside the keep, added to the royal apartments and provided comfortable confinement for the gentle prisoners who were soon to inhabit the castle: Eleanor, the damsel of Bretagne, was captured after the siege of Mirabeau in Poitou and, after her brother Prince Arthur's murder at Rouen, was kept at Corfe until after her uncle the king's death. She was joined there by Margery and Isobel, daughters of William of Scotland, and the queen herself honoured them with her unwilling presence for a time. The Mayor of Winchester and the Constable of Corfe were frequently ordered to supply garments and other necessaries to the royal prisoners and their ladies-in-waiting. Quantities of linen, cambric capes, caps trimmed with miniver, scarlet cloaks, thin shoes, boots and gilded harness for their horses suggest an indulgent form of house arrest.

Meanwhile, knights captured at Mirabeau had not been so lucky, especially after Savary de Mauleon had inspired his fellows to seize the tower. From 1202 to 1204 the west bailey with its three towers was built around the old hall. The towers Malemit and Sauvary were prisons and the most prominent, or *bout-avant*, of them was called Butavant, or The Dungeon. Its upper two storeys are pierced with arrow-slits, but the lowest storey, underground on its inner side, has no windows and, as access was limited to a trap in the floor above, was surely a place where undesirables could be dropped into oblivion. Twenty-two of the French knights were starved to death at Corfe while the female prisoners took their exercise on horseback. Every castle or kingdom must preserve the visible splendour of its Gloriette with a corresponding dark, barbaric oubliette.

In 1207 eleven miners spent seven months demolishing the bailey wall and digging the great ditch in its place. Later, the king's own miners and masons worked on ditch and bank by the outer gatehouse, for from 1212 the construction of the outer bailey in stone was under way. In that year Peter de Pomfret was committed to Corfe for prophesying that the king's reign would not exceed fourteen years. Although, on 15 May 1213, John bowed the knee to the Papal Legate, he had Peter the Hermit and his sons dragged to Wareham and back on hurdles, and strung up on gallows before the castle. The constable was charged with the custody of rebel barons in the strife succeeding the king's repudiation of Magna Carta, but on 15 May 1216 John wrote to Peter de Mauley, telling him to entertain one of the royal prisoners, Robert, Comte de Dreux, in "our Hall in the Ward" and to give him access to the tower, prior to his exchange with William Longspée, who had been captured by the French king. William, Earl of Salisbury, son of Henry II and Rosamund the Fair, had been both loyal and hospitable to John, but allied himself with Prince Louis soon after the exchange and may have assisted in the capture of Corfe Castle by the rebels.

In the fourth year of Henry III, Peter de Mauley carried the royal regalia, including the crown of the Saxon kings, from Corfe to London for the Coronation; but, on the death of the Protector, he usurped Crown property, was arrested for treason and only released when he relinquished Corfe, with Eleanor and Isobel, jewels, ammunition and military engines. By the time Simon de Montfort demanded the castle from Henry III, walls had been built, to replace palisades, between the keep and the Martyr's Gate and across the outer bailey. Simon died at the battle of Evesham and his son Almeric was incarcerated at Corfe.

Edward I's reign saw flamboyant reinforcement of the castle. By its close the gatehouses, the First, Horseshoe and Plukenet towers and the outer bridge were complete. The Great Tower's attics had been inflated into a full third storey with a chapel of St Mary. The Gloriette area was remodelled around the King's Hall, the King's Presence Chamber or Camera, and two towers, Cockayne and Plentye. Edward II's time was marked by dissolution. Piers Gaveston is said to have found temporary refuge in Purbeck. Robert de Walkefare murdered the Constable of Corfe and escaped his custody to join the future Edward III across the Channel. And this despite the castle's garrison, which in peace-time comprised sixteen cross-bow men at 4d a day, ten bowmen at 2d, and four men-at-arms at 12d; while in troubled times each tithing of Purbeck was required to furnish one able-bodied man for ten days, and twelve Corfe men had ½d a night and their keep for mounting a watch for forty nights. A watch was kept over Gaveston's liege-lord, the king, when he was held here. Edward had a dread of Corfe, perhaps because of his Saxon predecessor's fate, and one account maintains that he too was murdered within its walls. John Mautravers, of Langton in Purbeck, was one of the regicides, but Berkeley Castle was the place of execution. The mystery surrounding the death was exploited by Isabella and Mortimer: an elaborate charade, with all the pageantry of state, was mounted at Corfe to help convince Edmund that his brother was still alive, and the letter he wrote to the dead king brought him to trial for treason, and to the block.

The charade was mounted amid dilapidation at the castle as well as in the kingdom. Clearances of rubbish and repairs were carried out spasmodically, between waves of the Pestilence, in Edward III's reign. Timber and iron were imported through Ower and Wareham, chambers were refitted and kitchens rebuilt, roofs were newly tiled and leaded, a lime-kiln was built to make mortar from stone rather than chalk, and work on a new bridge, founded on stone from Lynch, and a new tower, la Gloriet, of stone from Quarr, overlapped the new reign. Richard II gave the castle to his brother, the Earl of Kent, and after that it passed to many owners, and many times reverted to the Crown because its custodians had a talent for high treason and other capital offences. Elizabeth ended the Crown's interest in the property when she sold it to Sir Christopher Hatton for £4,761 18s 7½d.

As we have seen, Francis Hawley, Hatton's deputy, ruled the piratical roost from Corfe Castle with the co-operation of Purbeck gentry, and imprisoned brigands who would not toe the line. Clinton Atkinson was one of these; Hawley offered to procure his release for a consideration, but matters were taken out of the hands of the local Commission for the reformation of piracy, and the trials of Atkinson and many other Purbeck men took place in London. In revenge for the executions and fines that followed, Hawley's deputies Uvedale and Ayres, his servant William King and a gentleman of Langton Matravers, whose man was imprisoned at Corfe for poaching, stormed the castle, ostensibly to free the poacher. They filched glass and lead, and stone for Uvedale's house, as well as demolishing the hunting lodge on Creech Barrow, for which crime Hatton took action against them in the Star Chamber. Hatton was careful not to be implicated in his deputy's activities, and Hawley, though roasted by the Privy Council, survived until 1594. Hatton's nephew William inherited the castle, and on his death it passed to his widow, the redoubtable and scandalous Lady Elizabeth, who eventually, after some notable matrimonial battles, sold her "Purbeck Castle" to the Bankes family in 1634.

An account of 1635 says this of it: "It is so ancient as without date, yet all her walls and towers, the maine castle called the King's, the lower castle called the Queen's, the large roomes therein, and the leads aloft, are all in very good repayre. . . . The walls round about her are very strong and large, and have faire walkes, secure platforms, and good ordinance," though it adds, referring to Lady Elizabeth, "but their chiefest guns, wch were goodly brave brasse pieces, were lately broken to pieces and sold by one (you may imagine) rather of Venus than Mars his company, much to the weakening of the whole island". The Bankeses certainly aimed to make the old fortress comfortable, and perhaps never imagined that their home would very soon become the object, once again, of a prolonged siege. They furnished it with hangings of red and green gilded leather, damask and fine tapestry; with Turkish and Persian carpets, crimson velvet suites of furniture, finely wrought beds and hangings, quantities of linen, trunks, a rich ebony cabinet and many other things including books and papers to the value of £1,300. Inventories of the contents survive, ironically, because they were dispossessed of them by Parliamentarian soldiers, and Ralph Bankes listed the family goods in his efforts to reassemble them after the Restoration.

Sir John Bankes, Lord Chief Justice of the Common Pleas and Privy Councillor, was serving Charles I at Oxford when the first attempts on Corfe were made in 1643. Every tactic was employed, from trickery to main force to blockade; a colourful, if Royalist-biased, account of Lady Bankes' defence is given in the contemporary *Mercurius Rusticus*. The Roundheads made their first sally on May Day, in the hope that the castle would be deserted, as it was the tradition that all the local gentry and the Mayor of Corfe were permitted to hunt a stag in the island on that day. Lady Bankes shut the gates and took in a small garrison. She refused to hand over her cannon to Poole Republicans. She smuggled goods in to circumvent the Wareham blockade. Artillery was sited on the hill above the castle. Siege-engines called the Boar and the Sow were advanced.

Corfe church served as stables, its lead was made into shot and its organ-pipes employed as ammunition cases. The assailants were reinforced with mariners, cart-loads of petards, grannadoes and scaling ladders, but Lady Bankes, her daughters, her women and five soldiers poured stones and embers on to the heads of the "pot-valiant" force.

So it went on, for four months, until news of an imminent Royalist advance scattered the Parliamentarians for a time. Nearly all Dorset was in Roundhead hands by 1644, and in December Sir John Bankes died in Oxford; but Corfe remained an island of Royalist defiance in a Parliamentarian sea throughout the next year. It was a stalemate, punctuated by dramatic alarums and excursions, until Lieutenant-Colonel Pitman turned traitor and tricked Colonel Anketil, governor of the castle, into allowing him to go and fetch reinforcements from Somerset. He came back with a hundred men from the Roundhead garrison at Weymouth, and more from Lulworth Castle. The castle was taken from within and without at once, and only a cool-headed Lady Bankes, willing to treat with her enemies, avoided the spilling of much blood. She was not the only loser. At least one man of Corfe, who stood for the Parliament, complained mightily that his property had been destroyed by the Royalist garrison and the stones thrown down upon the besiegers' heads. But, on the day, only one man on the Parliament side was lost, and another contemporary account concludes, "thus the Lord every way mightily showed himself for us, to the glory of his own great name, the good of us his unworthy servants, and the great dread and amazement of all our implacable and incorrigible enemies".

Lady Bankes was such a foe, but the castle itself was the most recalcitrant, and on 5 March 1646 the House of Commons voted to slight it. Lady Bankes is said to have deposited her valuables within the well by the chapel, but she was powerless to save the furnishings or the stone shell of the castle that remained after its gutting. Much money was raised for gunpowder and mining works; the £40 county rate due from Robert Cullyford of Encombe House, for instance, was diverted for the work, but Captain Hughes, governor of Lulworth Castle, found the fabric steadfast enough. The present state of the structure witnesses to Hughes' determination to fulfil his task, and to its difficulty. Breaches were made in the walls, but towers would not be dislodged and either lean outwards or have slipped bodily into the mines beneath them. The Martyr's Gate is neatly split and the western tower has subsided, so that one half of the old arch misses the other by six feet or more. The keep stands, like a broken

Above, Corfe Castle; *below*, Barnston manor

Above, Corfe Gap from Kingston; *below*, Brickworks, Godlingston

In Tyneham village   Swanage Town Hall

Quarr, one of the "marble farms"

Opposite above, The Priest's Way

Opposite below, A "ridden-hole" near Swanage

Above, A quarr-hut, Swanage

Centre, Crabstones and collar

Below, A quarr-shaft

Emmetts Hill and Hounstout

Below East Man, Winspit

Cliffstone quarry, Winspit

Above, St Aldhelm's Chapel; *below*, St Aldhelm's Quarry

"Donkey" and Clavel Tower, Kimmeridge

Brandy Bay, Broad Bench and eastwards

pillar symbolising a life ended before its time; passages, doorways, a twisting stair and a gaping fireplace open on to air.

If Parliament wished to restore Castle Hill to the turf-covered mound it once was, they were sadly disappointed. Its bones were not so easily interred. The massive relics draw pilgrim sightseers to them now, who wonder how such a self-important structure came to be raised and destroyed in such a quiet, uneventful corner of England. If its strength and beauty have been sapped, the terror its walls contained has also been exorcised. Its ruinous remains figure largely only in the strategy of the tourist industry. As a small boy, I first clambered around the perilous path that skirts the walls on the scarps' top. Beneath the ivy-clad overhanging masonry, haunted by grey-cowled, glossy-coated jackdaws that seem to live upon the memory of Lady Bankes' abandoned jewels, I saw my first adder unclasp its coils at my feet and flow away into the undergrowth. I was chilled and excited at the same time, sensations which the castle must have once evoked to the full. The last time I took that same path, a black cat, fat with kittens, followed me on the switchback tour of the old stones, all six hundred yards or more, sometimes almost tripping me up as I looked down to the roads and streams below, or padding ahead as I stopped for a moment to finger all that Purbeck stone, burr from the old limestone quarries, or bits of sandstone from Holme Mount. She was its familiar, a friendly, purring, pregnant guide to the harmless wreckage of medieval architecture. Neglect completed the work that Parliament began, and a poor skeleton is left that no post-mortem can re-instil with the power that brooded in the heart of Purbeck.

The castle was lived in for a time after its demise. The rear part of the south tower in the west bailey was enclosed, a fireplace installed and a garden laid out, but the small additions are now as ruined as the rest. On the night of 11 February 1866, a violent gale that followed unremitting rain did what Captain Hughes could not, and toppled a great chunk of the Butavant Tower down into the river. The vandalism of man and the elements must be added to the destructive forces that have taken Corfe Castle, in the words of the chronicler Heath, "without any offer of terms, by violence and policy mixed together".

14

HOLLOW-WAYS AND BANKERS

FROM THE CASTLE ramparts you can catch a glimpse of the undamaged keep and fortifications that dominate the model village in the village below. From that perspective the real place is as neat and tidy, as clinically picturesque, as its Lilliputian counterpart. Two charming streets, called East and West, run in from Corfe Common to the south, skirt the church-yard's raised banks and converge upon the market-place that lies just beyond the gatehouse and moat; then, as one, around the foot of the great mound to St Edward's Bridge. The village is mostly founded on the Wealden clay, but it owes its special character and prestige to the gap in the chalk hills.

North of the bridge and across the railway embankment, in sites not disturbed until clay-working began, Romano-British burials in stone cists were discovered, together with a fine collection of urns and other pottery, gathered together by Lord Eldon and subsequently lost. Stone paving, chalk-and-limestone floors and the hard-core of a probable road suggest a well-established site; while the pottery, bronze dividers, and shale from armlet manufacture, as well as elaborately carved table-legs, indicate that it was a place of industry. Our view of the long-dead inhabitants of any settlement, gleaned as it is from graves and artefacts, may be wildly distorted. Tradition and the veneration of the past associated with death ensure that graves have never been in the van of technical innovation; they have no need to be. And objects made, perhaps, by a small minority in a settlement, may have been incidental to the mainstream of life there. But we may conclude that, in the first few centuries of our era, Corfe was, if nothing else, a place of craftsmen.

It was granted a charter under the Saxon kings and came to maturity in the shadow of the Norman castle. If the castle was Purbeck's political and judicial hub, the village was its commercial centre, its trades- and excise-man. It owed service to the Crown in the person of the constable, who also collected the annual rents. In Edward I's reign one water-mill rendered 6s 8d, thirteen free tenants of the town paid 36s 7d, while rents of cumin, wax and horseshoes valued at 1d were collected from cottagers. The owners of carts were required to carry two tuns of wine each year from Wareham to the castle for the constable's use, and to supply him with bread and beer every Saturday. Corfe men had the duty of escorting prisoners to and from Wareham bridge. No doubt they were as jealous of the jurisdiction as their master, for by virtue of such service they held privileges by ancient custom. Tenants of the town were called barons, with the same freedoms as barons of the Cinque Ports, and were empowered to elect a mayor, a coroner and bailiffs. The mayor could graze one lamb in the king's pasture called Castle Close, and had pesage, the right to weigh goods, such as cheese and wool, throughout the island in return for the payment of two pounds of wax, worth 12d, per annum.

The Town House, built in the late eighteenth century to the right of the churchyard gate, literally oversees the market-place. Its central bay is filled, at first-floor height, with the great window of the Mayor's Robing Room. Below it, the front door led into the domestic portion of the house, now a bank, but the Robing Room can only be entered by a door from the steeply-banked churchyard. Just around the corner in West Street is the Town Hall, rebuilt about 1770; the Council Chamber, with its long table surrounded by paintings and prints of Corfe, is entered in the same way. The street door led into the lock-up, now a museum, below.

John Uvedale was a mayor of Corfe, and one of Hawley's deputies. Pesage was a poor sort of income compared to piracy. His house of 1575, between the garage and the public lavatories on East Street, was a fine building whose stone was supplemented by the revenge raid on the castle that I have mentioned. Almost all the fine building is late sixteenth or early seventeenth century, when the prosperity of the town was at its zenith. Morton's house on East Street, distinguished by its two west wings set either side of a courtyard, was built about 1600 as a fine residence for the Daccombes. Across the road, an attic storey was added to a fifteenth-century house of one or two rooms and a hall; it still boasts two medieval roof-trusses, though the timbering is mostly eighteenth century, and the north room later became a smithy. The Greyhound Hotel, in the market-place, took over two cottages and later outbuildings, but, in general, the trend has been otherwise until recently; as the town declined the quality of building declined too, and existing houses were divided up; Morton's house was split up into three, and Uvedale's residence into six tenements.

The bird's-eye view of Corfe, drawn in 1586 by Ralph Treswell, surveyor to Christopher Hatton, shows a number of hawes, or closes, to the west of West Street, which survive, with a number of their mere-stones, to this day. It is no accident that the largest plot belonged to Uvedale, the second largest to Daccombe, and two of the remaining strips to Bonville: they were prominent among those who profited from contraband. The church and the stocks in the market-place are also prominent on Treswell's plan, but neither of them deterred such men in the prosecution of their business.

Hawley tarnished and diminished the castle's rôle. The big fish of Corfe fouled their pool, and though we can be grateful for the results of their prosperity, it was based on greed for illicit trade, rather than on the larger concerns for which both castle and town were fitted. When Purbeck's charter was endorsed by Elizabeth in 1576, its inhabitants were exempted from the county musters. But this only exacerbated their traditional insularity of mind, their outlaw mentality, at a time when patriotism was demanded; they refused to pay muster taxes or to be trained for military service. So, in 1588, Hawley, Uvedale and all were overlooked, and Sir Richard Rogers of Bryanston was charged with raising a force of one hundred men in the island and, on the Privy Council's orders, with taxing the landlords who, like himself, had made big money from piracy and then moved inland when their Purbeck estates were under threat of Spanish aggression. However, by the 1590s we find that the islanders had reassumed their responsibilities under William Hatton. They found time for more honourable activities, now that their favourite trade had withered away, and looked seawards with different eyes: 367 trained men were prepared for Purbeck's defence, under the command of Williams of Tyneham, Clavell of Barnston and Uvedale of Corfe Castle.

A mess of motives and interests raised the grey and honey-coloured stone of the Corfe that we know. As its life-blood thinned in the next two centuries it grew more sober and stood on the dignity of its Corporation, having no other footing. In the face of its turbulent history it is strange to find the churchwardens presenting men before the Court Peculiar for being "drinky" during the time of Divine Service. It continued to send, with less and less justification, two MPs to Westminster. The seal of the Corporation, with its three-towered castle surmounted by ostrich feathers and surrounded by the legend "Sigillu maoris et baronu ville de corff castell", and the mace with its chained portcullis and the arms of

William and Mary, preserved the myth of the town's importance. But to
Hutchins, in the eighteenth century, "the appearance of misery in the
town is only too striking"; the people were of a "supine disposition" with
"a propensity to idleness". By now they were ready to hear John Wesley,
who preached to an attentive congregation in a meadow near the town;
he found the society of the island "artless and teachable, and full of good
desires. But few of them yet have got any farther than to 'see men as trees
walking'". The town had lost its way. Its rôle was no longer a distinguished one. In 1832 its rotten borough was disenfranchised, and the
following year the Corporation was abolished.

When Wesley or anyone else took horse or coach for Swanage they
went across Corfe Common and up the hill to Kingston to join the upland
route west. Not until the middle of the last century was direct link
made from the end of East Street, whose boggy destination had been
filled in for the present roadway. The main street had always been West
Street, which now peters out on the common. It contains the secret of
Corfe's medieval greatness, a cornerstone more enduring and more
honourable than the Elizabethan fabric that was raised upon it. Elizabethan
stone survives, but the stone trade of earlier centuries was its real foundation. Tracks and footpaths fan out from the southern end of West Street:
to Burberry Lane and Blashenwell Farm, to Lynch, and to Scoles Gate
where old roads meet. Hollow-ways are still scored across the ridges and
between the tumuli of the common, where ponies graze still, but where
horse-drawn stone-sledges made up the immense traffic between the
marble and freestone quarries and Corfe. Ten feet or more of stone "scars"
or chippings are said to underlie West Street, where many bankers stood,
stone benches upon which masons worked on commissions for the
churches of all England, and sometimes Europe too. Ambitious craftsmen went with their stone to work it *in situ*: in 1292 Edmund Corfe,
Peter Corf, Hugo de Corfe and John de Corfe were among the
masons at Westminster. Adam de Corfe—otherwise known as Adam le
Marbrer, the marbler—owned a tenement in East Street, but lived in
Farringdon, in the City of London, where the name Stonecutters Street
persists.

One vestige of Corfe's reputation remains to remind us of what the
trade meant to the island: the Ancient Order of Marblers and Stonecutters
still meets in the Town Hall on Shrove Tuesday. Beer swills stone-dust
from quarriers' throats at the Fox Inn, from whose small front parlour a
squint, like a hagioscope, looks on to well-stocked shelves, and stairs

descend to the bar. The traditional progress is made to Ower Quay across the heath, and the payment of a pound of pepper and a football is presented, not at Ower Passage House but at the farm, for the use of it. Ower is no longer any sort of port, and West Street's wide paving no longer resounds with the chime of mason's hammers, but Corfe is still a town of stone. Brick made some inroads, but all new building must now be of local materials, or the equivalent. So it preserves itself, and is annually revitalised with a little of its old spirit.

By 1865, the chief employment of the men of the parish was clay-cutting; labourers looked north instead of south. Masons survived in Corfe, alongside carpenters, tailors, cobblers and innkeepers, but its composition was much more like that of any small country town. A maltster, a wheelwright, a builder and a brick-maker, a plumber, a glazier, a painter and an ironmonger added to the tally of trades. Andrew Dyer, doctor, was classified, in the Directory of the time, under both Commercial and Gentry. The Revd Eldon Surtees Bankes was firmly entrenched as Rector and Squire, while the Revd George Hubbard fed his independent flock in the Congregational Chapel. Samuel Evans was fellmonger, saddler, harness-maker and agent for the Atlas Fire and Life Office. There was a registrar and a relieving officer, and Mrs Sarah Jenkins was the local officer of the Inland Revenue.

The church of St Edward, King and Martyr, set on its mound at the confluence of streets, is all of Purbeck stone. The fifteenth-century embattled tower is vigorously surmounted by pinnacles and gruesome gargoyles. Church and churchyard contain thirteenth-century coffin-lids of Purbeck marble, the material chosen for the beautiful piscina, the font and the reredos, fragments of which lean, redundant, against the pillars of the tower. Apart from the west tower, the church was rebuilt in 1860, using much of the old fabric, just as much of the castle's stone has been incorporated into walls and houses in the village. Parliament ordered, in 1646, that the damage the church suffered in the siege of the castle should be made good, and made a grant for that purpose, but of that period only the Royal Arms of Charles II, dated 1660, the year of his restoration, survives. Memory preserved in stone—fragments of fine old work, the half-truths of wall-tablets and floor-slabs, and the jig-saw of old and new created by the reconstruction of the past—is notoriously selective.

Today, the village presents just such a partial picture of its history. Its wealth was not so much in the stones that were raised or dismantled here, but in those that passed through. Its prettiness and its peaceful atmosphere, which draw people to it now, cannot convey anything of its past virtues and vices. Learn a lesson from the garage by the bridge near Uvedale's house: there, an eighteenth-century barn or store-house has been converted, petrol-pumps stand in the yard, and the building is filled with bric-à-brac, spare parts, antique machines, accessories, curiosities for the very curious, junk of possible use shored up against the future. Look too at the tiny museum in the old lock-up beneath the Town Hall: implements and domestic fittings of all kinds crazily confined behind the wire; a wittily-contrived curator's nightmare, including the remnants of twentieth-century civilisation found within the castle walls—a pile of litter.

In summer, visitors pour from cars and coaches, over the four spans of the old bridge across the ditch, and through the stunted gatehouse in whose stone grooves a portcullis would once have crashed down to bar their way. They charge their hold-alls with souvenirs and craft-goods from village shops, their stomachs with refreshments at the Castle Café, and re-charge their cameras with celluloid that will preserve for them a flimsy memorial of that much-photographed ruin on the hill. The village seems, as of old, to serve its fortress. As the banked-up graveyard is tended, so the grass is mown between the old stones on the castle's mound; so Corfe serves the dead.

Things survive because they are valued; or are valued because they survive, even if they were abandoned or discarded in the first place. Such is the ambiguous nature of the jackdaw-hoard that is Corfe's history. Out of season, though, when visitors are gone, it continues a vigorous life of its own. It is not all tourist-trade and retired immigrants, but stays close to the farmland which surrounds it and the resources which it taps. In December, life retreats indoors out of the cold, and preparations are made for the festivities. Every niche and pillar in the church is decked with holly and ivy; bales of straw are built into a stable for a life-sized holy family, and on Christmas Eve the village will celebrate something much older than itself.

Meanwhile, in the quiet of the damp, deserted market-place, where all the threads of Purbeck life once knotted themselves together between castle and church, the ancient vill seems to compose itself. It is like some-one fallen from grace, whose power and position used to command attention. Now it must rely entirely upon its charms; it cannot afford to tire of popularity, and yet it yearns to retire from the attentions of those who demand to see it. On a winter's day, near the site of the stocks, a model crib thatched with straw stands beside the pump and braves the rain. Such a symbol of new birth might have been placed here before the castle's first stone was laid, and, though frail, promises to survive long after the ruin on the hill has fallen away.

15

OFFENCE AND DEFENCE

SEEN FROM SWYRE HEAD, the western half of the Purbeck range sweeps gracefully from the old castle at Corfe to the ancient fortress of Flower's Barrow above the sea. The elegance of such a long view is beguilingly simple, and deceptive. A walker along the ridgeway is continuously delighted by new land-shapes and landmarks. Though his close view may be crystal clear, unencumbered by mist or heat-haze, he is confounded by the hills' flux and might as well be trying to interpret the configuration of the clouds that mass and fly above his head. Beneath his feet rock-strata lie, layer upon layer, and might be simple to understand if their folds, faults and superficial deposits did not play time-tricks under crop, turf and scrub. The outcroppings of history, successive man-marks densely overlaid even upon the hill-top, are cut and built into the one thin layer of soil between rock and air. The old green road is firm enough, but in one vertiginous step the hiker in history may tread from one millennium into the next. At first sight, man's testament appears both indelible and indecipherable.

The hiker is, practically speaking, trammelled and confined by public rights of way. West Hill is forbidden, but recent cultivation has blazoned its south slope with corn, and a Bronze Age tumulus on its narrow summit, together with Romano-British remains up there, circumscribe a period of considerable Durotrigian occupation. At the south foot of the hill, a deeply-rutted track traverses more ragged country; steep, scrubby slopes, pocked by an old chalk-pit, give on to rough ground with gnarled trees. The roots of an apple orchard and the shafts of wells plumb the history of a recent, vanished homestead.

A gate in the fence that marks the parish boundary lets the track through from Corfe Castle to Church Knowle and up on to Knowle Hill. Other fences graze barrows whose excavation has revealed successive burial customs: a contracted skeleton, with antler, pottery and shale fragments, in a chalk-cut grave; crouched bones in stone cists; cremations, one with a whetstone and one with a bronze dagger, also in cists; and later interments at full length, protected by rough stones, or simply by earth dug from the barrow's ditch. A ditched dyke, which runs across the ridge between the path and the boundary fence, was probably dug in the early Iron Age when the barrow which it abuts was already ancient. Boundary stones, elderly in a modest way, run westwards with the fence that restrains Norden Wood from conquering the summit, and then drop downhill in a line to the clay-scarred territory below. Another sort of stone dots the crest, and south foot, of the down: mere-stones dating from the enclosure of Knowle Hill in 1856. Initials carved on them denote private ownership of the open spaces, for field-fences did not enmesh the turf until World War Two, when sheep were again grazed up here. Where footpaths that run up from Church Knowle and down to East Creech cross the ridgeway, another dyke marks the entrance to a settlement of four and a half acres. Cattle graze here now, but many finds show that the Iron Age economy was also based upon the cow; the outer dykes, behind and at Bare Cross to the west, may be the remains of a cattle fence, rather than a defensive structure. Within the inner banks post-holes mark the site of at least one building, containing Iron Age pottery and evidence of shale-working. Beside a sixty-foot-long mound, probably contemporary with the settlement, I recently came upon signs of the modern shale industry: a seismographic survey control van, perched on the ridge, supervising a line of holes drilled from Furzebrook in the north towards Orchard Hill Farm near Swyre Head. Explosives set off in their depths sent up plumes of dust both sides of the ridge, and miles of cables fed information from sensors that read the rocks' tremors into the van in order to produce maps for oil-geologists to study. Though they delve more deeply, the configuration of the underground deposits that they seek is more easily charted than the human strata that lie upon the surface of the hills.

In the road cutting and chalk-pit at Bare Cross, just south of the westerly Iron Age dyke, a neat line of graves cut into the rock was discovered in 1859. As all the skeletons had belonged to women or young people, and as the arrangement suggested a Roman date, it is tempting to imagine a rout or reprisal raid inflicted by imperious legionaries upon the British of Knowle Hill. Tempting but unwise, for the ordinary far outweighs the extraordinary event. Perhaps they died of food-poisoning while the men were away hunting.

The tarmac road that crosses the hills does a zigzag detour to reduce the gradient, and runs down the fault gap to the north where the tongue of Knowle Hill slots into the groove between Stonehill Down and Ridgeway Hill. Old workings have long dishevelled the turf beside the road, and Cocknowle Quarries supplied marl to the Wareham Cement Works at Ridge. A grassy track that carried a tramway seven hundred feet down the steep slope now faces a much more extensive wound. For, across the road, the face of Stonehill Down has been stripped and plundered along some three hundred yards of its length; an unexpected white cliff in a fold of the hills, whose terraces supply hundreds of tons of road metal every year for clay-pit tracks. Compared to a mere century or so of cement production from chalk, the practice of surfacing wet tracks in this way is a venerable one, but modern earth-moving equipment has so increased the scale and speed of inflicting such scars that, despite English China Clay's relatively modest exploitation of it here, the potential both for profit and the destruction of the landscape are equally obvious. As it is, you can still walk above the quarry cliff and flush flocks of partridge from the scrub, their chestnut plumage glowing orange in the sun, whirring and cackling "it-it-it-it", or silently gliding on down-curved, delta-wings into the cover of Creech Wood and Furlong Coppice.

At the point where Barnston Manor's medieval strip-lynchets stopped stepping up Ridgeway Hill, there are some earthworks more enigmatic than any on Knowle Hill. They are called pillow mounds because that is what they look like, and nothing whatever is known about them. Above, the ridgeway climbs steadily westwards until, two hundred feet higher, it makes a cross-roads with an old route across the chalk. The White Way winds up from the direction of Whiteway Farm, beside disused chalk-pits, crosses our path and runs between improved grassland and arable land to the old chalk-pit and lime kilns this side of Creech Barrow's bulk. Ahead, though, is the boundary stone, crudely inscribed with "K" and "S", for Church Knowle and Steeple, and the path, still climbing, beside a jungle of scrub where, if you stumble through that way, a swallow-hole may take the ground from under you, and where, at about 650 feet, Grange Arch stands up just off the beaten track. It was built about 1740, just north of the hill's spine, on exactly that principle which Neolithic men employed in siting their long barrow on Ailwood Down: it was to be seen from below. When Denis Bond had it erected, its castellated central arch, and two stepped bays at either side topped off with pyramids, dominated he skyline when viewed from Creech Grange, and its two-dimensional grandeur gave the acquisitive eighteenth-century eye the illusion that it mastered all it surveyed. Called an "eye-catcher", it symbolised the catchment area of ambition, with open portals encompassing even the wide sky. From the ridgeway its shell looks inoffensive; its battlements face Grange; its ashlar is carved and scratched with numerous initials, though fresh white stone demonstrates the care that the National Trust take of their folly and its two acres. They try, not altogether successfully, to prevent the old prospect becoming obscured by natural growth, for Great Wood, like Birnam, advances upon it in dense ranks and threatens to overwhelm it.

Beyond, Grange Hill climbs out of the wood, joins the ridgeway, and tarmac replaces turf for a mile and a half westwards. The road is not always open, for it traverses the Royal Army Corps Gunnery Range whose perimeter is marked by well-maintained fences, white gates on roads and tracks, monotonous notices warning of unexploded shells, and flagpoles flying red rags to dare-devil youngsters, who have died quite often enough to lend weight to the army's admonitions. A picnic area is provided for those who want to park their cars and survey the landscape whose wildness is at once preserved and desecrated by those who practise to defend the realm.

A hairpin bend doubles back down the south scarp towards Steeple, passing a small coppice on the way which, with the adjoining field, bears and preserves the name of Hasler. Purbeck comprised two Hundreds: Rowbarrow, or Roughbarrow, whose western boundary followed the Corfe River from Wytch to Corfe, and then the Wicken for a short distance, until it broke away and made for the coast just west of St Aldhelm's Head; and Hasler, or Hasillor, whose western limit was that of Purbeck itself, Luckford Lake. Rowbarrow may mean, literally, line-of-hills; and Hasler suggests, perhaps, hazel shore or bank. Hazlor Hundred Moot met in the parish of Steeple, probably near the spot where the name persists.

The army may bar the ridgeway now, but there are far fewer gates than there used to be. Until after the First World War the journey from Steeple to Tyneham, via West Creech Hill, meant opening and shutting no less than eleven gates, but the motor-car's feud with livestock was ended when miles of fencing were erected, and the era of the open road ended too. Only the names of gates are left. Alms Grove Gate stood, just before the road branches off for Tyneham, at the edge of Alms Grove, a beech wood which is heady and hazy with bluebells in spring. Through it is Tyneham parish, and the boundary runs on the north side of the road until it turns abruptly north, towards Povington Wood, at Maiden's Grave Gate. Nearby, an ancient oak bears in its bark the carved shapes of two coffins, one old and one more recent, which gave it the name of Coffin Tree. With Maiden's Grave, it commemorates the burial of a girl who hung herself in the cowshed at Baltington Farm. Though there is no cross-roads, she was interred as nearly as possible in the no-man's-land between the parishes. Baltington Farm is a ruin. But blood-guiltiness has a way of staining a landscape, and although no-one knows how long ago she committed suicide, the girl's act, if not her name, is still remembered.

Povington Hill, at 625 feet, is the highest point on the hill after Nine Barrow Down and Ridgeway Hill. But here, a fenced-off picnic area and car-park serves the brilliant view. Immediately below is a narrow strip of woodland whose name, Limekiln Plantation, reminds us that lime-burners exploited the chalk there. Under your feet, however, and along the tops from Ridgeway to Rings Hill, is not chalk but a drift deposit of angular flint gravel that was worked for road metal on West Creech Hill. Although glacial ice sheets never extended this far south, the fractured flints in their matrix of crushed chalk suggest that local snow and ice mantled the hills in the Pleistocene period, only to slide and grind their way downwards at the spring thaw.

Early evening is the time to walk up here. Sea air, earth's heat, sky and weather always conjure a different landscape out of the dying light. To the north, the heath darkens, pools glint in the boggy ground of Earl's Kitchen, curlew and snipe quieten, and oblique light throws barrows into relief. Povington's great clay scar is livid and luminous in the setting sun. Furze and heather blossom fades and dies, bringing to mind the Dorset superstition that when they wither they are translated from the darklands up to heaven, the gorse flowers to be transmuted into the golden pave-ments of the celestial city, and the heather, by miraculous alchemy, into gates of amethyst. Scrub casts its shadows on the hill-top despite fairly recent ploughing, but one hundred acres of the north slopes of Povington, Whiteway and Rings Hills are covered with the remains of regular and irregular Celtic fields, the first sometimes imposed upon the even older pattern of the second. These fields, uncultivated since British times, are still delineated in places by lynchets running unbroken for more than five hundred feet, although shell craters pepper much of the landscape.

Southwards, the scarp falls more steeply away to the smooth curve of Tyneham valley, which climbs again, as limestone, and breaks off jaggedly

at Gad Cliff above the sea, or presides, like Tyneham Cap, over the shelves
of Kimmeridge Clay that run eastwards along the coast. In spite of some
grazing livestock, and visitors' cars negotiating the road down to the
village, the whole valley looks unkempt; fields and hedgerows are
ragged, farm buildings are overshadowed and hidden by unlopped
clumps of trees, and whole areas near the cliff are often scorched black.
The place has good reason to look derelict, but the view westwards is
magnificent: the woodland of Tyneham Gwyle and the stream it conceals
run down to the valley's curved rim, where, between the protruding
buttress of Worbarrow Tout and the natural ramparts of Flower's
Barrow, lies a bay, shivered and glistening in the low western sun.

At Lawford Sheard, or Lawfordshare, Gate the tarmac road winds down
around the bulk of Whiteway Hill and on to East Lulworth, but the
ridgeway continues, climbing again to six hundred feet. The view from
there is even more spectacular, and the Rings, the fortifications that guard
the westernmost point of the Purbeck Hills, can be picked out; although
it is only from the road below that the long, ridged profile of the hill-fort
stands out against the sky, and that the drop from Rings Hill to Arish
Mell Gap can be seen. A herd of Friesians crops the turf beside Flower's
Barrow but is powerless against the brakes of gorse that have become
established. When Sir Robert Newburgh of East Lulworth died in 1515,
he left 4,000 sheep on his land, and roughly 400 years later a daring Mr
Bond of Tyneham introduced a Shropshire flock to these hills, instead of
Dorset Horns. Whatever the breed, the grass up here was grazed close and
sweet for centuries.

Beyond East Lulworth, the bulbous, fortress-like residence, now a
ruin, called Lulworth Castle, purchased by the Roman Catholic Weld
family in 1641, still dominates the park where they have recently completed a new pseudo-Georgian house. The castle, finally burnt to a shell
in 1929, was seized by Parliament during the Civil War and stripped of
its lead and iron. In the year of the plague, Charles II visited it, accompanied by the Dukes of York and Monmouth. Dinner-services of gold
and silver, patriotically inscribed, greeted George III and his family, and
in 1786 Thomas Weld was given leave to build a Roman Catholic chapel
in his grounds, as long as it did not look like one—the first in England
since the Reformation. Even so, Charles X who as a refugee from the
Revolution in France, should have felt at home there, exclaimed on first
sighting the castle, "Voilà, la Bastille!"

Between an overgrown hole, like a giant crater, in the chalk, and

Flower's Barrow itself, a ditched bank crosses the path and perhaps once barred it. The parish boundary bisects this dyke so that half of it lies in Tyneham and half in East Lulworth, and a boundary stone is fixed, apparently precariously, in the landslip halfway down the cliff, below the south-eastern ramparts of the fort. Early Iron Age men heaped up a ring of earth on the hill-top and probably topped it with a wooden palisade; later in the same era a second line of defence was added, outside the original bank to the east and west, but inside it to the north because the scarp there is so steep. Four hundred feet below, pigs root around Monastery Farm, which Thomas Weld built as a refuge for French Trappists. The southern defence of Flower's Barrow is even surer now, for more than a third of the fortress appears to have fallen down into Worbarrow Bay, banks and ditches stop abruptly at the cliff edge, and a third of what remains has slipped twelve feet or so. The whole earthwork still covers more than fifteen acres, six of them within the inner enclosure, and about a dozen levelled platforms have been identified as the sites of huts or work-places. A refuse pit gave up fragments of bone, slingstones and sherds of Iron Age pottery, while in the nineteenth century the skeleton of a giant is said to have been dug up from the inner rampart.

Before the cliff-falls, before centuries of exposure to rough weather and the hooves of countless sheep, Flower's Barrow's marvellously rounded and dramatically curtailed contours must have presented an even steeper, more rugged challenge to an enemy. It may have been one of the twenty strongholds that the future Emperor Vespasian's Second Augustan Legion had to fight so hard to take, in order to subdue the Durotriges, whose final defeat was suffered at Maiden Castle near Dorchester. Now the challenge is an imaginative one: to see the palisaded, chalk-white defences, the small fields of growing spelt blowing in the wind on the slopes of Rings Hill, and men and animals busy about the settlement within the walls. Time, more than the sea, has robbed us of the place. It is half-lost, half-real, a place of illusions.

Rings Hill resounded with the marching of militia keeping pace, along the coast, with the Armada. In 1678, when Titus Oates was fomenting the Popish Plot scandals, Captain John Lawrence of Grange, his brother, four clay-cutters and more than a hundred heathland inhabitants, saw an army of thousands marching, with military commotion, from Flower's Barrow over Grange Hill. They rushed to Wareham to sound the alarm, all craft were drawn across the Frome, the bridge was barricaded, and three hundred militia were mobilised. John and his brother rode post to

London to break the news, on oath, before the Council. But oaths are worthless in the face of a phantom army, and only the Lawrences' known loyalty saved them from disgrace. A farm-worker alerted Wareham for the same reason early in the last century; and in this one, army officers have sworn that they, too, have seen the forms of a Roman legion and heard the thud of hooves, the tramp of feet and the clatter of arms as it advanced along Bindon Hill, down to Arish Mell Gap, and up Rings Hill to the camp within the old earthwork. On those nights, it is said that rabbit and fox lie low, and though a man may dare to reconnoitre, his dog will not.

Arish Mell is a magical name for the small bay that marks the western bound of Purbeck Island. Although the area is occupied by a quite unghostly army whose Centurions are tanks that pound the hills, Flower's Barrow is a magical place. There, where the chalk ridgeway steps off into the sea, is a man-made no-man's-land whose ramparts shelter the harebells, thyme, viper's bugloss and ploughman's spikenard that justify its ancient name of Florus' Byrig.

PART FOUR

PLOUGH

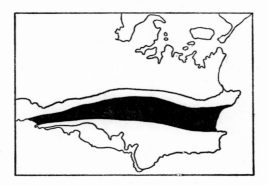

The island's lap: submissive soils,
plush copse, nesh grass and furrows' grain
each cropped in its own season; ordered
between deep hedgerows, Domesday's skein
unravelling between the hills.

Unharnessed from their mill-races,
dwarf streams that once carved clays and quartz
drain inwards to the island's heart;
and weed-grown railway ballast skirts
the common's horse-grazed calluses.

The summer strikes its garish tents,
retires in tints of Swanage brick;
sea-port whose sweated stones resort
to fun, and winter in the wake
of fake arcadian amusements.

But wildfire is the west's weather;
guns' thunder above ancient tillage.
Nature corrupts the laid-out dead,
roots and vermin mine the village,
carrion stoop to the vole's crater.

16

COLONISTS, EVACUEES

EARLY ONE MORNING I stood on the ramparts of Flower's Barrow. Not even sea-birds disturbed the air beneath my feet. The guns of East Lulworth were as silent as the rusting hulks of target-tanks behind Bindon Hill. The crumbling concrete of a war-time pill-box seemed less built than disinterred by a fall of the fort's flank. But Worbarrow Bay below harboured the neat grey bulk of a vessel whose helicopter deck's white bullseye was fixed on the vacant sky. Beyond it, Worbarrow Tout rose steeply from deep waters, slab upon slab of the Purbeck beds propped against Portland Stone. This rocky mound jutting into the sea, joined to the mainland by a narrow neck, is the last limestone in Purbeck. Banks and ditches seem to have fortified it at one time, and a circular earthwork on its summit was once adapted for a battery, and as a coastguard look-out, but any remains were destroyed in the last war. As I watched from my look-out, the hum of ship's engines broke the spell of the place, and she went slowly astern out of the bay, went hard to port and steamed westwards for the Isle of Portland, leaving her wake to lap against the deserted pebble beach.

The view from water-level, as you float in the bay's embrace, is a panorama spanning the upper Jurassic and all the Cretaceous strata. From Cow Corner, beneath Rings Hill, the pebbles shrink in size to shingle that meets the reddish marble outcrop at the foot of the Tout, while towering white chalk and stubborn grey stone are linked by vivid clays and sands from which the sea has taken a long, lazy bite. Landslips below Flower's Barrow have masked the strata of Gault and Greensand and mixed a geological cocktail of greens and greys mixed with pinks, ochres and darker loams. The path from the fort descends steeply on to Wealden Clays and sands whose alternating oranges, reds, purples, greys, yellows and blacks are bisected by a seam of coarse quartz grit. Cottages on the cliff-top and at Worbarrow itself, where the track from Tyneham meets the bay, are all in ruins: overgrown footings, or roofless half-walled shells whose hearths are colonised by weeds. Garden plants gone to seed and roses rambling over derelict walls are the only evidence of how recently they were inhabited. The homes of Millers, Minterns and Tizzards, and coastguards' cottages will soon be little more than the Iron Age remains on the cliff and at the mouth of Tyneham Gwyle. We know that Kimmeridge shale was worked here in the Roman period, that marble was probably dug and brine boiled, but there are only memories of the fishermen who so recently set their nets for mackerel as soon as "Balaam and Balaak" was read in church, or put out lobster pots woven from withies in the winter months. Coastguard and boatman no longer watch out for ships or shoals, or wage unofficial war over the flotsam beached along the bay.

The watchers now are Army Range Wardens, and their eyes are focused inland. They patrol their shell-ridden preserves, to ensure that hikers and bathers keep to prescribed paths bordered with red and white notices repeating ad nauseam the warning, "Danger. Keep Out. There are bombs and unexploded shells inside. They can kill you." Both beach and cliff-top are cleared before the Range is opened to the public, as is the gravel track that runs up to Tyneham Farm beside the gwyle. There, out of bounds, buried in the thicket of stunted oak and hazel, tangled ivy and clematis, fallen fungus-infested timber, hartstongue and fern, the little Tyneham stream threads a way down the valley. Its elvers baited many a hook, and the gwyle's writh, or brushwood, baited cottage fires. Pre-war Tyneham woodsmen would weep to see the valley now: tree-stumps or mocks, once coppiced in strict rotation, are all grown to waste, timber stands are over-ripe for felling and replanting, and the ornamental trees around Tyneham House are left untended. Arable and pasture have reverted to rowaty grass and scrub, though ponies, sheep and cattle are still turned out here by arrangement with the military. Badgers, never victimised by Purbeck farmers, give birth and bury their dead within their sinuous, subterranean strongholds, but now carry the threat of bovine tuberculosis, which makes grazing cattle here a risky business. The whole cultured valley has assumed the complexion of moorland. It is as if a once-civilised face has, through neglect and degradation, been forced into a grimace of wildness.

Baltington, the farm nearest the bay, stares from its window-sockets across the valley. Its buildings are resigned to the vegetation it once regimented, its hedgerows invade the fields they guarded. But Baltington was already old when the Conqueror's inventory was compiled; Celtic fields, of which traces persist, surrounded not just a farm, but a settlement. The Domesday Survey records four Tynehams, known in the thirteenth century by their present names of Baltington, Tyneham, North Egliston and South Egliston. By that time, East Tyneham, on the site of the House, was a fifth unit, distinguished from the older Church Tyneham. Centuries of occupation and husbandry have made their mark in each of the old manors; strip-fields and lynchets, often neatly superimposed on Celtic fields, cover two hundred acres; broad-rig ploughing has cut across field banks, while eighteenth-century narrow-rig, mostly on higher ground, marks the expansion of arable land at that period. Raised or hollowed tracks run between closes to the south of Baltington, Tyneham and North Egliston, with Chapel Close at the latter said to be the site of St Margaret's Chapel, showing that all three were hamlets supporting a considerable population.

The track from the bay turns left at Tyneham Farm, across the bridge, to Tyneham village; a bunny carries the stream underneath, and the gwyle continues towards Tyneham House and Great Wood. The house is inaccessible now, hidden amongst trees that once preserved its elegant privacy, but which now cover its shame. War-time vandalism by the WAAF and the RAF started a work completed by neglect and demolition. The Conqueror's half-brother, Robert of Mortain, held the manor. Thomas Bardolfe gave it into Russell hands, where it remained for 150 years; they built the fourteenth-century, timber-trussed hall which formed the south-west wing of the house until its evacuation. It passed, by marriage, to the Chykes who provided MPs for Wareham borough for many years; and, in 1532, to John Williams of Herringston, who divided the old hall into two floors, added the main gabled east range and the north-west wing, both of fine ashlar. Only the old part of the building was worthy of Celia Fiennes' attention; writing in about 1608, she says, "at Tyneham there is a pretty large house but very old timber built, there I eate the best lobsters and crabs being boyled in the sea water and scarce cold, very large and sweet". The house was never sold again, and through the female line came into the Bond family, who retained it until 1952.

During the war, more than half of Purbeck was taken over by the military and closed to the public. In 1943, Tyneham parish was requisitioned and 225 people were evacuated from 102 properties. The War Department stated that when they had no further use for it, the inhabitants would have every right to return, and a notice was planted in the village to this effect. It was plucked up at the end of the war and the promise was never kept. Tyneham's population, or those who survived the uprooting, are exiles for ever. Visitors' cars are permitted to park on the undulating site of its medieval closes, before walking the mile to Worbarrow Bay.

Bones and samian ware of the Roman period were found in the diverted stream-bed at the head of the gwyle, and seven sets of bones, a separate skull and a black, unbaked Iron Age vessel were found in the sandy barrow, called the Mount, near the Rectory. The Rectory burnt down in 1966, but the village's Edwardian telephone kiosk, in classical white concrete, which the rector of the twenties so heartily abhorred, still stands. Houses around the church, suffocated by trees, gape from behind barbed wire and exhale a smell of rot; lichens, mosses, ferns and liverworts thrive on their stone tiles, or what is left of them, and a notice exhorts us, "The buildings are dangerous. Keep Out". Until recently, the churchyard too was out of bounds, and the army advertised bombs and shells among the Tyneham dead.

The medieval church of St Mary was restored in 1744 and augmented in the last century. When the fourteenth-century south porch was dismantled and reassembled at the west end, burial cists of Kimmeridge shale slabs were found at its foundations. Now that the shutters which blinded the church have been removed, the elaborate Williams memorial can be glimpsed in the north transept and, less predictably, a black marble tablet of 1769, within a freestone moulding, erected to the memory of Elizabeth Tarrant, "servant to Mrs Bond of Tyneham, in which station she continued 34 yeares". Outside, near the chancel's east wall, a large stone commemorates Nathaniel Bond's coachman. Bond headstones, including infant burials marked only by initials, share the earth along with all the other Tyneham and Worbarrow names, and with a line of graves under the chancel wall with no names at all. These belong to unknown seamen who "came ashore", who are hardly more lost to their relatives now than native bones. The dead, unlike the living, cannot be dispossessed.

Representations were made to the War Department in January 1945 by Wareham and Purbeck Rural District Council. They were concerned at the number of evacuees still in temporary billets, and though they thought that Studland would be handed back, they expressed grave doubts about the Tyneham area. They feared that its one-time inhabitants would "remain exiles to the end of their days from their native place and their Parish Church and Churchyard", and would therefore suffer a "worse fate than blitzed people in towns who can at least return to rebuilt or new houses". They quoted NFU estimates that 419,750 gallons of milk were lost annually, and that 1,100 head of cattle, hundreds of sheep, scores of pigs and thousands of poultry had had to be sold at the time of the evacuation. Their eyes were also fixed upon the future of the tourist trade: "The Isle of Purbeck is easily accessible to centres of population and it is anticipated that, if it remains open to the public, visitors to it will still greatly increase, especially having regard to the advent of universal holidays with pay." How right they were. But it was not until 1974 that Nugent's Defence Lands Committee initiated the action that has led to the Lulworth Range Walks being opened. In 1976, work began to make the buildings of the Tyneham valley safe, a combination of demolition and restoration aimed at creating a sound, orderly set of ruins. In 1977, the army leased the church for twenty-one years, for use as a museum. Time and their own public relations have so blunted the military conscience that they are now proud to offer the week-end and holiday-time visitor a wilderness protected, as they say, from the ravages of human occupation.

They are right when they assert that wildlife thrives, despite the tens of thousands of armour-piercing, high-explosive and phosphorous smoke anti-tank shells that rend the air each year, and shake the ground for miles around; some areas are scored with track-marks, but there is no ploughing and no pesticides. Those who mourn Tyneham, and not everyone who lived there wants to return, must not imagine that some valley idyll, some picture of unblemished village life, some ideal community would have persisted unchanged. The Bonds might have resisted the commercial temptations of the tourist trade, and contained its garish trappings, as most other Purbeck landlords have done, but the costs of maintaining an estate and the mechanisation of agriculture would have precipitated the same migrations, the same re-colonisation by outsiders, and the same fraying of the fabric of life that other rural communities have suffered. Wareham merchants would long since have given up the trek over the hill to buy Worbarrow fishermen's catch, and many memories enshrined in the earth's shape would have been obliterated by the plough. In the spring following the battle of the Somme, the churned and blood-fed earth brought forth its agrimony, saffron, self-heal, fumitory, traveller's joy, rest harrow, gipsywort and nightshade once again. Though its Second War trauma was not so bloody, Tyneham's ground has blossomed with a wild harvest. But here there is no sense of victory or resurrection.

To walk its trammelled paths between the wire is to traverse no-man's-land during a brief cease-fire. The valley's beauty gives an added edge to

its sense of desolation. When the beach and village are populous with
tourists it is more painfully clear that no-one is at home, that everybody is
a stranger. On a fine day sometimes, suddenly, the infamous Purbeck
sea-mist sweeps up from Worbarrow between the chalk and limestone
hills to chill the air and steal its fragrance, as befits a hant, or haunted place.
The battle for Tyneham's future is still waged, though hopes were lately
dashed by Nugent, and its campaigners fight to harass the army into
sounding the retreat. But, for those who lived here, the war is lost; it was
lost to a perfidious army in 1945. For what is defeat to a man, if it is not
the enforced loss of home, of territory, and of his history.

17

FROM STEEPLE TOWER

THE CHURCH OF St Michael and All Angels at Steeple squats in the valley, on rising ground, as befits its dedication, two miles east of Tyneham. Perhaps it took over a sacred site of the old religion, and symbolised the Christian exorcism of Durotrigian tribal gods. The present nave is of Norman foundation, with additions and restoration of almost every century since. Its walls of random and squared rubble, roughly coursed stone and finished ashlar stand, almost lost, up a little lane off the Tyneham to Church Knowle road, with Manor Farm, Steeple Manor House, a nineteenth-century rectory and a cluster of trees. Though it presides over so little, and despite its out-of-the-way site, it stands at the cross-roads of history in the valley; its fabric represents and bears the marks of the successive claims that were made upon it; the prospect it commands makes it the involuntary crux for much that passed away or bore issue under its eye.

After absorbing the contents of the church it is good to climb the dark, narrow spiral stair that ascends the tower in a turret at its corner. This dates from the early sixteenth century, but older, rougher stonework from an earlier tower can be seen in the ringing chamber. Soft, honeyed light filters through slats in the chamber above and casts the great bell that hangs there into dark relief. The huge beam from which it depends was salvaged from a seventeenth-century bell-frame which was unmanned by death-watch beetle. The bell must have been installed when the tower was first finished, and is inscribed SANCTA ANNA ORA PRO NOBIS, while its post-Reformation fellows, by Anthony Bond 1634, have been relegated to the west end of the nave. There, the bells of St Mary's, Tyneham, have joined them; one a sanctus bell of about 1500 inscribed IN NOMINE DOMINE.

The tumults of the Reformation have left little visible mark upon the fabric of St Michael's. There is no doubt that the hanging bell not only summoned men and women to the Latin mass, but also brooded, as they

did, over the new Great Bible in the vulgar tongue set up in the nave
following the injunctions of the 1530s and '40s. We do not know how
long votive candles flickered here before they were extinguished, only to
be re-kindled with a vengeance in Mary's reign. In 1573, new communion
plate was ordered from the silversmith Lawrence Stratford of Dorchester,
identical to that of Church Knowle and Tyneham, to the same pattern as
the larger vessels of Lady St Mary's, Wareham. On a stand paten of 1716
the arms of Bond of Grange impale those of Williams of Tyneham,
prefiguring a later ecclesiastical union: the shot-gun, or Centurion tank,
marriage that was to be forced upon the twin livings.

The vestry in the south transept is furnished with a cupboard that was
the case for Tyneham church's barrel organ, together with the mechanism
from the Steeple barrel organ that used to pipe and throb as the metrical
psalms were ground out of it. After about 1890 the barrel mechanisms
were replaced with keyboards, and in 1943 Tyneham's organ came to
Steeple, and Steeple's was rebuilt in St Peter's, Church Knowle, as part of
the present organ. Tyneham's Jacobean pulpit is now occupied by the
army chaplain at Lulworth camp, but the simplest memorials to the
abandoned St Mary's lie in Steeple's pews: hymnbooks, some with the
name of Bond inside their covers, and others bearing the legend
"Tyneham Church. 1930. Not to be taken away".

It is just possible to squeeze through the tiny turret hatch that opens on
to the roof of the tower. Over the western parapet is the unkempt,
uninhabited, occupied valley. Invisible in the stream valley to the south,
Steeple brook flows from Tyneham, reinforced by little tributaries from
North Egliston and Lutton. An abandoned track runs past those settlements and joins the Creech Hill to Steeple road. Lutton manor, one of
four in Steeple parish, had belonged to the Abbey of Bec; but after
Henry VI deprived alien orders of their tenures in England the Bond
family acquired it in 1431. Now a deserted farm, it was a medieval hamlet
whose buildings covered at least five acres. By the seventeenth century
Steeple village had been largely taken over by the farm, but the place
where it sank out of sight is marked by the ripples of hollow-ways, banks
and house-sites around the church, with a likely windmill mound to the
south-west. In 1540, after the Dissolution, Sir Oliver Lawrence bought
Creech Grange, due north across the chalk ridge, and Steeple. In St
Michael's Church the Lawrences' *argenta cross ragulé gules* quarters the
argent two bars and in chief three mullets gules, or stars and stripes, of the
Washingtons, for the two families intermarried in the fourteenth century.

John Washington later settled in Virginia and his great-grandson George became first President of the United States. It is an attractive notion that he democratised the noble arms from the old country by giving them to the people as the Union flag. The Lawrences erected the wagon, or barrel vault, roof of the nave, and its panels are punctuated by their shield-of-arms, while the corbels in the chancel bear Bond shields for, though the chancel was replaced in the last century, Bonds replaced Lawrences as lords of the manor in 1686.

Steeple Manor House had already been sold to the Clavells in 1567. Seen from the church tower, it is an elegant, unassuming, very private residence with small windows, whose building started in Elizabeth's reign and spanned the years of reaction, regicide, commonwealth, restoration and revolution. There are modern additions, but the north-west front bears the Clavell crest, the initials $R^C R$, for Roger and Ruth Clavell, and the date 1698. If Wareham and Stoborough were rife with radical dissent, this parish seems to have stood for moderation. William Bolde became rector of Tyneham in 1682 and preached and printed a "Plea for Toleration against Dissenters" which did not endear him to James II, and for which he was fined and imprisoned for a time in 1685. Steeple and Tyneham livings were united in 1721 and Bolde held both until his death. Over the hill, the south front of Creech Grange, added in 1738, has a doorway surmounted by a bust of William III. When the chapel-of-ease of St John the Evangelist there was consecrated in 1859, the unfortunate curate of Steeple had to tramp his way over the hill in all weathers to celebrate communion for the Bond family, and he is said to have spent all one summer cutting steps up the ridgeway's flank to make his winter progress a little easier.

If you turn your back on the desolate valley and look across the eastern parapet, vivid with lichens, the scene changes dramatically. Chalk downs to the north and limestone downs to the south frame the same Wealden Clays, but the prospect is one of nurture rather than neglect. Corn-fields and cattle pasture pattern the undulating floor with cadences of emerald and gold, linked to the army's territory by dark fragments of woodland and copse, descendants of the thick forest hacked down by our distant ancestors in the struggle to cultivate the valley and make its shelter habitable. Their names comprise a litany: Lutton Withy Bed, Hasler, Ash Coppice, Thornhill Coppice, Steeple Leaze Wood, Pole Coppice, Horse Coppice, North Withy Bed, Blackmanston Withy Bed, Alder Bed, Beach Coppice, Higher and Lower Withy Beds, Whiteway Withy

Bed, Yellow Withy Bed, Horseground Coppice, Hop Yard and Madgrove. At Blackmanston, either side of the Corfe River at the foot of the hill called Devil's Staircase, are traces of the third Domesday settlement in the parish, where rough and worked limestone footings have been unearthed. The Elizabethan manor house, now Blackmanston Farm, has spawned modern barns with corrugated roofs, while beyond Hyde Cottage, Hurpston, Domesday's Herpere, is now a Georgian ruin among medieval remains.

William Bond of Blackmanston built the south transept of the church, probably as a family pew. He and his were to outface the Lawrences of Creech, who sat in the north transept. He did not live to see the turmoil of the seventeenth century, or the execution of his aged grand-daughter, Dame Alice Lisle, at the hands of Judge Jeffreys. The first victim of the Bloody Assize, she was accused of concealing John Hicks, a dissenting minister, in her house at Moyles Court near Ringwood, convicted, and sentenced to be burnt. Jeffreys allowed her to petition King James, who gracefully commuted the sentence to one of beheading. By that time the Clavells had bought Blackmanston, and though Steeple Manor has been sold several times, the farm's landlord is a Clavell descendant to this day. The family claimed their place in Steeple Church as the Lawrences and Bonds had done; a tomb in the floor of the chancel which was barely legible at the turn of the century, and quite indecipherable now.

The north wall holds a medieval coffin lid of Purbeck marble, with a trefoiled cross carved in relief. It is less than two feet long, and may be the resting-place of a cherished, but anonymous infant, or one of a number of heart burials in Purbeck. Facing it is a memorial which unwittingly represents a change in the fortunes of the island; a slate tablet of 1641, framed by the then fashionable alabaster, which superseded the more expensive Purbeck marble, richly carved with cherubs' and lions' heads, scrolls and doves. There is nothing cheap about the sentiments recorded within it by William Chaldecott. The youngest son commemorated his parents thus: "The righteous shall be in everlasting remembrance. Psalm 112:6. In this chancel under a marble stone doe lie the bodies of Francis Chaldecott Esq & Edith his wife younger daughter and coheire of William Chaldecott of Quarlston in Dorset who were liberall constant housekeepers, bountifull relievers of the the poor, careful breeders of theire children in piety and virtue, diligent devout comers to the church though it were very painful unto them in their later times by means of age & other infirmity. 53 year & upwards they lovingly lived in chaste wedlocke

& had issue 15 children whereof 3 sons & 7 daughters came to mature age & were most of them in the lifetimes of theire parents matched into antient families of worship, most of them having fayre issues. Thus having lived to see their children to ye 3rd generation they meekely dyed in ye fear & favor of their God, He on Thursday ye 19 of May 1636 aged 85 She on Thursday ye 23 of August 1638 aged 75."

This is the kind of memorial that a visitor might expect to find in such a church; but after discovering something of Steeple's history, after watching the swell of earlier tides still breaking around the foot of the tower, after hearing within the church's walls the echoes of rival claims, both spiritual and temporal, it comes as a shock to read those words. Imbued as they are with peace and joyful stoicism, they epitomise the virtues of rural life which a fond son chose to record: deliciously, they feed our nostalgic appetites. But they are also true, as true as the changing values which surround them, and which they throw into relief.

Whiteways, the gentlefolks' manor, was soon to be taken over by a tenant farmer. This was to be the natural fate of many of the demesnes in the valley. Others had shrunk almost to nothing at the time of the Great Mortality and through migration to the towns. Some later landlords let leases fall in to be rid of unwanted tenants. Memorials to the manner of life, to the peaceful or ignoble deaths of the parish's inhabitants lie without as well as within consecrated ground. As grass grows over everyman's grave-mound in the churchyard, so it thrives on the bones of his house. As hollow-ways become overgrown and closes rank with weeds, so the ligaments and sinews that knitted the life of this populous valley together have fallen away.

Long-lived churches remain to tell the tale, though the living of Steeple, under Bond patronage, merged with Tyneham in 1721, and has more recently been united with that of Church Knowle and Kimmeridge, under the incumbency of the rector of Church Knowle whose patron is Major Mansel of Smedmore, heir to the Clavell estate. The view eastwards from Steeple tower is rich and various, but the triangle of green before the church is emptier than it was. Despite the well-stocked garden and mature trees of the Rectory nearby, the place is pervaded by a sense of vacancy, of memories fossilised in the church's stone or locked irrevocably underground. It demands that the imagination should re-populate it, should flesh out the ghosts which haunt the hamlet. That we can choose to do it as we will is history's misfortune, but represents a grain of future hope.

18

MANORS AND CUSTOMS

ONE DAY, WHEN the Steeple to Church Knowle road was buzzing, as much as it ever does, with summer traffic, I decided to make my pilgrimage down into the deserted valley bottom, to the Steeple brook, and across it to the Harp Stone which stands just north of Hurpston Coppice, even more lost than Rempstone stone circle. The public right-of-way leaves the road and passes between the modern Whiteway Farm and the medieval settlement remains—house platforms, a terraced track and banked-and-ditched parish boundary—in the field immediately to the west of it. Whiteway was owned, with East Orchard, by the Abbess of Shaftesbury. The modern farmhouse dates from about 1600 and, with the slightly later dairy-house, was never built for beauty, though their pedigree is betrayed by the hollow-chamfered stonework around windows and doors, and in the practical relieving arches of rubble that take the strain above many of them. A four-square granary of about 1700, with its pyramidal roof, a barn, a byre, and cottages of the eighteenth century add their bulks to the cluster of grey stone near the pond.

When William Hatchard, yeoman farmer, died intestate in July 1704, twenty-six acres of barley, oats and beans, and fourteen acres of wheat stood in his fields waiting for harvest. His wheat mow, waggon and ploughtacklin stood idle. Sixty bushels of oats were stored in the granary, and eighteen hundred of cheese, probably blue vinney made from skim, of the pale sort of cheese ironically called Double Dorset, matured in the dairy-house loft. Seven swine, who turned skim into pork, rooted in the yard, three yoke of oxen stood in their stalls, five horses and colts, twenty-six cows and two bulls grazed leaze and fallow, and three hundred sheep, which had yielded their wool at the shearing, of which eighteen waits remained unsold, dotted pasture and downland.

Now, later buildings, outhouses, animal houses and coops add to the apparent confusion that has grown up among thistles and rusting machinery around the old manor house. A squad of jealous geese, whose green droppings made the going treacherous, massed themselves, raised ramrod necks and opened garish beaks to hiss defiance; but they retreated in disgruntled disarray with no trace of discretion, amid cackles and the beating of wide wings to compensate for their lack of valour. I advanced to find that the gap where the public path should pass through the fence had been wired across. I climbed through, but only to find that in the next gateway, at the boundary bank, the way was more thoroughly guarded; attended by his cows, a massive Hereford bull stood his ground. It was my turn to retreat, with the utmost discretion, and eyes that watched from within the farmhouse, alerted by their white-feathered watchdogs, must have smiled to see me making back towards the road with the high-pitched blearing of the bull and the mocking scritching of geese in my ears. The Harp Stone would have to wait.

Barnston, lying below Bare Cross and Cocknowle, is the next Domesday settlement along the road. The manor house looks out over its stone-banked lawn from leaded windows in a magnificent Elizabethan bay. Farm buildings to the east are later additions, in use until recently. Today, goats and domestic animals are the only livestock, and the eighteenth-century barn across the courtyard has, in recent years, been the setting for the summer theatre season. Its great doors open on to a raked stone floor, the auditorium for plays, concerts, dance and one-man shows. Exhibitions are mounted in the house, and food is served there in the intervals of shows. Mrs Brinsley Sheridan was one of the ladies responsible for the supper when Richard Brinsley Sheridan's play *The Critic* was performed in 1976. It is a brave venture, to import professional theatre into the heart of Purbeck, in the hope of encouraging, and at the risk of outraging, local support; but it is a far cry from the amateur shows and concerts that were put on in, for instance, Tyneham's schoolroom or village hall.

Since the demise of its farming life, plaster rendering has been removed from Barnston's walls, and some internal partitions have been taken down, so that the house looks almost as it did in the time of John Clavell. With his brother, William Clavell of Smedmore, John was more than ready to deal with pirates such as Clinton Atkinson. His sources of income may have been dubious, but his expenditure on the remodelling of his house was impeccably employed. The original Hall was built in the thirteenth century, probably by the d'Estoke family whose knightly effigies of the

period recline in the chancel of Lady St Mary's, Wareham. Though a
first floor with windows under the eaves was inserted in the sixteenth
century, the Hall's collar-beam roof was still visible until the Second
World War, overlaid with ancient soot from the fire that had burned in
the middle of the Hall floor. The great chimney-stack which replaced it
was built against the south wall in the fifteenth century. Though its bay
window is Tudor, the Solar Wing is of the same age as the Hall; on the
first floor, reached by a later spiral staircase and flanked by stone window-
seats, is the solar window. It is of two trefoiled lancets, and hinge-pins
and bolt-holes that once fixed the shutters survive inside the glass. In the
sunlight, the pale honey of the house's walls, pierced with window-
openings large and small, its stone-tiled roof, stacks and huge east buttress,
are warm and welcoming. Delicate details everywhere seduce the eye;
its bone structure is craggy, but its features are refined and sensitive.

Across the road from what was the demesne farm, terraced remnants
of Barnston settlement spread dying ripples over two acres on the east-
facing slope. In Edward the Confessor's reign the manor was Bern's tun,
or enclosure, one of about fifty estates of the time whose boundaries are
still preserved in almost unbroken banks and hedges today. It is said that
it was with these parcels of land, firmly founded on the British pattern,
that the Saxon king Cenwalh, successor to Cynegils, rewarded his
veteran thanes when they finally entered Purbeck, fifty years after
Cynegils started his advance into Devon. Four hundred years later,
William the Conqueror granted estates, in his turn, for services rendered,
and Walter de Clavill was Bernston's tenant-in-chief, that is, he held it
directly from the king. In 1086 it was a forty-shilling manor with eleven
cattle and fifty-seven sheep, but by John Clavell's time it had come a long
way. It comprised six messuages, two hundred acres of arable, three
hundred of meadow, one hundred of pasture, forty of woodland and
three hundred of heathland, with the right to graze four hundred and ten
sheep in East Creech.

The Clavell floor-tomb in St Michael's, Steeple, has been worn to
oblivion, but John Clavell left a magnificent memorial to himself in
St Peter's, Church Knowle; possibly the more magnificent for having
been commissioned and executed nearly forty years before his death.
Barnston was known also as Cnolle, while the village and church made
up the manor of Glole, and numbered among its owners Robert de
Tybovill, the Mortimers, Henry VIII's three Katherines, Sir Oliver
Lawrence and William Clavell of Smedmore. The Conqueror had

honoured Roger de Belmont with it, and he had inherited the only resident priest mentioned in the Domesday returns for Purbeck. St Peter's, on its knoll, is mainly of the thirteenth and fourteenth centuries, and was perfectly cruciform until the north aisle was added in the last century. A stone mural screen with pointed, painted arches divides chancel from nave. Coffin lids lie in the south transept, together with a medieval altar slab salvaged from the north aisle floor; John le Frank of East Creech was granted arable land in Church Knowle in return for providing two wax tapers for the altar; his deed, written in French, is dated 1558, the last year of Mary's reign during which the mass, the altar and the Latin liturgy had been reinstated and the English Bible suppressed. In the same year, John Clavell gave his chaplain an extra twenty shillings a year to say Jesus Mass every Monday in the north aisle for himself and his friends departed. Above a richly-carved altar tomb there, sheltered by an intricate soffit and canopy of white Purbeck stone, the brass of the kneeling knight is flanked by those of his two wives, Myllicent and Susan. How long the family chantries continued and when the stone altar was hidden in the paving, or the holy water stoup, now restored, was buried in the stonework of the porch, we do not know.

Just as the apparently timeless fabric of churches has weathered a turbulent past, so the fabric of fields may appear seamless when, in fact, it conceals the rents and patches that accrue from centuries of changing ownership and use. A history of husbandry is betrayed by groundswell not yet ploughed out, and by names preserved only on old maps and in the memory. Two fields that flank the road from Barnston cross-roads to Puddle Mill, both called Row Barrow, are memorials of Rowbarrow Hundred that covered half Purbeck, sister to Hasler in Steeple. "There appertayneth to the Castle of Corffe 2 lawdayes yearly to be kept at the castle gate, called the oute lawdayes, being of the nature of a wood courte, or swannymote courte, the one kept at the ffeast of Saint Michaell the Archangel, the other at the ffeast of the Annunciation of our Ladye, whereunto doth appear all the freeholders of the island, and all the tithenge men of all the 2 hundreds of Roughbarrow and Hasillor . . ." This, from a sixteenth-century manuscript attributed to Sir Christopher Hatton, demonstrates the persistence of Saxon custom time out of mind. A tithingman, originally the representative of a group of ten who stood security for one another, in Norman times became a deputy-constable appointed by the Courts Leet or, later, by the Vestries.

EP

At the manor or parish level, reeves of villein status co-ordinated the agricultural work of their fellows. The coppices and withy beds were supervised by the hayward who allowed housebote for building and haybote for fencing; oak supplied the cooper who made barrels bound with hazel or iron for all kinds of liquor, while alder was employed for the dry-coopering of grain and feed-bins. Bent birchwood was formed into corn measures, and the manufacture of dairy pails and churns was known as white-coopering. In the 1270s both William de Clavill and the Abbess of Shaftesbury brought actions against Elyas de Rabayne, constable of Corfe, for misappropriating oaks, ashes, maples, and thorns for his own use rather than for the works of the castle. The thirteenth-century vandal was amerced for damaging two hundred acres of the Abbess's woods at Kingston. Cowleazes and horsegrounds, permanent downland and temporary valley sheep-pasture were managed by the hayward or hedge-looker, whose moveable fencing provided folds and driftways on waste, fallow and stubble, according to the season. Champions were open fields, while Shotts Meade and Farlands, from furlongs, signified their division into shotts and strips stinted among the inhabitants of the manor. Lanty, from Lanchard or lynchet, refers to the field-banks by which such holdings were divided.

The field-master, sometimes synonymous with the hayward, was set over the open-field system and oversaw its rotation: the breaking up of fallow with beetle and maul between Lammas and Hallowmans, the sowing of barley between Hook tide and Pentecost, oats between the Feast of Purification and Easter, beans on St Valentine's Day and potatoes on Good Friday, when the Paschal moon was waxing. Herdsmen often had their land cultivated for them, or were paid in kind. Peas Plot, Oate Meade, Hay Moor, Orchard and Vineyards are self-explanatory titles. Foul Field and Jack-me-lads or Noman's land were more or less useless, while wet ground was known by such names as Sedgeups and Withy Lakes. Dry or Coath Plot provoked sickness, or cothe, in livestock. Inhooks near Bradle was fenced in during the fallow year, while the long history of permanent enclosure, from the Dissolution of the Monasteries onwards, is reflected in Common Closes, New Close, Crab Close, Egg Close, Crate Meades and Oakey Close, along with fields bearing the names of farms or persons, such as Weston's Cowleaze or Freddie's.

At the time of the Great Mortality, stock died and crops rotted in the fields, but it was labour shortage which strained the fabric of feudal social life to rending and, despite legislation to prevent it, serfs hired themselves to the highest bidder. Those who once subsisted, clothed in grey fustian, now feasted and bedecked themselves in colourful clothes. But this excellent state of affairs did not last long, and the subsequent fate of the farm labourer, victim of poor law legislation and the steady encroachment of enclosures, may be seen as a regression down the old social scale, from villein to bordar to cottar to little more than thrall or slave. In the 1790s, William Morton Pitt, then of Encombe in Purbeck, inveighed against the landed interest, against the law which forbade the poor to leave their parishes, or punished them as vagabonds, and against the wretchedness of poor-houses. In the 1820s, labourers' wages were seven or eight shillings a week, while a loaf of wheaten bread cost a shilling or more. Even barley flour was expensive and barley cake was made from meal, though long days of leazing on the landowner's harvested fields might enable a woman to make a wheaten loaf. Nitches of gorse baited the bread ovens, and potatoes grown on the farmer's fallow, nettles and perhaps a little blue vinney cheese and pickled pork eked out the diet. Pennies could be earned by children who spent long hours stone-picking, bird-scaring or minding sheep. Rents were low, but wages were often paid in kind, in cider or in ale, opiates that could not for ever drug labourers tied to the land, but landless. Game-poaching and sheep-stealing were rewarded with penalties that made the medieval verderer's laws look humane. The noose, or Bridport dagger as it was called, that threatened lesser thieves, depended from the hands of greater thieves. Cottage ruins in the Purbeck valley, subjects of deliberate dereliction in order to lessen the burden on parish relief, mocked single men and women who were forced to live in, on the farm, and swelled the ranks of bastards in Wareham's orphanage.

In June 1830, George IV died and was succeeded by William IV, who created enough peers the following year to pass the Reform Bill, and presided over a stillborn revolution. It is hard to know what the presence of Charles X in Lulworth Castle, refugee from revolutionary France, meant to the peasants of Purbeck, but dicontent was rife enough within the island. That summer, the whirring sound of hay-mow and thresher, within banks and walls and hedges that spelt legal theft, was no signal for a joyous harvest-home. Labourers, who should have known better than to learn to read, had plucked from Goldsworthy's Ingoldsby Legends a name that was soon to be whispered abroad, the signatory for many a petition or threatening letter aimed at parson, yeoman farmer or gentleman. From the pages of *Babes in the Wood*:

> ". . . Captain Swing came in the night,
> And burnt all his beans and his barley."

Landowners were granted good consciences, if they needed them, by churchmen with glebeland in mind, and together invoked the names of God and King against the humble poor. Mostly the labourers came cap in hand, tugging forelocks, even if they refused to disperse, but Atheism, like popery, might spread from across the water, and be strangely transmuted in nonconformist hearts to anarchy. As George Loveless, the Tolpuddle martyr, wrote, Dissension was regarded by some as the sin of witchcraft. Where "congregational" had once been a term of ecclesiastical mockery, now "mob" was the prevailing political epithet applied to the people. Footguards patrolled Wareham's walls, and forty horsemen acted as sharp-shooters to try to suppress riots and to apprehend those who fired Purbeck farms. In December, for instance, Bradle farm, now a prosperous-looking place with new barns and silos, suffered two conflagrations. Special Assizes at Dorchester dealt with seventy-one prisoners the following month. Many descended the narrow stairs from the dock into the squalid cells which still survive beneath the offices of the National Farmers' Union. 1831, in the heat of Reform and Reaction that accompanied the county elections, saw the yeomanry hold Wareham against a Poole mob marching on Corfe Castle and Encombe where the illiberal Lord Eldon had succeeded Morton Pitt. In the succeeding years, Purbeck folk who never came to trial, who were not shipped to the Antipodes, opted for voluntary transportation—emigration to a New World. It was a continuing story: many of the Tizzards of Tyneham Farm sailed for Canada, in the wake of Tolpuddle men, when the farm was let before the First World War.

Peddlers of nostalgia who mourn the past must remember that much of it should be mourned. The man-marks they venerate are also scars. Ancient banks across the Wealden valley were also weals raised on the backs of Purbeck men, and ditches ran always with sweat, and often enough blood. Just north of Bradle, however, were marks of quite a different sort. Innocent or sinister, the name Mizmaze preserves the memory of the old Troytown-type maze of earthen banks that once stood there. Was it scrupulously sited by a dowser along spring lines, did the warping hazel-fork dictate its shape? Were the youths who trod it on holy days retracing pagan steps in a ritual or game of life? Was it simply a game, or the site of an old fair? If Troytown is a myth, East and West

Bradle hamlets certainly covered at least seven acres around the present farm, and a chapel is recorded there in 1326.

Thomas Bastard, epigrammatist of Blandford in Dorset, wrote a verse petition to Elizabeth in these terms, appraising her of the results of farmers' greed:

> "Howses by three and seaven and ten he raseth,
> To make the common gleabe his private land;
> Our country Cities cruell he defaceth;
> The grasse grows greene where litle Troy did stand;
> The forlorne father hanging downe his head
> His outcast company draws up and downe;
> The pining labourer doth begge his bread,
> The plow-swayne seeks his dinner from the town."

Customs die when places die; when properties are sold to outsiders and switch allegiances; when innovations oust old habits of mind; and, sometimes, when reformers or puritans outlaw them, as it is said they outlawed the treading of the Mizmaze. Not that men think of their customs as customs. Practices long embedded in the memory are simple common sense; those written into charters or by-laws, which means farm-laws, often enshrine unwritten law obeyed time out of mind, though imposed customs may die when the authority that requires them fades or is deposed. Purbeck men and women can marry outsiders without the Constable of Corfe's permission, because there is no Constable of Corfe. Such things are seen as customs by foreigners or, in retrospect, by those that once adhered to them.

Just as cuckoos, or guckoos in Purbeck, always came in time to buy new breeches at Wareham fair, so men ploughed, planted and reaped, dipped and sheared sheep, hunted and fished according to the weft of lore woven in and out of the warp of holy days, a tapestry whose pattern encompassed and organised labourers and craftsmen into necessary unity. Now, the fields are white with an earlier harvest, thanks to herbicides, pesticides and new strains of corn; and though there is a slight drift back to the land, machinery ensures that the labourers are few. Rapid changes in agricultural practice have expunged traditional wisdom from all but old men's memories. And old men die.

Who now would insist that oats in stitch must hear the bells chime thrice before going home, that three Sundays must pass before stacking? What hunter with his gun spares pa'sons, black rabbits, by ancient

custom when they are hardly, if ever, seen? Elder trees still thrive beside
the dairies and larders of old farms and cottages, but refrigeration and
Ministry of Agriculture regulations reduce the perils from the flies that
they discourage. Their crooked growth adorns a wall of Purbeck stone,
but few keep them because they guard against lightning and evil spirits.
Foresters do not like the elder's inferior timber, but perhaps some still
will not cut it because it is God's Stinking Tree, upon which Christ was
nailed and Judas hanged himself. It is not burned in hearths because it
spits, and not because its fire will conjure the devil on the chimney-stack.
Silgreen, the house-leek, Sempervivum, the ever-living Jupiter's plant,
grows on many a stone-tiled roof. It too protects from lightning and from
fire, and Silgreen ointment has long been made in Purbeck as a cooling
salve, a preparation against all kinds of fire in the body. Hares that haunt
woods and downs at night are never despatched by silver bullets, the
surest way of killing a wise-woman in that incarnation; nor are charges
of common assault brought by witches against a person overlooked, who
wanted to draw blood and break the spell. Bottles of urine with corks
stuck with pins, ox-hearts or bacon joints similarly impaled, were thrust
up many a chimney to prevent a witch's entrance. Fishermen used to tie
hagstones to staples in the bows of their boats, and coiled the ropes in the
stern in such a way as to avoid ending up with empty nets in a bewitched
boat surrounded by a shoal. In Purbeck, men suffering from epilepsy who,
like bewitched horses, might be hag-ridden, were advised to collect one
penny from each of thirty friendly virgins and to change the pence for a
half-crown freely given in the church offertory; the coin was worked into
a silver ring and worn as a reliable charm. Superstitions are not always
what they seem: one farmer tells how the occasions when his father's
horses were lathered up in the morning, as if hag-rod, always coincided
with the appearance of a barrel of smugglers' brandy in the hedge.

Like roads, new ways gain acceptance, and tarmac fixes main routes in the
mind of native and tourist alike. But beyond them, in the hinterland,
there is the mizmaze of ancient tracks which must be trodden for the
richer sights and sounds of Purbeck, and whose banks yield an historical
harvest as well as nuts and berries. Hazelnuts which once fed tanneries are
gathered by holiday-makers or left for rodents; twin-nuts may be
exhibited as curiosities, but are not treasured as specifics against toothache.
Blackberries too fill tourists' sandwich boxes, and are rarely picked after
Michaelmas because the school term has long since begun; not because

after that time they are spat on by the devil. But old customs, like hollow-ways long trodden in the mind, die hard. Overgrown through disuse, old tracks still shape the mental landscape long after origins and destinations are less than shadows in the turf.

The summer fête at Church Knowle takes place in the gardens of the Victorian Tudor Rectory, rebuilt by the Revd Owen Luttrell Mansel who held the advowson for the second half of the last century. By the house, a huge box painted with devilish faces is rotated by an electric motor, as though the church presided over a modern-primitive rite it has not seen fit to exorcise. But only raffle-tickets are drawn from it, and names called span the length and breadth of Purbeck, admixed with those of settlers and visitors. Second-hand books, home-made jams, pickles, clothes and toys vie for custom with pottery, jewellery and paintings by local crafts-men. Hoop-las and shies, skittles and darts encourage commonplace fair-ground talents. At one side-show rats emerge from their hole and weave their way down a zigzag run, while each competitor, poised with a flail, frenetically attempts to slash their tails off. Those that achieve the tally get their money back, in memory of the time when church-wardens would pay 2d for a dozen real rat-tails or, in a bargain not preserved in the fun of the fair, a dozen sparrows' heads.

Colonel Mansel built paired cottages in the village during the 1840s, but the family's property was sold off bit by bit early this century. Despite Purbeck valley's nineteenth-century decline there were, towards its close, a brick-maker, a mason, a miller, two cobblers and two smiths in Church Knowle. Now these have gone and arts and crafts are sold instead, though a tea-shop for tourists was recently suppressed by village opinion. Bungalows have sprung up and cottages have been modernised in olde worlde style by the outsiders who have settled in them. Sometimes these newcomers become pillars of the local community, but, however vital their function, they are like concrete beams shoring up old stone, never to knit with the ancient village fabric. They prop up the bar of the New Inn, together with old Purbeck men who will tell you of the time when the public bar was the farm dairy.

I remember the inn when it was a less sophisticated place, all of wood and stone; when beer was drawn from wooden barrels propped above the flags against the back wall of the bar. Now, unlike most Purbeck pubs, it is an upholstered, glossy place where horse-tackle on the walls and brightly-painted model wagons and caravans only emphasise its aliena-tion from the old ways. Brasses were the property of carters who vied with one another to equip and groom the finest turn-out in the island, and the smith's shoes and farm implements were for use not ornament. The latter's craft persists in decorative wrought-iron work; the bar itself is a show-piece, got up for tourists, self-consciously rural in a way that the farm it so recently was part of could never be.

19

BRICKS AND CANVAS

IN THE SHADOW of East Hill, a road climbs out of Corfe Castle under the railway bridge and along the chain of manors, now represented by Little Woolgarston, Woolgarston, Ailwood, Knaveswell and Knitson farms, that shelter to the south of the hills; a delightful, sinuous, switchback route coinciding with the narrow belt of greensand beneath the chalk, from which springs issue and supply a line of wells. Knaveswell Farm—in turn the property of Milton Abbey, of the Cullifords of Encombe, of Benjamin Bower, Poole apothecary, and, after the stormy eviction of Mr Bower's family, who seem not to have conceded that the place was sold, of John Calcraft of Rempstone Hall—is supplied by its own reservoir. The road curves south towards Windmill Knap, meets Burnham's Lane at Marsh Copse, and as Washpond Lane runs towards Godlingston Manor. A reservoir in Godlingston Wood feeds the farm and the manor house, which is older than Barnston, and more secretive, set amongst ragged woods and wet cattle-pasture. Men digging drainage trenches near the stream to the south-east, in 1961, discovered three almost undamaged Durotrigian jars which, with fragments of later Romano-British ware, demonstrate the longevity of the habitation.

Some authorities maintain that Godlingston Manor is to be identified with Moulham, where Durand, carpenter to the Conqueror, held a tenement in return for maintenance work at the Great Tower of Corfe Castle. If so, it is appropriate that the owner of 1300, who built the Hall, also constructed a thick-walled tower at its west end. Lit by loop-windows, with no entrance on the ground, it is an aggressive gesture softened by the inclusion of stone nesting-boxes, above the original first-floor ceiling, where doves sighed peaceably.

We do not know whether the manor house, thus equipped, ever figured in any military engagement; but we can be sure that it was a refuge in Elizabethan times, the subject of spirited, or spiritual, defence.

John Rogers, youngest son of that Sir Richard who figured so largely in the landed pirate empire of Dorset, farmed two-thirds of Godlingston for the Queen, because it was owned by the Roman Catholic recusant Henry Wells. Henry refused to bribe the Clerk of the Pipe Rolls and staunchly declared his allegiance at a time when many rich recusants bought immunity rather than surrender land to the Crown and fines to the Exchequer. We do not know what rôle he played in the religious underground, nor whether he harboured priests in Godlingston's tower, a crime for which his activist brother, Blessed Swithun Wells, was lynched at Gray's Inn in 1591. However, it is certain that discretion was not a Wells virtue, for another brother, Anthony, was to set sail with Raleigh in 1595 on the *Delight*'s abortive mission four hundred miles up the Orinoco in search of the fabled El Dorado. Looking at the house now, it is tempting to imagine stealthy comings and goings through the trefoiled door-arch, camouflaged now with climbers, although anyone who approaches it today is greeted by the barking of dogs and the blearing of cattle. Seventeenth-century dormers in the low-pitched roof and a two-storey east wing do not detract from its demeanour; if, unlike Barnston, it is close, defensive, content to remain undiscovered, it is undeniably the more resolute.

Godlingston Manor is solid stone, but a little way down Washpond Lane, past the cemetery, is the turning into Brickyard Lane. As nearby Ulwell, with its mill cottages mission and hall, and Swanage and White-cliff Farms are threatened by the tentacles of Swanage's development that reach out along old and new roads, there are those who hold that brick is a hideous innovation in the landscape of Purbeck; but a brickworks, that once served the Bankes estate, has stood on this corner for about 250 years. A band of ferruginous quartz grit, that outcrops in the Worbarrow cliffs and forms an upswelling that runs past Tyneham, Steeple, and across Corfe Common to Windmill Knap, is dug here and ground up to give texture and brown colour to the Swanage Brick and Tile Co's products. The body of the multi-coloured, multi-textured bricks is scooped from the red, purple and grey marls of the Wealden Beds exposed just north of the works. Blended and packed by hand into wooden moulds, the raw blocks are stacked within the kilns, oil-fired now, whose iron bracing and arched apertures give them the appearance of a fiery, hellish colonnade surmounted by a stepped chimney tower of their own blackened brick.

A sunken way north of Marsh Copse once ran across country to New

Buildings and Harman's Cross. When the turnpike fixed East Street as Corfe's main road and pushed diagonally across the valley to Swanage, the old way to Godlingston and the brickworks fell into disuse. Later still, Harman's Cross spawned a ribbon of undistinguished red brick, and the railway became even more influential than the turnpike. The iron road provided an easy route to and from the outside world and the other roads within the valley became more and more orientated around Corfe and Swanage stations; north–south tracks, especially those that climbed the chalk ridge, became more densely overgrown. Farms in Purbeck desperately needed to reorientate themselves at a time when American wheat and, later, animal feed was undercutting a market already chronically subject to depression. The railway encouraged a new race of dairymen whose produce could be rapidly and systematically exported from the island, and with which imports could not compete. Milk, sold locally until then, became a cash crop, and butter, once heavily salted and kept down the farm well, suddenly produced a quick return, while skim was still used for fattening pigs and making cheese.

Swanage's reputation as a salubrious watering-place, studiously cultivated by William Morton Pitt in the eighteenth century, now drew steam travellers to it. What they lacked in quality or money, they made up for in numbers. The railway also brought cement and lime and bricks that rendered most of the kilns and works that had furnished the estates redundant. Harman's Cross was born, and the small town of grey stone that was Swanage, successively fishing village, stone-port and select resort, began to sprawl across the valley towards Ballard Down. Now the railway that brought new growth, both benign and malignant, to Purbeck is dead. Like the heathland's clay-lines, its rails have been ripped up and only an embanked earthwork remains, an immense rabbit run patrolled by rasping pheasants, no-man's-land for linnets and goldfinches, where swallows scythe the air, harvesting insects above the weathered ballast that bore the glinting metal road.

Road-metal now bears all the weight of Purbeck's traffic. Lorries carry stone that once left Swanage by sea, or trundled heavily over the tracks to Ower Quay. Livestock transporters carry loads of sheep and cattle that used to be driven across country to Wareham. And coaches, cars and caravans bear down upon the beauty-spots with their loads of travelling people, and the casual labour that floods in to serve and entertain them. Tarmac has simplified and concentrated the network of highways, lanes, drongs, cart-tracks and footpaths that once linked a more scattered

population. Tractors and combine-harvesters now share the main roads
with other traffic, but it is not so long since steam threshing machines
braved the rough tracks between barns—on one occasion at least somer-
saulting down the chalk scarp and breaking up in the fields below—
lumbering with their loads of itinerant labourers between tight hedges.
The hedges were kept in trim by travelling strappers who regularly
plushed them: selected saplings were allowed to grow into good hedge-
row timber, but the majority were cut and laid to make a dense stock-
proof barrier, while ditches and banks were cleared and repaired at the
same time. If stools were growing close, all the plushers would be laid one
way: either up the slope, or from east to west with the sun. Sparse hedges
were plushed in both directions, with the stems held down by crooks
driven into the bank. When flocks lay thick as snow upon the Purbeck
Hills, the spring thaw came in the persons of itinerant gangs of sheep-
shearers, while the reddle-man picked his solitary way on donkey-back
over the downs and among the farmsteads peddling the ochre with
which the beasts were marked. Within living memory, Stanley and his
wife Lovey, an antique pair, made a virtue of the daily grind, sharpening
knives and honing scythes in all weathers. Rectors, curates and doctors
on horseback, in dog-carts or on bicycles wove careful webs across the
island in the cure of bodies and of souls. Gipsies, who now trade in the
steel detritus of the highway, peddled luck and woodwork around the
lanes, outraging settled inhabitants by poaching and by impertinent
grazing of their stock. Greeks with mangy dancing-bears, mountebanks
with their merryandrews, hurdy-gurdy men, travelling quacks and
preachers provided regular diversions, while choirmen, like the stalwarts
of Church Knowle, took to the road once a year to bring seasonal cheer
to village and isolated farm alike.

Today's travelling people are summer folk. They come to buy entertainment, to purchase a short season of rural life, to procure rest for their
souls in the salve of the sea. At the time of the French wars, signal posts
were set up on Ballard Down and St Aldhelm's Head and volunteer
yeomanry were enlisted for the protection of the coast; wagon routes and
drove-ways were fixed for the evacuation of men and animals in the event
of invasion; and lists of persons and inventories of stock were compiled in
accordance with the plans proposed by William Morton Pitt and William
Clavell. Details of similar secret schemes were circulated to landowners
in 1914, and to the Rural District Council in 1940, but they were never
implemented. It was rumoured that Bonaparte himself landed at

Lulworth to spy out the land, but any subsequent invasion was by our own, or allied, forces; and, since 1945, by ever-increasing tides of tourists. They are billeted in boarding-houses and hotels, in rank upon rank of caravans, or bivouacked in hundreds of tents pitched in the Wealden valley. At Woodyhyde Farm, where an old drongway runs under the the railway, over the Byle stream, and up past disused marble workings to the pocked stone tableland, a colourful harvest thrives in the valley fields; orange and blue canvas is a valuable cash crop, and the barn fills of an evening with holiday-makers hoping for a full house at Bingo.

From Ulwell Gap to Prospect Farm to the quarry-scarred territory south of Swanage, camps spring up like heat-rash on Purbeck's hide, and trailers supplement permanent caravan sites and the incomes of farmer, landowner and local authority alike. Those who do not profit from them tend to despise the flimsy no'thern hulks and the no'thern folk that fill them, for northern, in Purbeck, is a synonym for uncouth. Permanent settlement by furriners has caused Swanage's red-brick expansion that elbows its way between the bay and Cauldron Barn Farm, and up towards Whitecliff under Ballard Down. Domesday's Whiteclive is said to have been one of King John's hunting-lodges; remnants of strip-lynchets barely hold their ground nearby, and the ochre cliffs that fell away in 1877, uncovering child burials in stone cists, are increasingly interred, with all the signs of earlier life and death, under New Swanage's foundations. The town's population has swollen from 1,200 at the close of the eighteenth century, to 7,000 in 1925, and over 10,000 today, tripled or quadrupled in summer. Some old names survive, or have been appropriated to label roads: Ballard, Cauldron Barn and Rempstone Roads place the suburbs in Purbeck, while Wessex Way, Anglebury Avenue and D'Urberville Drive self-consciously write their own kind of fiction.

John Mowlem of Swanage, possibly of De Moulham blood, saw in the railway age and supervised the expansion of his town, after making his pile as a stone contractor in London, in much the same way as he erected the monument to himself at Northbrook cemetery: partly with his own hands. His pyramid of Guernsey granite, not local stone, was originally raised over the bones of his wife in the graveyard at Kingston. John Mowlem must have thanked Providence that the increase in population which he abetted required the opening of a new burial ground with room enough for his mausoleum, and that he lived long enough to be buried, alongside his re-interred Susannah, under its stepped plinth in his native town.

Due east, beside Shore Road, is the less imposing war memorial; a truncated pyramid of local stone, now absurdly enclosed by a stone wall and incongruous wrought-iron gates. But there is not a memorial to beat the one beside the Mowlem Theatre on the sea-front. If modern cliff-dwellers, or the inhabitants of Battlemead and Battlegate Road, look out across a bay studded with pleasure-boats, their counterparts of 1,100 years ago might have rejoiced to see a more momentous sight. Contrary winds, that used to prevent the packet from Bournemouth landing her passengers, and kept coal-barges offshore, sometimes for days, aided the island then. A granite column stands, after one fall in 1883 and a change of position in 1965, upon a base inscribed, "In commemoration of a great naval battle fought with the Danes in Swanage Bay by Alfred the Great, A.D. 877. Erected by John Mowlem, A.D. 1862". When ships returned from the Crimea complete with Russian bomb-shells embedded in their hulls, Mowlem acquired four of the balls and piled them, another pyramid, on top of his memorial to the Saxon king. Swanage offers weightier oddities than this. It dispenses souvenir booty to summer-time invaders. Its fortune is built with a bucket and spade upon the sands.

PART FIVE

BIDDLE

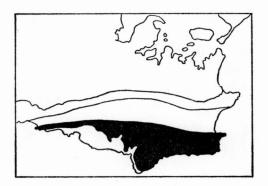

Black holes, stopped throats of stone; barren well-heads
—whose buttressed capstans groaned at drawing rock
up into daylight—sound successive beds
and teem with fossil dead of sea, swamp, lake.

Old mammals, dinosaurs' tread, crocodiles
congealed between the cliffstone's ammonites
and marble's burnishable snail-whorls.
Time, unmanned, in the rocks' mirror distorts.

Sea-walls and city streets, churches, headstones
excised, exported; here, still monuments of air
erected underground. Open-cast mines,
like pores, sweat rocks from rising strata:

an ancient virgin face at heart, composed
by wedge and biddle, stern chimes from quarr-shop.
Sea's tongues speak in hacked caverns, which no glazed
tallow-light or music now lick into shape.

Lanes founder beneath turf, and at cliff-edge
dry stone unpicked; man's strata, walls' web stutters
surf-wards, the plateau's net that, plucked, would dredge
a catch of crops, herds, flocks and stonecutters.

20

MARBLE FARMS

King Alfred had his successes against the Danes, but the *Anglo-Saxon Chronicle* suggests that this was not one of them: "the pirate host sailed west about, and they were caught in a great storm at sea, and there off Swanage one hundred and twenty ships were lost". Alfred chased the mounted host from Wareham to Exeter, but could not overtake them. The victory was for the waves and the rocky promontory of Peveril Point, where contorted beds of the Upper Purbeck limestone stubbornly resist the sea.

In 1868, a clock-tower memorial to the Duke of Wellington, in the Perpendicular style, was erected on the Peveril side of The Grove, now the Grosvenor Hotel. It had been removed from the southern side of London Bridge and shipped to Swanage by Mowlem's; for pseudo-religious reasons its slim spire was replaced by an absurd cupola; and it has never contained the fine clock which was its original justification. The fishing boats drawn up beside it, with their coiled ropes and floats and lobster pots, are refeshing after the pretensions of the town, the amusements of the sea-front, the miniature golf-course above the hotel and the pleasure-boat pier beneath it; while the nearby life-boat house, coastguard station and look-out on Peveril, or Perilous, Point, bring a sobering taste of reality to Swanage-by-the-sea. The look-out keeps a weather eye open northwards across the sandy bay to the chalk mass of Ballard Point, and southwards to the grimmer Durlston Bay whose stony shore is fed by cliff-falls. The name Sentry Fields, where a gun-battery was sited near the look-out, reminds us that the sea was not the only threat to Swanage's peace of mind.

In 1086, the manor of Suuanwic was the property of the predatory wife of the hated Sheriff of Dorset, Hugo Fitz Grip, and the adjacent Sonwic belonged to Ida, Countess of Boulogne. It has been suggested that the *Anglo-Saxon Chronicle*'s name for the place, Swanawic, may refer to a swannery that once reared birds for Shaftesbury Abbey. Certainly, the area of Peveril was part of the manor of Kingston held by the Abbess, but she may have been more interested in keeping a look-out for littoral income; that is, in her right of wreck of the sea.

If so, under her nose was the easternmost outcropping of the stone which was to adorn so many abbeys, churches and cathedrals in medieval times. Two seams of the hard, intractable limestone known as Purbeck marble, dense with small shells of the freshwater snail Viviparus, outcrop into the sea at the Point. Scoured by the tides, they are smoothed and their colour is unmistakable; greyish-green at the top of the Purbeck Beds, followed about ten feet south by the red stuff. Some hold that the red and green together with the blue and black types found elsewhere, are distinct beds, but men who have worked it say that one or other of the colours may be missing in a pit, and suspect that they are the result of impurities or local chemical processes. What is certain is that marble seams run westwards, the length of Purbeck, and emerge on the north flank of Worbarrow Tout.

The distribution of marble above ground is somewhat wider: loom-weights and mortars made of it by Romano-British craftsmen have been found in the Tyneham valley, and burial cists at Studland were fashioned from it. It was made into tesserae for paving Dorchester villas, and used for the tombstone of at least one Roman there, whose memorial inscription translates as: "To the spirits of the departed: for . . . Carinus, Roman citizen, aged fifty; Rufinus and Carina and Avita, his children, and Romana, his wife, had this set up." The marble found its way to Chester, Lincoln, Corbridge, Caerwent and Verulamium; and to Colchester by the middle of the first century. It is one of the stones used in the mosaic floor of the Roman Christian church at Silchester, but a millennium was to pass before it took the ecclesiastical market by storm.

If the marble is quite easy to spot near the coast, it is not so easy to find inland. Its seams are four feet thick at most, and even when exposed it does not wear its heart on its sleeve. It is no good going to the working quarries of today, for the old marble pits are buried beneath copse and scrub and pasture on the northern slopes of the limestone, before it disappears under the clay valley floor and its streambed. W. J. Haysom dug marble for the restoration of Temple Church, after the blitz of 1941, just west of Swanage Modern School. At Combe the Swanage road forks: the relatively modern valley route to Corfe branches off for Harman's Cross, and the eighteenth-century turnpike for Langton, Kingston and

Corfe climbs up on to the stone plateau; between them, the track that once connected the chain of marble workings in the Middle Ages has long since degenerated into fragments of footpaths or less.

Wilkswood farm derives its name from the Walshes, sometime patrons of the Priory there and lords of Langton Wallis. We do not know when the Priory was founded, but there is a record that "Alice, once wife of William de Ponsont & relict of Sir Ingelram de Walleys, by a charter sans date, constitutes William Bonet, chaplain, to celebrate an obit for the souls of the said William and their ancestors, at Wilcheswode, for life." The oldest walls of the farmhouse date from the seventeenth century when the Havellands, commemorated by a brass in Langton Matravers church, were lords of the manor. They leased the property until the Dissolution of the Monasteries, when they received a grant from the Crown of all the lands of the Priory at Walsheswood, and continued to live there until about 1730. Wilkswood's shallow pits are probably the oldest in Purbeck, still worked for Purbeck stone in 1942 when schoolboys found, below the faint shapes of Celtic fields, sherds of pottery of the first century, fragments of lathe-turned shale armlets, flint tools, iron slag, nails, coloured glass, a bronze dolphin brooch, stone slabs from some sort of building and a piece of weathered, but sawn and polished marble.

Little is left now, to indicate its former industrial and religious prestige. Chunks of unworked marble are hidden in a haze of tall grasses, among briars, brambles and rusty dock, and in forests of spiky teazels. Continuing westwards, Langton West Wood is a dank, overgrown coppice of hazel and oak, that could be aboriginal but for its web of banks and ditches, in which a log-cabin hide squats like a rustic Tardis amongst time-warped trees. Only badger setts rival marble workings for age here, and the woods that punctuate the marble vein between Combe and Steeple Leaze farm were probably planted to mask and employ quarry-scarred ground. Emerging on to the ragged slopes of Primrose Hill, one can see the small farm of Quarr, whose name betrays its origin. Now it is a humble building with a wavy stone-tiled roof and rendering falling from rubble walls, fronted by a heap of old timber, old iron and antique machinery overrun by nettles, and framed by oak and willow; but fragments of wall, and hollow-chamfered window-frames and mullions, suggest that it was once part of a larger, grander house. Quarr it was that supplied marble and masons for work on Winchester Cathedral, and Purbeck burr for Corfe Castle.

Purbeck marble is very hard to work but, during the twelfth century, it flooded in increasing quantities from the narrow seams. Marble was never cheap; its extraction, even from surface outcrops, was hard work, and in places pits were cut down through the clay to where the stone lay, often under water; it was winched up, dried and cleaned of mould over a bracken fire. It seems not to have been worked at the quarrs themselves, but transported along the marble road and across the clapper-bridges and hollow-ways, that can still be found on Corfe Common, to West Street where the masons, or marblers, shaped it. It has to be worked tenderly, for it clouds imperceptibly and weathers badly later on if it is too roughly handled. Surface joints show for several inches into a block, making its working a tough, wasteful business; and if the punch is driven too near the final surface it will bruise or stun the marble. Perhaps the skill and discipline required to cut it properly was the reason why apprentice stonecutters were traditionally assigned the task of making a clock-case or other delicate object from it.

A stream of worked and unworked marble flowed through Corfe Gap and over the heath to the stone-ports on the Harbour shore. Fonts, like those at Corfe, East Lulworth and Swanage; altar tables, like the one at Church Knowle; and floor-slabs, as at Corfe and Wareham Lady St Mary, fed an enormous market in England, Ireland, Normandy and even Italy, following the Crusaders' new taste for marble. William of Sens ordered it in 1174 to embellish the choir of Canterbury, and shafts like those of St Edward's Chapel in Lady St Mary's became the fashion among cathedral architects. Coffin-lids, like those at Corfe, East Holme, Wareham and Steeple, left Purbeck in vast numbers, while effigies became all the rage in the thirteenth century. That of King John at Worcester gave "marmor regis" its ultimate sanction, and the tiny but magnificent medieval church at Tarrant Crawford received a marble effigy for the tomb of Queen Joan of Scotland in 1254, at a cost of one hundred shillings. Anyone who doubts the quality of the material or the finesse of the marblers' workmanship should look at the beautifully-preserved effigy of a bishop, perhaps the Patriarch of Jerusalem, Heraclius, that has lain in the choir of Temple Church in London for more than seven centuries.

West of Quarr, Downshay Farm and Dunshay Manor are hidden from fields of tents by a wood where an old track runs between wide banks. The present manor house was built by John Dolling in 1642 and partly rebuilt in 1906, but beyond it are the scarped platforms of a much older settlement stepping down towards the stream beneath a quarried hillside.

George Dolling heads the signatories, who also included two John Dollings, of the articles of agreement of the Company of Marblers and Stonecutters dated 3 March 1651. Leland tells us that Alice de Briwere supplied marble from her quarries at Dunshay during the 1220s as a free-will offering for the building of Salisbury Cathedral. The drums of the colonnade and the polished piers there stand as a magnificent memorial to this medieval lady, and to the material which she championed. The tall pinnacles of Dunshay's gateposts and the elegant curve of its white gates and flanking walls are reflected in a round pond where mallard brood in a floating nesting-box. A swan squats by the water's edge, wrapped up in itself, a brute bird delicately sculpted in stone. Faces in burr and thornback, either side of the gate, are subtly composed, and the stable block contains a host of beasts and human figures in wood and clay and stone. On the lawn, between two aged cedars, a girl of onyx stands, whose flesh and hair is, at once, flowing and translucent, and opaque and secretive as stone. Aboriginal figures of freestone crouch in the garden, watchful, wary, knowing themselves and their completeness. Stone, though not marble, is still worked here by Mary Spencer Watson, whose training in sculpture began in the Purbeck quarries when, at the age of twelve, she was given her own banker and tools by Titus Lander. One of her favourite stones is the grainy, porous Purbeck burr, the next workable seam beneath, or uphill from, the marble veins. It is hard, and hard to work, and though it was extensively employed as massive building and foundation stone in the Middle Ages, the only recent large-scale use of the water-worn burr from Downshay Wood was for large ornamental rockeries. Mary Spencer Watson's figures populate house, outbuildings and grounds, enrich private collections and adorn public buildings and new developments all over Britain; products of a strenuous magic, they emanate from an ancient site whose sweated labour was the source of so much craftsman-ship.

She has worked in alabaster too, a material that was to oust Purbeck marble from the mass market in the fifteenth century. Some was dug in Durlston's cliffs, but most of it came from the Nottingham area. It was cheaper to dig and took fine detail with more grace; the marble seams were still worked for another two hundred years, but in smaller and smaller quantities. Woodyhyde's veins were re-opened in the 1840s to restore Temple Church, where so much Purbeck marble had been employed six hundred years before. But such small revivals hardly touch the picture of decline and abandonment that the marble farms present.

Next in line, Afflington was the Domesday manor of Alvronetone, held by Aelfrun in Edward the Confessor's time. Immediately to the east of the farmhouse are ten acres of settlement remains, with embankments against the stream, platforms, closes and a hollow-way from which a two-field system of agriculture was worked. Looking now at the damp pasture, it is hard to imagine it as the site of the market and fair that Henry III granted, and just as hard to re-populate it with the modest fifty persons who lived there in 1800. Just as modern members of the Company of Marblers present a pound of pepper annually at Ower, so William de Scovill rendered the same rent to the Constable of Corfe in the thirteenth century for his holding at Scoles Farm. There are the remains of a ruined chapel there, portions of a medieval hall survive in seventeenth-century out-buildings, and bee-boles were rebuilt to house the bee-skeps that mead-brewers raided. To the north, Scoles gate now leads out on to Corfe Common beside a deep, wooded streambed, through the garden of a picturesque cottage. At Lynch, the stone roofs of farm buildings grow out of the hillside below Kingston. Its brew- and bakehouse is no longer filled with ferment and very little remains to tell of its medieval and Roman ancestry. Its pasture is quietly grazed and the scars are overgrown that spoke of the industry, enterprise and ingenuity of marblers.

Further westwards, Blashenwell's roots plumb far greater depths. Friesians chew the cud between streams that feed the Corfe River; ponies, that have to be licensed with the haywards, mow burial mounds or the marblers' roads that rut Corfe Common. A large stone-rimmed pond, just north of the farmyard, is fed by a spring, dammed at source by a wall at the south, that drove the great iron water-wheel beside the barn within living memory. This water supply, and the nearby tufa deposit with its whitening properties, combined to give the place the name by which it was known in 955: Blechenhamwelle. The track to Corfe cuts through the tufa, whose lime was excavated from a large marl pit; in and around it, contracted burials in cists of Purbeck stone, Kimmeridge shale waste from armlet manufacture, pottery spanning Iron Age and Romano-British times, paved floors and herring-bone masonry suggest a busy hamlet. But the tufa has preserved, as it precipitated out of the spring water, signs of settlement from about 4500 B.C.; embedded early Mesolithic flint tools, shellfish, and the bones of red and roe deer, ox and pig. Hollow-ways, closes and a mound to the west of the farm are much more recent; they belong to the period when marble was dug here in a

big way. Marks of medieval quarrying can be seen beside the track uphill
to Kingston.

Bits of marble can be picked up in the fields where the pits yielded it so
prodigiously, and beside the roads where the stone carts rolled. By close
scrutiny of its buff, weathered outer shell you can select pieces of red,
blue, grey and green stone. My amateurish efforts at working it left me
full of admiration for the craftsmen who shaped it so finely. With much
sweat I sawed it through; slowly the deep colours of its heart revealed
themselves, and polishing produced the rich, glowing surface of the real
thing. Despite its hardness, it does not weather very well, although the
red variety is the most durable. Coffin-lids such as those in East Holme
churchyard have suffered badly from exposure and reverted to a dull,
crumbling state. Shafts, cut along the plane of the sediments because of
the narrowness of the seams, may flake and decay in damp churches. But
under good conditions, polished to a dark glow with oil or preserved
with varnish, Purbeck marble sustains its full medieval glory. I oiled my
crudely-worked mementoes and watched the greens, blues and reds grow
luminous around the glinting fossil shells embedded in the stone; and felt
something of the satisfaction that marblers must have experienced when
they brought their carvings to perfection.

The Blashenwell quarrs were re-opened in the 1870s, when the new
church of St James at Kingston was built. Stonecutters well used to
other Purbeck seams must have learned a fresh satisfaction, and frustration, in working the material on which their ancient company was
founded. The old church of St James, at the east end of the village, built
by the first Lord Eldon on the site of a twelfth-century chapel, had stood
for barely half a century when the new one was begun. The third Earl
commissioned the architect George Edmund Street to build it of stone
from the Encombe estate and timber from his land in Gloucestershire. It
was to be an exemplary piece of craftsmanship; the foreman is said to
have insisted that the beds and joints of the stonework should be as well
executed as the exposed surfaces, exhorting his men, "Let your deeds be
done as well in the dark as they are in the light." The steps and base of the
chancel screen are fine examples of the marblers' art, and the extravagant
Gothic-style pillars and pilasters look back to a time when Purbeck was a
vital centre of both stone and skill.

The marble rests now, between Peveril and Worbarrow. Where
mining hamlets were once forged into an industrial chain, linked to each
other and to Corfe by busy roads, isolated farms now lie apart, lost

between more recent routes. Beneath strip-lynchets that step down limestone slopes, gorse and blackthorn grow over medieval scar-heaps. Coppices that hid the workings and supplied hurdles for the shepherd and pit-props for the quarrier, grow rank and wild, and muddy paths above the marble seams are printed by badger and roe deer. Time has gone into reverse, and fame has deserted the marble farms.

21

FANTASIES, HARD STUFF

THE NEW CHURCH at Kingston is a fantastic building. Above the backdrop of Kingston Plantation its huge tower rises, built to house a full peal
of eight bells which ring out across the valley, a landmark for half
Purbeck and a focus of pilgrimage for campanologists from far and wide.
Its rounded apse with a conical roof, its gables and its fairytale pointed
turret with criss-cross mouldings are unlike any other church hereabouts.
In Purbeck, built from Purbeck's rocks, it is not of Purbeck. Finished in
1880, it served as a private chapel to the Eldon family until it was conveyed
to the Church Commissioners and consecrated in 1921. The not-so-old
church of 1833 became the church hall; ivy-leaf details in stone and vine
tendrils in its stained glass anticipated the rife growth that has overtaken
and smothered its mean shell. The gate is chained and entry is forbidden.

Kingston village, built high above Lynch and Blashenwell, looks like
everyone's idea of an olde worlde hamlet, with its high pavement and
cottages of stone, its inn glowing with Virginia creeper and, beside it
until recently, a scarlet and yellow gipsy caravan. Inside the bar there are
tables and wall-slabs of polished local stone, but the Scott Arms—named
for the Scotts of Encombe, sometime Earls of Eldon—is no stonecutters'
resort, for Kingston is an estate village, almost entirely rebuilt in the last
century. Quarrymen are an independent race, and though they may have
been grateful for Scott patronage at first they found that, during seven
years' regular employment on the church building, good orders went elsewhere and their traditional trade withered away. The tough time that
followed the Kingston job has died hard in the memory, and it is not for
nothing that some still look along the stoneland to that monument to
their craft and think that it resembles nothing so much as a white elephant.

The road towards Langton runs eastwards along the uplands, above the
secretive line of marble farms and the wooded valley whose floor ripples
away to the chalk ridge. From here you can look down on Corfe Castle

guarding its distant gap, backed by black heath and the steely reaches of Wareham Channel. The old stone track from Woodyhyde climbs to the top road and continues across it as the tarmac road for Worth Matravers. That way the fields are stitched together with miles of stone walling; an almost treeless patchwork covers the plateau, cleft only by the valleys of Combe Bottom and Hill Bottom running down towards Chapman's Pool and the sea. White stone-dust rises in a pall from Swanworth Quarries' blasting, where Purbeck-Portland rocks are crushed for aggregate to feed a haulage business—a far cry from the mason's craft.

North of the road the ground is lumpy with mole-, or 'oonthills, and with heaps of scars or spawls, the left-overs of stone working, overgrown with close-cropped grass. Scars were used to surface estate roads, and a celebrated court case decided that they were the property of the quarrymen, being a product of their labour, rather than of the farmers or landowners from whose ground they were dug. They fetched 3d a ton as road-metal, until they began to be sold to concrete manufacturers. Gorse thrives in the hollows, and you almost tread on the great dark-eared hares that make their forms on the pocked fields.

A fantastic sound begins to infiltrate the ears near Gallows Gore. A magical music as from a manic gamelan whose notes are struck from every crevice of the scale, bell-like, chiming, or brittle and metallic. There, among clusters of huts and stacks of stone, is its source: masons shaping blocks of different sizes, timing their rhythm to the task, striking in concert with well-tempered tools. Nowadays, a transistor radio is the most likely accompaniment, but two brothers of Gallows Gore were famous for the words and music of the carols they composed, sung for years at Worth Matravers. Songs still precede burials there; but what sort of music, what ritual was it that followed ancient bones into their graves here between Gallows Gore cottages and Downshay Wood? For quarrying has uncovered interments of the first century amongst the black debris of occupation that overlies the rock. A child was entombed in a stone cist, with surviving coffin-nails, a bronze wire brooch, a bone knife-handle and, relics perhaps of the Durotrigian equine cult, half-a-dozen horse's teeth. Two women, old and young, were laid side by side and head to toe in an earthen grave, with two Durotrigian bowls of black earthenware and a red beaker. Other graves too were dug amongst Iron Age and Roman storage pits and hut-sites littered with the signs of industry. Drystone walls, floor-slabs and roof-tiles belonged to buildings no less substantial than those that stand here now; spindle-whorls, weaving combs and loom-weights are the cloth-worker's legacy; shale remains and flint tools span the eras of hand-cutting and lathe-turning; stone blocks set into the ground were probably the lathes' foundations; hobnails from leather boots and Romano-British brooches are the only personal relics, while coins of the third and fourth centuries are the currency of the long-lived, long-dead business that was conducted here. Twentieth-century bulldozers have unearthed them, but the essentials of today's trade are the same: men, stone and tools with which the one shapes the other, making music from morning till night.

In total contrast to Wilkswood in the valley to the north, the Domesday manor of Acton is an exposed, bare place on the limestone plateau. Its earliest building is a humble, late sixteenth-century house, added to in the last century when most of the cottages were built by quarrymen. It lies between the Langton road and the grassy, stone-walled, beaten highway, called the Priest's Way, which runs through the heart of the stoneland from Worth Matravers to Swanage. But Acton is off the beaten track; it seems not to welcome visitors for, exposed as it is, it is a close place, squatting in a huddle of stone around its narrow lanes, aloof, wrapped up in its own business. And yet, outsiders have moved in and some quarriers' cottages have been taken over by week-enders. Even so, there is no fantasy about these dream-houses; Acton is all business-like stone set on its own rock, only fifteen feet thick in places, undermined by its own workings. Sometimes these quarrs, or quarry mines, are broken into by the open-cast workings, or ridden-holes, of today; sheep nudge at the field-fences to get at the rough grass of the scarred wares that run down to the cliff; hens strut among the quarr-huts, rabbits and their young venture out of their own shafts, nagging partridges hurry their broods into the scrub, redstarts and stonechats patrol their rock-strewn territories, and men drag freestone out wholesale beside the once-dark lanes where their fathers worked. Walking there is like invading a family hearth whose stony faces conceal ramifications which an outsider can never plumb. Old shafts became wells for the settlement, into which effluent from communal closets filtered back through the limestone layers. Often overgrown now, their insignificant entries insinuate the ground's bowels; passages push out along the seams where men crawled and sweated in the humid atmosphere to fetch up the hard stuff that was dressed in the light of day, building the grey-green scar heaps that survive to tell the tale.

In contrast, Langton lives up to its name, straggling out along the road and the spring-line from Acton to Combe that fed its wells. The western half of the parish, once owned by the de Walleys and known as Langton Wallis, is now controlled by the Bankes family; while the eastern half gave its name to the village, for it belonged to the Mautravers family, of whom John Mautravers, one of the murderers of Edward II, was a member; the remains of their manor are in the hands of the Scotts of Encombe. Langton Matravers' spacious properties and shoulder-to-shoulder cottages are unified only by the main street that links them. Housing estates, like the one at Capstan Field, named after the capstans which wound stone out of the quarrs, and the award-winning Council scheme at Three Acre Lane, have edged their way out of the village to north and south along old stone roads and sheep droves. Langton's population is equally diffuse: quarriers and farm-workers, schoolmasters and retired immigrants, tradesmen and professional people live together in its grey stone, cleft often enough in the past by factions violently opposed or holding their ground in uneasy truce. The village owed its medieval expansion to the success of the stone trade, and its eighteenth- and nineteenth-century cottages, often built of paving waste, to the time when the industry moved uphill once again from Swanage where over-mining was a serious danger. But the crown of Mount Misery, over-looking Wilkswood and once grey with intensive quarrying, is now green again to match the Celtic fields and lynchets on its northern slopes; and Mount Pleasant, once covered with quarrymen's houses, is flanked by playing fields and a swimming pool.

Education is Langton's largest industry. A National School was founded, opposite the church, in 1845, and six private schools were established between 1893 and 1929. The first, Durnford House, offered superior educational facilities to the sons of gentlefolk in what had been the De Derneford manor, long bitten out of the Langton Wallis estate; the first headmaster, Thomas Pellat, used to drive his boys down Durnford Drove to the sea, where he had had a swimming pool blasted out of the cliff quarry-shelf called Dancing Ledge. The village primary school survives in its buildings of 1875; Spyway House, a grand establishment off Durnford Drove, caters for boys and girls; another preparatory school, the Old Malthouse, began its career in the old maltster's premises and the Sweet Content alehouse; while Leeson House is now a field study centre, set in its own park, where teachers may bring pupils for a working holiday, applying themselves to the rich geology, ecology and intensely varied land use of Purbeck Island.

The schoolroom in the cottage-style Wesleyan chapel of 1845, that stood beside the existing chapel of 1875 until recently, was a mean place in comparison to the National schoolroom that superseded it and the later private schools; but its meanness was a reflection of the poverty of quarriers and farm labourers, not of the quality of their zeal. Nonconformity appealed to those who wished to be responsible to God alone, to learn and give their children a little learning, and to organise in their own way, rather than be overlooked by the rector and landowners of the village. That their independence of spirit issued in political radicalism is not in doubt, but, behind that, it was their theology, their knowledge of God that renewed their vision of man, fed by a religious tradition with deep roots in Purbeck.

Views on education, worship and class figured largely in the mind of Mrs Frances Serrell of Durnford, in whose veins the landed blood of Bankes and the new-blue blood of Scotts was mixed. Her late husband had donated the building for the National School, but an argument with the strong-willed Revd Trotman over the appointment of a master caused Mrs Serrell to set up a rival school in two of her cottages next door. The National School had to close in 1870 for want of pupils and the following year, to add insult to injury, Ma'am Serrell walked out of church with her Sunday School, because their usual seats had been usurped by a newly-constituted choir, and she began to hold Anglican services in her school across the road. A new rector, the Revd Lester, tried to heal the schism, and it was only in 1878, when Mrs Serrell complained vociferously against Jane Bower, a working woman, for holding an open-air service at Acton, that the rector let fly in a sermon against both women's usurpation of his authority, against the rich lady's attack on the poor woman, and against disunity within the church of Christ. Until her death in 1884, Mrs Serrell's services continued, accompanied by a brass band whose strains cannot have blended very harmoniously with the singing of the official choir.

St George's Church has a squat fifteenth-century tower that used to dominate the medieval church whose roof-line can be seen on the west wall of the nave. The nave was rebuilt twice, in 1828 and 1875-6, and now its roof is taller than the tower. Though full of interest and fine detail, the present church is most notable for its sense of light and space. Many of its memorials have been lost in the rebuildings, and stone tablets inscribed with the Ten Commandments lie face down in the path to the south porch. In 1946, the south chancel aisle reverted to the original rôle of the south transept in the medieval church, being dedicated to St

Leonard, and Walter Haysom carved the saint's statue there. The chapel had been linked with the priory at Wilkswood, where Cluniac Benedictine monks probably tended lepers during the 1200s, while in 1373, after its appropriation by the Crown during the Hundred Years War, Edward III "gave Henry Attechappelle, chaplain, his chantry of Wilcheswode, that he might find maintenance for himself and two fellows in victuals and clothing, in the chapel of Wylcheswode and Saint George of Langton, there serving God and Saint Leonard". The restoration has undone, physically at least, the work of the Reformation when St Leonard was deposed. A new rector was appointed at that time who would implement the services of the English Prayer Book, but he nimbly reverted to the mass in the reign of Mary, and back again on the accession of Elizabeth.

Adaptability, as well as stubbornness, is very much a Langtonian virtue, or vice. Thomas Hayward, who rented the cliff quarry at Dancing Ledge from Mrs Serrell, was also sometime sub-postmaster, sexton, parish clerk and warden to Rector Trotman. But his stone-carts that laboured up from Dancing Ledge were often laden with more than one sort of hard stuff. The quarries were ideal landing- and hiding-places for contraband; Spyway Barton's bull is said to have done his share of sentry duty around the barn; Mrs Serrell's cottages at the head of Durnford Drove had communicating roof-spaces; and it was not only at the Priest's Way that smugglers' and churchmen's paths crossed, for barrels of liquor were humped up the church tower and into the roof-space above the domed ceiling. The parish clerk supervised the operation, whose son-in-law was, perhaps conveniently, an exciseman.

Whatever the cause, the roof of the church of 1828 became most unsafe, and the whole structure was ugly and unsound. Two of its bells had been cracked by newly-admitted members of the marblers' order, nonconformists no doubt, who were traditionally allowed to ring the bells with their hammers to announce the Shrove Tuesday Kissing Day festivities and marblers' meeting at Corfe. Two of the bells that survive were probably installed when the tower was built; another, also of the fifteenth century, was presented in 1973 by Old Durnfordians in memory of the school's founders, and a fourth, of 1602, was transferred from Kingston's old church to commemorate an Old Durnfordian—Lord Tovey, Admiral of the Fleet and first Baron Langton Matravers. The rebuilding healed the splits in the fabric, but not the schisms; the new roof, pitched higher than the tower, shelters the memory of the village's worthies and hides a multitude of sins.

It is all too easy to fantasise about the romance of rural history, but the fine series of exhibitions mounted in the tiny village museum give the visitor something much tougher than vague picture-postcard notions to chew upon. Across the road, the King's Arms, once the Mason's Arms, traditionally served quarriers; its thick walls and Purbeck marble fireplace match its reputation; it does a brisk tourist trade today, while locals linger over serious games of cards. Down the hill, past Putlake Farm, and up again, opposite Langton Manor Farm, the Ship Inn serves an agricultural clientele. It is a bleaker, more basic place whose furniture is worn almost to blackened matchwood, yet whose tobacco-stained walls bear proud trophies and rolls of honour of its sportsmen, a bare chantry or place of pilgrimage for darts-players and footballers. Its local name, The Steps, and the name Steppleshill, appropriated by a modern house, refer to the steps cut into the switchback road down from Langton to give cart-horses a firmer footing.

When the route to Swanage was made a turnpike in 1761, the stone traffic was confirmed in its shift eastwards and the roads to Corfe and across the heath no longer bore their ancient, weighty loads. Carters blowing horns proclaimed their unstoppable progress down the dangerous new gradients, and when the first steam locomotive came to Swanage it was drawn there by cart-horses up Kingston Hill, through Langton, up and over Steps, and down to the resort and port whose water-borne traffic it was soon to supersede. The old settlements of Leeson, Combe and Herston were firmly linked. Yards Lane, just north of Combe, ran to the great woolyards of Herston, for the stone plateau yielded the soft stuff in great quantities, as well as rock. At Gully, Bonfields are again digging stone just south of the road, and old quarr huts have been renovated with new, raw drystone. Land not swallowed up by housing is pocked with the remains of old shafts alongside tracks running to South Barn, Verney Farm and Belle Vue Farm on the Priest's Way. It is to the south of Swanage that Purbeck stone workings are thick upon, or in, the ground; but these and the rock they delved must wait until the next chapter.

Our road continues into Swanage which is the craziest town I know. It has the sublimity of long history, the charm of a fishing village, the ambition and pragmatism of a port, and the calculated grace of a watering-place. Architectural absurdities were imposed upon it by John Mowlem and George Burt, hard-headed men with the avaricious appetites and eccentric tastes of jackdaws. It sports the artistic pretensions of a poor man's St Ives, the garishness of a fun-fair and the red-brick boredom of a retirement haven. It contains modern buildings of flair and style, like the library, as well as block-busting monstrosities like the Mowlem Theatre.

The High Street runs along the ridge of the Upper Purbeck stone beds, past the site of John Mowlem's Herston House to Newton Manor, now a girls' school, behind whose castellated façade Sir Charles Robinson, director of what was to become the Victoria and Albert Museum, assembled a private museum that was mostly dispersed on his death in 1913. Some say it has no right to the title of manor, but it was the seat of the Cockram family, of whom Brune was rector of Swanage in the seventeenth century, while his son Thomas farmed Whitecliff. Scores of Dutch gin bottles were discovered in the foundations, but it is said to be haunted by the sober spirits of three men hung, drawn and quartered in an adjoining field, by order of Judge Jeffreys, for the edification of Swanage dissenters. The neo-Gothic Methodist Church further down the road has the spacious air of establishment about it, however, as do the twin Congregational chapels that guard the corner of Church Hill. Turning down the hill is like entering a clinical eighteenth-century film-set; pretty cottages are graciously disposed about a mill-pond adorned with ducks, as though designed for the picture-postcard rural life enjoyed by the prosperous twentieth-century townee. The long Mill House at the bottom is inscribed "BEn BARLOW Mill Wright of Southampton fecit 1754", proving that the fabric of the dream is real however much nostalgia has subsequently faked it. Beyond the church, Swanick House, once the Rectory, a fine rubble building of ancient ancestry, has been split into two, and new houses have been built to the east, forming a close reached from King's Road by a series of little willow-draped bridges over the Swan Brook. Sound investors have long since seized the old town, and Swanage's working parts have seized up.

The parish church of St Mary the Virgin, once a mere chapel-of-ease to St Nicholas, Worth Matravers, preserves thirteenth-century work and Norman mouldings in the fourteenth-century tower which was heightened when the church was rebuilt in about 1620. The tower was a refuge, as at Godlingston Manor, with no ground-floor access, but an arrow-slit in its east wall is now a squint into the nave of 1859, later extended in 1907. The airy Victorian church contains brasses and monuments to Cockrams, Serrells, Welles of Godlingston, to William Clavell and his two wives, to naval and military men, and to Chinchens, a name closely associated with the stone trade. In the churchyard there is a glorious headstone of 1781 to Katherine Henrietta Chinchen, lovingly executed by a mason relative. Fourteen windows were blasted by enemy action in 1943, and one of the new ones is a war memorial to the boys of Hill Crest School, while the font cover was one of the last things made at Swanage Grammar School before it moved to Wareham.

Here, again, the educational connection is a strong one. Early in the last century, Andrew Bell became rector, on his return from missionary work in Madras where he initiated the monitor system in his schools. He published a pamphlet on the scheme, which was taken up by the Quaker Joseph Lancaster for his non-denominational British Schools. In 1807, Andrew Bell relinquished his living to help establish the Anglican-inspired National Schools. William Morton Pitt, better known for his attempts to furnish Swanage as a resort, had founded some of the first Sunday Schools in the area in the 1780s, but philanthropic and educational objects were by no means new. A commission of 1548 "for the contynu-ance of Scholes and preachers . . . and for money and other things to be continued and paid to the poor" links Swanage and a school near Bridport when it states, "We . . . have assigned and appoynted that the said Grammar Scole in Netherbury aforesaid shall contynue And that Martyne Smythe Scolemaster . . . shall have for his wages yerelie Cvis viiid And that the said xs xid shalbe paid yerelie to the mayntennance of the Sea Bankes in Sandwiche aforesaid as heretofore it hath been accustomed", all this to be paid "out of certyn lands within the parishe of Sand wiche".

Stone bankers on the sea front were the foundation of Swanage's later wealth. John Mowlem's nephew, George Burt, who headed the firm that his uncle founded in London, built Purbeck House to command the High Street at the point where it runs down towards the water, a place where he could retire and brood over the town he so dearly wished to hatch in his own image. It is constructed like a monumental puzzle from fragments gleaned from his London contracts. Cornish granite trims walls faced with colourful chippings from the base of the Albert Memorial in Hyde Park; columns and a balustrade came from Old Billingsgate; a reproduction Parthenon frieze graces the stable block; and an arch, worked by the brothers Burt and first erected at Hyde Park Corner, stands in the garden, together with statues and busts, often the worse for wear and weather, from the Royal Exchange and other places. Tiles and stone from the Houses of Parliament and Doric columns from Waterloo Bridge contributed to the temple in the grounds, while the circular summer-house contains the only major relic of the Purbeck stone trade: a rotating table-top built upon one of the six-foot diameter wheels from a stone-cart that used to ply between the bankers and the boats in Swanage Bay. These, and many other London relics, were inherited, after Purbeck House had stood empty for many years, by the convent and school that now inhabit it.

George's grandmother might not have approved. It was she, so claims the inscription on the Wesley Memorial Church, who walked to Salisbury to bring the preacher to Swanage in 1774. The cottage opposite Purbeck House where he briefly sojourned was known as John Wesley's Cottage until it was destroyed by a bomb in 1941. His judgement of the town was this: that three or four persons, all of one family, "seemed really to enjoy the faith of the gospel. Few others . . . appeared to be convinced of sin. I fear the preachers have been more studious to please than to awaken, or there would have been a deeper work."

If Swanage clergy made it their business to gratify rather than to stir their patrons, it appears that both were concerned to stem the tide of lawlessness with which certain elements of the lower orders threatened to engulf the town. A House of Confinement, or lock-up, was built north of the church tower; small and solid, with a barrel-vaulted roof, no windows and an iron-studded door surmounted by the legend, "Erected for the Prevention of Vice & Immorality By the Friends of Religion & good Order AD 1803". A poor substitute for the deeper work at which Wesley aimed, it was moved eventually from the shadow of the church to its present site behind the Town Hall. It was from this, his King Alfred's Hall in the High Street, that Burt must have hoped that his town would be re-ordered. Into the design of Crickmay's sober building of 1882 he incorporated the frontispiece of the Mercer's Hall in Cheapside, an elaborate, voluptuous stone fantasy of 1670, whose City grime has been scoured by Swanage's weather.

Meanwhile, it was William Morton Pitt who was studious to provide work and to please, the first to prevent crime, and the second to make money. He tried to establish fisheries and a herring-curing industry, but it failed, and his factory on King's Road West became a brewery before it was burnt down in 1854. At the same time he wanted to transform Leland's "fishar town" into a watering-place comparable with Weymouth or Lyme Regis. In 1825, Billiard and Coffee Rooms were built above Baths, and named the Marine Villas; the Manor House on the front was given the sobriquet Hotel, proudly renamed the Royal Victoria after the Princess stayed the night there in 1835. Pitt died the following year, having lost his fortune by his good works and before he could recoup it from rich visitors.

At that time, the area between the hotel and the fine sand so admirable for sea-bathing presented a very different appearance. Teams of horses dragged lumbering loads of stone from the quarrs down through the narrow streets of the town to be stacked up in the merchants' depots between Pitt's old quay and the Swan Brook. The tall heaps of dressed stone were called bankers, and derricks, operated from stone-tiled winch-huts, lowered blocks of building stone, tiles, flatteners or flags, pitchers and setts for road-laying, troughs, sinks and pillars into high-wheeled carts in the water; the horses waded out to stone-lighters in the bay, which in turn transferred the stone to ketches in deeper water. The number of handling operations depended upon the state of the tide, but the labour and risk they involved is unimaginable today. John Mowlem, as chairman of the Swanage Pier and Tramway Company, headed the effort to streamline the procedure with a scheme to lay a line from Langton to the new pier of 1859. Rails are still embedded in the promenade, running back into the coal depot that is now an amusement arcade called Playland, and alongside it to the site of the bankers. They never got much further, and in 1885 the main-line railway reached Swanage, though the spur planned to service the bankers was obstructed by Mowlem's rivals. The bankers slowly dwindled, and horses carted stone direct to Swanage station. In 1896, a new pier was built, at a cost of £10,000, to serve paddle-steamers and the trippers which they disgorged. So it was that the face of Swanage finally lifted from the grind of the stone trade and turned itself whole-heartedly to the studious provision of pleasure.

Amusement has replaced the solid stuff of business. Bathers and hired boats have ousted labourers and working vessels. The bowels of the Royal Victoria reverberate now to the discotheque within. Anachronistic leather-boys still stack their bikes where the bankers stood. Good writers, painters and sculptors who work about the old town are far outnumbered in bars and at parties by talk-artists and has-beens who never were. Mariners and fishermen who have incessantly sailed the seven seas in pea-green boats navigate the narrow passages between the pubs. Posh bars and boutiques cater for the inhabitants of sea-front flats and dream cliff-houses. Retired people stroll in parks and gardens overlooking the sea, away from it all, while streams of holiday-makers clog the promenade and double-yellow-lined streets with their cars. Somehow the fantasies of today seem meaner, more prosaic than the bold, grand notions that possessed the town in the last century.

Perhaps, as Purbeck people say, new maggots stopped biting John Mowlem, for in 1844 he retired from his planning and scheming to Number 2, Victoria Terrace, where the turret of his observatory still dominates the roof-tops. There he got away from the fashionable soirées of the watering-place, from the bustle of the working town, and from the raw stone, worked stone, ambitious building stone that spawned him; away to the serene contemplation of the stars. My favourite experience of Swanage is of weaving through its strait streets in moonlight, making my way downhill through a stone maze whose curiosities, drawn from half London as well as its own ground, loom again and again out of the darkness; solid bollards from City streets, whimsical details in stone, and whole buildings and monuments I have not touched upon; past light breaking from bakery windows with the pungent ferment of yeast; and, at last, the scent of the full-bodied sea and the sound of its deep obscure rhythm pounding against the stone of the sea-wall. Then its air breathes full in your face, and its swell heaves the stars that burn in its depths, embraced by the ghostly white cliffs of Ballard Point and the long arm of Peveril pointing towards the dawn. For a while the works of man float away on the tide of night, until the sun erupting above the sea's edge salvages them; plastic, ephemeral fantasies, some of them, and others, both stolid and eccentric, built with a craftsman's pride out of the hard stuff.

22

ANCIENT BEASTS, ANCIENT ORDER

UPHILL TO THE south-west Swanage peters out raggedly, and with good reason. Sir Charles Robinson's first house above Peveril Down disappeared into quarry lanes beneath, and the end of Alexandra Terrace foundered above the Cowleaze workings. The full extent of the shafts that undermine the slopes cannot be known, for quarrying families kept close about the levels and seams they plundered, and knowledge of the old lanes died with the old men. Where Burt built a house or a hospital you can be pretty sure the ground is sound, but stonecutters were not exempt from disaster, for Seth Benfield's cottage was undermined by a fellow quarrier and collapsed into a hole, forcing him to move into his own quarry. Men will tell you that a number of Swanage dwellings, apparently founded on solid rock, are actually perched above a honeycomb propped by the stone legs with which the miners caught the ceilings above their heads.

A carvan site climbs steeply up towards the plateau, with mobile homes on plinths of glowing Purbeck stone; while the rough land that borders it is a range of overgrown scar heaps. The tops of scrubby woodland poke out like islands among the rough grass, concealing the quarry entrances that their roots plumb. On the otherwise barren, windswept stoneland, elder, blackthorn, bramble, sloe, briar and burnet rose find shelter enough in the quarr craters to germinate and raise their heads, lush with pale blossom or dark berries, hips and haws, to the light. Many of the shafts have been blocked in for safety's sake, but if you can penetrate the thorns, nettles and twining tangle of clematis and ivy, you may find yourself in no mere hole in the ground, but a scrupulously-built place, whose well-made walls and beautifully keyed arches to the underworld testify that you are in the province of workers, as well as getters, of stone. In some places the drystone of the quarr houses survives, hidden under dense shrubbery, and sometimes, between these and the heads of the old shafts, pairs of crab-stones stand like sculpture, outstaring one another, vacant sockets cut in their freestone where an oak collar slotted and held the elm capstan-post in place. Weeds have even conquered the hard-packed stony soil where men or beasts trod the capstan's ash spack round and around to fetch each load of raw stone up into the daylight.

Despite dumped rubbish and rusting debris deposited out of mind, life still thrives here. One day, with eyes intent on treacherous footing and on the stony face around the quarry's mouth, I suddenly found myself face to face with a collared dove reproaching me with soft eyes from her rough nest, long after the small birds had ceased gorging themselves on berries and had fled my crashing invasion of their subterranean woods. Signs are here too of badger and fox who revel in their usurpation of the palatial burrows bequeathed to them by man. They can dig their way, beneath rubble and rubbish, back into the forgotten territory, while bats, notably the greater horseshoe, are confined to unblocked haunts where they may hang deep underground in the thick darkness.

Down there, in the aboriginal dark, undisturbed by iron and muscle, lie ancient beasts, the dead whose bones and shells and prints give bulk and texture to the virgin rocks. Their fossils petrify time itself, freeing the imagination from the Purbeck uplands, and demanding unimaginable shifts of altitude and latitude in the tracing of their lineage. Most quarries between Kingston and the cliffs of Durlston Bay plumb the Middle Purbeck Beds, at whose base lies a thin layer of fossil soil, an old land-surface from which Beckles dug the remains of primitive mammals, cat-like, opossum-like and rodent-like, from a quarry near Hill Crest School in 1856. Marsh-loving crocodile species are abundant at this level, both full-sized and dwarfed. The freshwater Flint Bed, full of shells and black chert, is followed by the workable lower building stones called New Vein, Cap and Feather in quarriers' rather than geologists' terminology. Then comes ten feet or so of Cinder Bed, packed with oysters and other marine shells from a time when the sea conquered all; and after that, the marine and freshwater beds of the middle and upper building stones, separated by clayey dirt, often laid down in warm, brackish estuaries whose fishes, turtles and other reptiles are disinterred by today's quarrymen, and whose megalosaurs and iguanodons laid their tracks through the Roach beds of today's pits.

If it is hard to conceive of such creatures and such conditions, it is also difficult to imagine the race of men that worked their way underground so recently. Heathcroppers scratched an ephemeral living from acid soils; clay-cutters, with all their lore, were relative newcomers earning wages from upstart entrepreneurs; shepherds might lord it over the downs, but agricultural workers were peasants, only lately discovering some dignity in the struggle for lawful combination, who might be found in any valley in England; while stonecutters were freemen of an ancient guild, whose families could trace their ancestry as well as many of the gentry on whose land they dug. Unlike the dinosaurs, they have not become extinct, for they have adapted themselves to changing conditions. Some of the techniques and customs that distinguished them, that gave them the lineage and pride of an élite, have gone; yet in many ways their descendants are still a special breed of men.

Until the early years of this century they lived by sinking shafts fifty feet or more into the ground. This initial hole, paved as necessary, became the slide up which stone-carts were hauled. Its angle had to be carefully calculated: a shallow shaft required more props of stout ash, more likely to spew and destroy a huge investment in time and sweat; a steep shaft made harder work of haulage. Lanes were driven out along the chosen seams for perhaps a hundred feet, and legs were caught, that is built of stone and wedged against the ceiling. Wood wedged between leg and roof warned of any movement. To catch a leg in the wrong place might cause a fall rather than prevent it, so that an intimate knowledge of each seam's temperament was necessary for success and for survival. In 1268, a verdict of misadventure was recorded on Walter le Vel and Hugh le Mochel who were crushed in Peter de Clavile's stone quarry where they were digging with a pick valued at 6d; and there are enough recent stories of crushed heads and amputated limbs as a result of founders to inspire respect, in young apprentices, for the rock and the old men's knowledge of it.

Old men often worked their last years in the Lannen, or Laning, Vein which was fairly close to the surface, and whose three-foot lanes, although cramped, required less strenuous lifting to catch legs there. It is impossible to generalise about the depths of strata, for they rise from beneath the Corfe valley till they run roughly horizontal, but are plunged down once more by a fault that cleaves the centre of the plateau. More than that, the Portland and Purbeck Beds are tilted up, so that the older seams surface westwards. The seams vary so much in quality in so few yards that the desirable rock in one quarry may be shivered in the next. Consequently the names by which they are known also vary from working to working and from family to family. Nor are quarriers necessarily geologists; one man dressing stone at his banker earnestly informed me that the marble vein was deep beneath our feet and only outcropped down the hill. He knew where it could be dug, but as it is almost the top layer of the Purbeck Beds it peters out on the lower slopes. If millennia of weathering had not removed it it would have outcropped many feet above our heads. These factors, and the confusion of quarriers' and geologists' terms, may explain some of what has been said and written on the subject.

Below the marble, but uphill from it, is the burr, the great building stone of the eleventh century; then the marble rag and the Laper, Roach and Black Bed of the Laning End. The shafts were usually driven through the Laning Vein and the Rag, with its Devil's Bed, Royal Rag and Mead Bed, including blue stone excellent for memorials when consistent in colour, but more often crushed for road-metal or ideal in bulk for harbour infilling and otherwise obstinate to work and hard to sell. The top layer of the Freestone is the Grub, a hard stone that can be cut and polished, but which was often left as a ceiling above the Roach's layers. A hard, shelly conglomerate, the Roach makes good building stone, and splits into excellent cladding. Its Pink Bed bears the most abundant dinosaur tracks. Next comes the Grey-bit, the grainy Thornback or Sugar that Mount Misery was famous for, and the buff, shelly Wetson, or Whitstone Bed. The Freestone series was twelve feet or more deep, but the prize dug from its six-foot lanes was two to three feet of fine Freestone proper, ideal for building but notorious for falls on to its floor of White Horse overlying Dun Cow, and now dug out of ridden-holes at Acton. But in the early eighteenth century it was the products of the Downsvein beneath that Daniel Defoe noted; for 250 years paving of all kinds was exported from Swanage in a fleet of ships for London's roads, courtyards and alleys. Locally, it was used for tiles, or slats, and many a Purbeck cottage is built of its waste. Beneath Laper and Grey Vein, the Downsvein's seven thin beds cleave out of winding; they are separated by easily underpicked dirt, though the stone had to be cut small because a treacherous ceiling demanded close legs; the lanes were three feet high, cramped as well as deep, and Downsvein men were said to surface only in times of dispute.

The Cinder Bed is as real a boundary underground as anything above; it is hard, intractable, useless rock, and when all the Swanage Caps had been dug Langton quarriers had to punch or blast their way through twelve feet of it, or else dig the dip-slope of the Wares where it dies out. The Caps it covered consisted of Button, Feather and Cap itself, a two-foot layer dug from taller lanes than the Downsvein, but the shaly floor had to be paved so that carts could run along it, and so that crowbars could purchase enough leverage to shift the large creamy blocks that furnished kerb-stones for mile upon mile of city streets. Still further beneath are the Sky, Five or Six, White, Brassey and Tompson Beds of the New Vein.

The appearance of raw dry rock at the surface is deceptive. The lanes were pitch dark, but for a candle stuck in a dob of clay, slippery and damp with cold, dripping water, although the temperature might be a constant fifty degrees before men began to labour in the confined, humid spaces. A man had to be wed to his tools, alert to the feel and note of iron struck on rock. Dirt was underpicked with a paddle, a bar with a flat end, driven with a hammer until a man could tell when he had reached the rock's back joint; with the dirt removed, a hammer blow sang to tell him that the block was dying to come. Big stones were propped, or trigged up, with smaller stones that had to be extracted, by crawling underneath, one by one, in exactly the right order, for a quarryman wanted a worked block at his head when the time came, rather than an unworked block on top of it. The stone was heaved on to a cart or trundle of elm reinforced with iron plates, 4′ by 2′ 6″, set off the ground on four wheels in such a way that it could be tipped to receive its load. It had to be manoeuvrable to negotiate narrow lanes, for a cart-load of stone was just the job for sweeping legs out of its path. The quarrier ran backwards, with the chain biting into his hips, sometimes stopping to adjust the chained load to suit the gradient, until he reached the slide where he hooked the trundle on to the capstan chain. Then a man above, or himself if he was single-handed, could tread the spack, the capstan arm, around or let the donkey do the work until the load lurched out of the shaft's arched entrance. Buttress-stones braced the crabstones against the strain and a roller carried the chain over the groove at the slide's top. Some quarrs had rails down the shaft and along the lanes. The size of the capstan post and the length of the spack depended upon the depth and angle of the shaft, while a fistful of grease in the gudgeon-hole and round the capstan's neck kept the sturdy mechanics of the business in good trim.

Traditional dress for going to work was a top-hat and tail-coat hung on a hook in the quarr-house for the day. But this was not surprising, for clay-cutters, and many another self-respecting tradesman, sported bowlers. A few old men persisted with this uniform until the First War. Moleskin trousers of shaved fustian, and leggings, protected them; crops, or the crown of a hat, kept their hair dry and clean; sheepskin shielded neck and shoulders, especially in the cramped lanes. Only half the work was underground; quarr-huts were built opposite one another so that a man could

always work away from the prevailing wind. There, stone was cleft and
dressed, made up into orders and loaded, from bankers built of scars to
cart-height, for the bankers at Swanage or, later, for Swanage Railway
Station. Handling stone in the bay was hard on man and beast, and not
especially easy in the station yard; there, an old man might shift forty or
fifty tons of stone in a day. Quarriers went home from the shafts covered
in clay, or from the bankers impregnated with stone dust that filled the air
and often provoked lung complaints. A man would let his muscles sag by
his own hearth, and be washed clean of sweat and dirt. Not that quarr dirt
was dirty: newly disinterred from its ancestral seam, it was virgin dirt and,
though hardened, a quarrier's hands were not ingrained with grime. His
hands, his strength, the technique that made the most of what strength he
had and, as he grew older, replaced muscle with skill: these were his pride.

His pedigree could be traced on paper for a few hundred years and, as
likely as not, went back a good way beyond the records. He was a man of
the company whose latest charter, inscribed in the memory if not on
paper, dated from the reign of Anne, but which probably originated at
the time when Corfe Castle was in the building. The medieval construction industry was capitalist rather than feudal, and stonecutters moved
freely, for wages, from one master to another. They were thus freemen
who organised themselves into guilds to preserve their freedom and
protect their privileges, freemasons in the original, literal sense. When
nineteenth-century magnates, like John Mowlem and George Burt,
donned the ritual garb of latter-day freemasons they subscribed to a per-
verse anachronism. When the Company of Marblers was summoned to
the Shrove Tuesday meeting at Corfe the articles were confirmed to them,
including the obligations which freemen bound themselves to keep; if
broken, the company required the forfeiture of fines ranging from twelve
pence to five pounds, as set out in the ten articles, or commandments,
of 1651.

No man should set into his fellow tradesmen's quarr, nor come within
a hundred feet of it within a year and a day of his fellow working there.
Usually disputes were settled locally, but if this was not possible the
warden of the company was informed and his steward brought the trade
together for a meeting, often at Greasehead, half-way between Langton
and Swanage. For a time there was a rift between the two towns, and
rival companies were set up; even after the schism was healed, a Swanage
clerk and a Langton clerk recorded their own version of the proceedings
for a time. Arguments over underground workings were hot and hard to

adjudicate. Plaintiffs might have been aware that a rival was trying to annex the same underground territory for days, each hearing the other's labour reverberating through intervening rock. The meeting would vindicate one or the other, or draw a compromise boundary line. When a vote was taken it was customary for the Ayes to step across the capstan chain.

Selling stone under an alias and undercreeping, or undercutting, were forbidden. Partnerships with outsiders and the hiring of labourers were not allowed. Apprentices had to be taken into a freeman's house, uprising and downlying, for a full seven years, which in practice tended to confine the trade to quarriers' sons. Base livers, bastards or sons of loose parents were barred. A new apprentice had to pay 6s 8d, a penny loaf and two pots of beer. The Shrove Tuesday following his marriage every man was to pay 12d, and the last married contributed a football. New-born sons were registered at the meeting, and if a quarryman had died his widow was able to pay 12d for her freedom, and thenceforth could engage apprentices and manage her own quarr. Men forfeited 3s if, when so instructed, they failed to appear before the wardens, and those that hindered meetings were fined 12d. The stock of the company was given into the custody of the town warden, provided that he had the security for it. The company bound themselves, their heirs, executors and assigns in the forfeiture of £10 to these articles, of which the tenth forbade the revelation of the company's secrets.

The company was jealous of its quarrying rights. Once a man agreed with a landlord on the site of a quarry, and paid the fine on it which some still see as an unwarranted charge, he sank his shaft and founded his capstan; and, so long as it was not idle for a year and a day, it was his property, the landlord receiving royalties on the stone dug. Agreements between D. Alexander Esq. and the quarriers J. Haysom and Thomas Benfield Junr for workings at Durlston fixed the dues at 6d a ton in the 1840s. Other people too were jealous of their rights, resenting the arrogance and exclusiveness of the company. They did not respect a long-lost charter, and saw the stonecutters as taking unwarranted liberties and behaving as if they were outside the law. The influx of new blood into nineteenth-century Swanage confirmed these feelings and some landowners began to exact rents, demanding the signing of agreements such as those cited above. Some quarrymen went along with them, while others hotly resisted any signing away of rights which obtained to them time out of mind. In the face of an injunction, "Bosser" Lander opened a quarry and stubbornly worked it

until he was imprisoned for contempt in 1903, long before the case had
been settled in court. In 1889, the Earl of Eldon presented H. W. and
F. A. Burt with a notice to quit their Swanage quarry, which they con-
tested in a long correspondence concerning rights and customs, until a writ
was taken out in the High Court of Chancery. The Burts gave in, but not
before it was agreed that Lord Eldon's agents would pay £20, in 1897, by
way of compensation. By this time, quarriers were well on the way to
being ousted from the salubrious resort which had so recently been their
port. The Parade and Institute Road were built over the old bankers. Sir
Charles Robinson had stone posts erected to prevent carts reaching the sea-
front, but they were swiftly dispatched with sledges, and on one occasion
the enemies of the company bricked up the doors and windows of Corfe
Town Hall, to prevent the Shrove Tuesday meeting.

Little wonder then that their sense of solidarity persisted. They had a
reputation for closeness, and the habit of marriage amongst their own
kind continued, long after an alliance with an outsider required the Constable of Corfe's permission. However, the Langton schools imported
female blood which was not slow to course through future quarriers'
veins, and masons sometimes brought brides from London or Liverpool.
The old curse, provoked by a worker who urinated down the walls of the
Temple in Jerusalem, was that stone-workers should be restless upon the
earth. Their freedom was two-edged. When great cathedrals or municipal
monuments were being built men left their quarrs and travelled the
country to employ their finer skills. But migration also occurred in times
of slump, when stone piled up unsold at quarr-mouth and banker. The
Dissolution of the Monasteries and the Reformation both depressed
ecclesiastical contracts, and masons touted for work in the great houses of
new landowners and merchants. The First War and the use of concrete
threatened to bring the trade to its knees, but it was not until the thirties
that the slump bit hardest. Smartly-dressed masons from London were
jealously regarded, but insecure employment and temporary lodgings did
not suit an independent man who preferred to keep his quarr ticking over,
tending the gardens that often adorned the head of his shaft, and eking out
his income with a bit of poaching and beachcombing in his native island.
When work dried up in town, men returned anyway and many a new-
found wife discovered that she was married to a clay-stained quarrier
rather than the neat mason she had wed.

In the bad old days some men hardly touched money and shop-keepers
exchanged goods for stone, Swanage pennies as the slabs were called. A

man might go to buy bread laden with this currency, and pubs, like the Black Swan, acquired their own bankers to block the windows. Blacksmiths, like the Smiths of Langton and Swanage and William Combs of Court Hill who made cable chains for the capstans, were badly hit in hard times and bitterly complained of quarriers whose debts mounted on their slates. If he was lucky the smith could recoup his losses with ironwork for estates or tool-setting for farmers, but the mason was dependent on his punches, chisels and pitchers that were used up by stonecutting and dressing. Tools could be ruined by a moment's overheating; the temper on steel had to be straw-coloured, so that a chisel kept its edge, yet was not brittle. As smiths died out, more and more work was done on small forges in the quarr-huts, though tungsten steel and chisel claws with interchangeable blades have made it less important now. The forge, together with tools, spack, roller and pony or donkey, all locked away in the hut when the quarryman went home, were his major assets. Apart from royalties on stone, blacksmiths' bills and expenditure on candles and the hire or keep of his animal were the major overheads he had to bear. In the 1920s a number of co-operatives were started, both to share resources and to reduce profitless competition, but times were bleak for Purbeck's élite.

There were good times too, when the marbler's sense of ancestry was matched by his relative opulence. In 1793 Claridge estimated that 50,000 tons were shipped from Swanage per annum, and Mr Chinchen put the figure at 38,750 tons shipped and 150 tons carried inland for the years 1801–6. By the last quarter of the century the number of workers had dropped from over 400 to 264, working in 92 quarrs, and output had declined to little more than 13,000 tons. It is said that there were 500 stoneworkers in Purbeck before the last war, but the number of quarries has dropped to less than 50 with about twice that number of men working them.

Though the way to the brick Passage House, with its ancient stone foundations, at Ower is still kept open, many other traditions have withered away. February 2nd no longer sees the Kissing Day at Langton when freeboys, sons of freemen, claimed their rights from any girl they could catch. But the greatest change has been in the method of digging stone. All the quarries are open-cast now, regarded with distaste by the old men as mere ridden-holes. A quarrier's greatest expense is having the initial hole gouged out of the fields. At Swanage Quarries, the most versatile stone now dug is the relatively shallow Roach, which alone pays back the investment in building stone and cladding for breeze-block houses. Prints and casts of dinosaur tracks fetch a good price, treading as they do across the quarry floors, though parts of prints and the grooves left by the animal's dragging tail render the rock useless. In summer the emphasis is on getting the stone out and dispatching it, while in winter splitting, dressing and stocking up with blocks, rockery stone and cladding takes precedence. Quarr-houses of drystone are full of immaculately faced stone, graded according to size and colour, while outside unworked rocks take their chance in the hard frosts.

Rocks are cleft vertically by being put through a mangle-like contraption, a hydraulic rock-splitter with square iron bars whose angles exert enormous pressure at top and bottom; but many skills are practised just as they were when rock was first lifted from these hills. As a boy I bought myself chisels and a lump hammer, and spent hours trying to tame Purbeck stone in the back garden; by the time the tools were blunt I had learnt enough to admire the craft so briskly executed in every quarr-hut in the island. A man sizes up a stone before he sets steel to it, piercing it by eye and judging its clift. He knows its seams, and its lists or places that look like snail-trails on some beds. Skilled men can cut across the grain of a nor'eastern list, but not a nor'western that follows the main faults of the formation. In general the stone must be cleft centrally, for a break will run off to the lighter side, though wedge-pits cut with hammer and punch may be driven towards the heavier side, against the natural clift, so that when wedges force the stone apart the final cleavage will come right. Wedge-pits are cut deep so that the point of the wedge, or gad, does not touch bottom, otherwise a hammer blow will launch the lump of metal into space; one way, it is said, of bringing down a pigeon or two, but no good for breaking stone. Wedges are often slotted into grooves cut by power-saw these days, but the biddle, or heavy hammer, still comes into its own. It is brought down upon the gads in sequence with carefully judged weight, a matter of the note struck and the strain felt through its shaft, until the last blow on the last gad cleaves the block. Eye, ear, and the sense and rhythm of muscle combine with craft to prepare the way for punch and chisel, as they once combined to shape Corfe Castle's flanks, the calloused piers of London Bridge or the foundations of the Tower of London.

The quarrier's biddle and wedge and the mason's mallet and chisel are still in daily use, though the slatter's pittaway and slatting hammer are rarely seen, and many of the old mysteries are dead and buried in the darkness and secrecy of the old shafts. The Bankes family exact small rents and often neglect the collection of dues, while Swanage Council charges higher rents and royalties, surprisingly not unwelcome to those who want to maintain the Purbeck stone industry on a sound economic basis. Men there do not necessarily belong to the ancient company, which some see as an outdated, frivolous affair concerned with flogging bird-baths to tourists and doing nothing for employment in the area. Stone in its bed is exposed now, and a man can walk into a pit in sight of the sea and select and judge the seams that undulate along its length, while young men work with the old tools, never having crept along the lanes beneath their feet where the old men fetched out Caps and New Vein. Ponies and donkeys no longer wind the capstans, nor do horses lead stone-carts down the hill. The railway too has deserted Swanage, and lorries ship every ounce of stone from Purbeck Island.

The Priest's Way still runs across the pocked plateau, where the priest from Worth, self-important centre of the stone industry, trod to perform services in the little fishing village that squatted beside Swanage Bay. It is bounded by stone walls which, though it is open to the sky on the downs, give it an air of seclusion abetted by the wild roses, thorns, brambles and sloe that clamber and cluster over them. The road runs as a corridor between stone-hemmed fields, with lesser tracks, droves and ancient field-boundaries running off north and south. The courses of these walls are mostly built level, their stones tilted outwards to shrug off the rain, but sometimes they grow out of the earth as if they continued the strata that climb underground. Even though broken down in places by scrambling sheep and careless walkers, their flow southwards to the cliffs overrides the pattern of strip-fields that underlie their web. It was good wheat country, though its barley was not pale enough, but it is mostly pasture now. Working farms with their clusters of old stone barns and outbuildings outcrop along its route, while one, taken over and given a swimming pool, has been elegantly remodelled in fresh, honey-coloured stone. Less obvious are the broken-down, overgrown remains of quarr-houses, one sheltering a disused capstan post, that still preside over concealed shafts on both sides of the way. Near South Barn, unharnessed donkeys graze beside redundant crabstones and a lime kiln crumbles, whose chimney-pit packed with culm and limestone, used to glow at night like a dull beacon.

It is possible to sit down on the grassy track, at the foot of an over-spreading sycamore, the only tree in sight apart from stunted, wind-warped blackthorns frothing with blossom, with bees working the limestone flora and the sea's scent coming on the breeze, and be quite innocent of the intense industry that once undermined and underpinned the place. But the Priest's Way is essential Purbeck, its charm and secretiveness inseparable from its scars. Near Belle Vue there is a memorial stone to the old ways, and an invocation of the present peace; it reads, "Beneath this stone lie our mule. She was a faithful creature drawing up stone from this quarry for 32 years. Died aged 34 years. Also our little cat named Too Too who followed her master from this quarry to his home and back for 20 mnths. R.I.P. Also our little pet dog named Flossie who died of . . ." The latest inscription, cut there by Warren Bonfield in 1919, has weathered the worst and is indecipherable.

23

RIDDING AND RIGHT OF WRECK

ABOVE A FRINGE of sea-wrack and rocks plucked from every Purbeck vein, Durlston Bay's strata rise southwards, through faults and land-slips, building the island's bulwark against the sea. Gypsum and alabaster were extracted from the Lower Purbeck Beds, and building stone, cut from the cliff-face, slithered down ramps directly into stone-boats, guided by men who waded in the water below. At Durlston Head a great fault shifts the Lower Purbeck marls to the cliff-top, and the Portland Beds shoulder their way above sea-level. It is they that buttress the beachless, sheer shoreline between here and St Aldhelm's Head against the breakers broiling at their feet.

Swanage's gentle sands underwrote its success as a resort, and Burt dreamt of founding an idyllic estate called Durlston Park upon the rugged cliffs. Elegant terraces were to crown them, and quarry land was to be transformed with trees and shrubs, paved walks and seats of stone into a pleasure garden cultivated with refreshment rooms and tennis courts. Burt's vision and Crickmay's plans conspired, against Sir Charles Robinson's aesthetic quibbles, to raise the monuments that survive as a testament of the uncompleted grand design. The only wares that Park Road Market displays are the game, fish and fruit of its carved keystones. A circular water-works once fed a cistern in the ecclesiastical water-tower with a turret at the top of Taunton Road. The Belle Vue Refreshment Rooms, which became the Tilly Whim Inn, stand at the top of the zig-zag path that led down to Durlston Head, punctuated by stone seats and interrupted by cliff-falls. Above, turrets outcrop in duplicate atop a bastion that welcomes visitors in need of refreshment, who approach its towers and balustrades between granite bollards which were patterns for those that stand in Trafalgar Square. Durlston Castle was never intended to defend anything except George Burt's reputation as a public benefactor. Its massive lower walls, and the walls that line nearby paths, are peppered

with plaques purveying instruction and admonition: tables of tides and
other vital statistics, maps of the world with Swanage at its pivot, and
signs to the Large Globe. This last phenomenon is hedged about with
great slabs inscribed with passages from the Bible, from Shakespeare,
Shelley and other poets, laced with scientific data, while scope for graffito-
artists was generously granted on two stones, blank but for the inscription,
"Persons anxious to write their names will please do so on this stone only."
The Globe has weathered well, with its deeply incised oceans and con-
tinents in relief. Made in Mowlem's Greenwich yard and shipped to
Swanage in fifteen sections, its forty tons of Portland stone stand as a
monument to the mason's craft, to his mastery of the most adamant
materials of the earth's crust which lie, old sea-bed, infinitesimally eroded
by today's ocean, beneath its plinth.

When I first visited them, the major attractions were, contrary to
Burt's wishes, encumbered with ironmongery in the form of turnstiles
which admitted paying customers only. Now that the County Council
has taken over Durlston Country Park all that has been swept away, and
one can walk as Burt intended, sheltered by holm oak and feathery
tamarisk that thrive in the salt air. Burt's exhortations, "No guns or
sporting dogs allowed" and "Look round, and read Great Nature's open
Book" are supplemented by requests not to pick flowers or disturb wildlife. Spindle trees, sycamores, elders and blackthorn provide permanent
homes for tits and robins, and landfall for migrants like willow-warblers
and chiff-chaffs. The path drops down a little, though gulls, guillemots
and kittiwakes still wheel far below, to the much-vaunted Tilly Whim
Caves. Railings and a pier from Pentonville mark the entrance tunnel that
Burt blasted through to the caverns below. Suddenly you are in the cliff's
bowels; floor, walls and roof are all of rock; here is where eighteenth-
century quarriers gouged their way into the rock face, where they worked
stone for the façades of great buildings, gate-posts and pillars, stone sinks
and rick-staddles, and on calm days, when the sea did not threaten to
shiver the boats below against the rocks, winched their work down and
away. Durlston, or Durdlestone, comes from the Anglo-Saxon "thirl", to
pierce, suggesting that a door of rock, long since digested in the sea's
juices, stood at the Head; but the name of the caves is a mystery. Some say
that Tilly was a quarrier, though Tilly Mead is a field-name north of
Swanage, and that whim is dialect for winch, although derrick, gibbet and
wink are preferred terms, and Durlston became a whim or folly only after
the quarrymen had deserted her. The caves open on to ledges of stone

above the water, salt and light sting the eyes, walled walks and cunning construction give way to rugged shapes and the crude mass of rock. Above, refugees from inland like pigeons and jackdaws nest in natural crevices, alongside indigenous rock-pipits. Fulmars find shelter on over-hung ledges. Lower down, guillemots make do with exposed platforms, while kittiwakes build nesting sites of seaweed with almost no support at all. Brigand herring-gulls patrol, on the look-out for unguarded young, around the man-made caves where many a load of brandy, rum and wine, of Bohea tea and gunpowder, silk and lace were winched to temporary safety and sometimes stashed in a stone safe concealed by an innocent-looking banker, before transfer to the stone cellars of gentlemen and parsons. Here, in more ways than one, was the negative of the good life. Men employed and displayed their wealth by raising houses and monu-ments of stone, whose reflection at the water's edge was the yawning cavern staring out to sea, the laboriously sweated caves of air that grew in the coast's flank.

Before John Mowlem left for London in 1807, aged nineteen, he is said to have worked as a poor quarry-boy in these caves, a Caliban styed in the hard rock. In the capital he prospered, and he and his nephew returned to Swanage in a different guise, having assumed the Mason's mantle, symbol of their Art. But it is likely that Caliban's caves will long outlive Prospero's grand design, and it is impossible to know whether Burt exuded senten-tiousness or humility when he caused that character's lines to be cut in the rock of Tilly Whim:

> "The cloud capp'd towers, the gorgeous palaces,
> The solemn temples, the great globe itself,
> Yea, all which it inherit, shall dissolve;
> And, like the baseless fabric of a vision,
> Leave not a rack behind."

Just West of Tilly Whim, a valley that once drained the stone upland runs off the edge of the cliff; here are thrift, sea plantain and samphire; on the downs are squinancy wort, milkwort, bird's foot trefoil and orchids which have been trampled and picked almost to extinction; the corn bunting's chinking, tinkling song comes on the sea air and the stonechat's voice breaks small rocks above the quarries. Whitethroats and yellow-hammers nest in the valley trees and shrubs, in the shade of mantling ivy, but the combe is dry, its bed cut from under it by millennia of breakers exploding into spume in an altogether other timescale. The waves return us to the beginning of *The Tempest* where we are directed, "On a ship at sea: a tempestuous noise of thunder and lightning heard", and the ship's master shouts, "Fall to't, yarely, or we run ourselves aground; bestir, bestir." The masters of the rear-masted stone-boats were intimate with the lie of the ledges and the constellation of wind, tide and current about the cliffs, and were skilled in standing off beneath the quarries. But the gibbets from whose ropes the stones hung were sinister reminders of the treachery of the coast; the massive timbers from which their pillars, arms and diagonal supports were constructed had invariably been salvaged from the sea, the flotsam of ships wrecked near or far, and capstans by which the stone was lowered away were sometimes wound by a ship's wheel. Wreck of the sea has long been the prerogative of Purbeck men, and many a house or barn is trussed with ship's timbers, while cargoes washed up along the shoreline were appropriated for local use, or for the turning of a quick penny. Technically, a vessel had to be abandoned before she became legitimate prey, and boarding parties had ways of ensuring that the crew did leave their sinking ship; goods and timbers were officially reclaimable by the owners, within a year and a day, but were usually "lost" within hours of a disaster. The Abbot of Cerne and the Abbess of Shaftesbury who controlled much of this coast before the Dissolution were often rigorous in the exercise of their right of wreck. The seaman's unlucky landfall was the shoreman's propitious windfall; "when my ship comes in" was an expression of far from innocent hope, and bodies that came ashore were quickly relieved of valuable ballast.

After the crew of the *Wild Wave* had almost been lost off the treacherous Peveril Ledges, the life-boat *Charlotte Mary* was launched at Peveril in 1875. But easterly winds which impeded Swanage's sea-borne trade and kept coal-barges offshore for days at a time also made the life-boat's deployment difficult in precisely those seas which drove ships like the *Constitution* and the *Anna Margrethe* on to Handfast Point and Ballard Head in the winter of 1878. These wrecks were the stimulus for the building of the lighthouse on Anvil Point, just west of the dry combe, in 1880–1, to supersede the Telegraph and Signal Station whose ruined walls and foundations stand above it on Round Down. Nevertheless, a southerly gale the following spring, said to have driven sea-salt overland into the depths of Wiltshire, ripped the canvas of the great sailing ship *Alexandrovna* into flailing flags of distress to which the coastguards on St Aldhelm's Head responded in vain. The tempest drove the vessel

against the Ragged Rocks to the west of the lighthouse. All those aboard
were drowned and about twenty bodies, some later interred at Swanage,
were recovered from the sea or found wedged between the rocks. As if in
mourning, the salt-blasted elms, the coffin-trees, of Purbeck withheld
their leaves until late autumn.

Beyond Round Down, kestrels hover above cliffs whose stone walls
stop abruptly, far above ledges where the black cormorant and the
metallic shag breed. On calm summer days the cliff-top bakes above a
blue sea; they mix their smells, the sea aster glows mauve, the crimson
and black burnet moth balances precariously on the purple knapweed
flowers, and the chalk-hill blue, common blue and marbled white
butterflies make sorties in the fragrant air. It is a day to make for Dancing
Ledge along the cliff-path, watching yachts and fishing-boats ploughing
gull-strewn furrows in the pacific Channel, while you tread turf-
cushioned rock which only sailors can see is undermined by the gaping
mouths of cliff quarries like Blacker's Hole. Natives, impatient with
tourists' demands for entertainment, have been known to direct those in
search of a glittering night-spot to Dancing Ledge. But the broad platform of rock there is rutted with the wheels of man-drawn horn-carts
with shafts like out-curving antennae, though it is an ideal place from
which to dive, not into Durnford School's rock pool, but into the sea for
a final swim as the sun goes down behind St Aldhelm's Head. I remember
warming fires on the ledge pushing back the dusk, but powerless to
disperse the dense blackness of the caves where the foolhardy, fearless of
rock-falls, capered. Then the sea bremmed with firelight and moonlight,
and strangely bleached rock reared up against the stars as if it floated,
liquid with sea-sound, in the flickering and steadfast lights or was
swallowed by the deep caverns. Songs cried out to be sung and you
could dance if you liked, so long as you conserved enough wind for the
steep smugglers' path up to Spyway and Langton Matravers.

Westwards, little paths fall away to Scratch Arse, Smokey Hole the
Topmast quarries, and the cliff-path makes a detour around the quarry
shelf of Headbury where an eighteenth-century cannon aims seawards.
The bones of a derrick hide in the caves which were worked on two
levels. Where the quarry ceiling has fallen and the cliff-top gapes like an
elephant trap, plants have been quick to grow up in their new-found
shelter. After Mike's Quarry and Pig and Whistle, a domed gun-
emplacement above Seacombe presides over a scarred valley whose upper

slopes frown with the ridges of medieval lynchets. In a dry summer it could be in the Middle East, with parched grass clinging to glaring rock, scrub panting for moisture and dead rushes standing up in a dried-up ditch. Here too are quarries abandoned between the wars, and rugged deep-cut ledges where the water laps invitingly or menaces with churning fury.

The Purbeck Portland Stone is a thicker formation than on Portland Island itself. The stratum that cliff quarriers cut down to, that forms the sandy-white, black-speckled ledges and cave floors, is the topmost layer of the cherty series which weathers unevenly. Between ledge and water is the Prickle, or Puffin Ledge, where puffins in great numbers used to nest in the crevices. From the quarry floor upwards, for eight or ten feet is the high-quality Under Freestone, full of fragmented shells which ensure good weathering qualities. Above it is the Underpicking Cap, for here there are no dirt layers, and this seam of hard stuff had to be shifted before the Under Freestone could be lifted away. Holes were drilled, charges packed and touched off so that two feet was blasted out, leaving stun-marks in the remaining rock. Charges had to be carefully laid so as not to shiver the ceiling or spoil the freestone beneath, while twelve-foot legs had to be left or built to bear the massive burden of the overlying beds. Gads or pyramids of iron mounted on stout wooden shafts were employed in splitting the rock, at the depth required for the blocks, away from the bottom and the surrounding rock. This process was repeated until the cherty floor was reached, and blasting prepared the next instalment, and so on until the cavern might extend for two hundred feet into the cliff; or be deliberately foundered so that the upper layers could be dug out as from a ridden hole. The caves were also quarr-houses where the stone was worked before being dispatched by winch into the waiting boats. Man-hours of shifting rock out of the cliff, called ridding, has given Purbeck's south coast its weathered, pocked aspect, its hollow sockets that peer above the tides.

If Seacombe boasted the most extensive quarries, those at Winspit, on the eastern flank of St Aldhelm's Head, are the most atmospheric. There, rock benches descend like giant steps towards the sea, and recent ruins, plundered for their stone, squat among unworked rubble, for Winspit was worked until the end of the Second World War. Tunnels honeycomb the cliff and scar heaps support a scanty turf before the eastern caverns. Legs, like the primitive architecture of a rock-dwelling tribe, prop natural lintels of House Cap, or Spangle, which sports casts of the giant ammonite Titanites, and is puddled and cracked on its underside like baked mud.

Its grey bulk is surmounted by a thin layer of the less shelly, easily fractured Listy Bed. Above that comes five feet of chert, or Flint Stone, followed by the same depth of good Pond Freestone, opened in places like an upper storey, and ten feet of Titanites bed, or Bluestone, capped by white, fine-grained Shrimp Stone, full of crustaceans and shells. At times this ceiling of solid rock did shelter men who chose the workings as a hermitage. One constructed a solid door to his cave, while another slept in a barrel to escape the wind and the water that dripped from the roof of his rocky cell.

Those men dwelt there, for their own reasons, within living memory; but in the early hours of 6 January 1786 there were others who were pleased to find refuge in the grim caves east of Winspit. The East Indiaman *Halsewell* set sail for Bengal from Gravesend on 1 January, with almost 250 souls on board. Her sails soon became sheets of ice, heavy with snow in a wintry storm, and the mizzen mast had to be severed. The seamen were "remarkably inattentive and remiss . . . skulked in their hammocks, and left the exertions of the pumps". The coxswain and four men were drowned trying to uproot the main mast. When the wind shifted to the south, the master dropped anchor to avoid being swept into the dreadful St Aldhelm's Race, but it dragged and the vessel was thrust inexorably towards the cliffs, until she foundered at 2 a.m. in darkness and gale-force winds. Most saw no hope in committing themselves to the waves only to be dashed to death; Mr Meriton climbed out on a spar, fell, and was washed, with others who dared to jump overboard, into a quarry, an unexpected whale's belly for the Jonahs among them. Mr Rogers clutched a hen-coop and was swept on to the stone buttress known to this day as the Halsewell Rock. Of the twenty-seven other men who clung there, seven or eight managed to scale it and join their fellows. Below them, the ship broke up, to the accompaniment of screams from the men and women still aboard, and sank. Some of the men in the cave tried to climb the cliff and lost their last footing, but the cook and the quartermaster succeeded in reaching the summit and found their way to Eastington Farm, where they roused Mr Garland, steward to the proprietors of the quarries. Quarriers roped themselves together and dropped a noose from the cliff-top; the wind drove it into the cavern and, though some could not keep their hold on it, most of the survivors were hauled to safety. The villagers of Worth tended to their lacerated bodies and broken bones, and the seventy-fourth and last man was saved over twenty-four hours after the wrecking. Meriton and Rogers, the two chief officers, were among those who "happily escaped the dreadful catastrophe" and lived to write a somewhat self-satisfied account of the affair in 1796. Another record is preserved in Worth parish registers, and Dickens elaborated the story in "The Long Voyage". Flotsam was salvaged, including a mirror that hangs over the door in Worth church, and a green hour-glass, that runs for a four-hour watch, survived unbroken in its octagonal frame when the sands had run their course for so many who had sailed with it. Of the 168 souls lost, those who came ashore were buried in Seacombe Bottom.

In rough weather the caves are dank, sepulchral places inhabited by the shades of mariners, fishermen and stonecutters. The sea still crashes outside, but they no longer echo with the rumble of blasting or the gentler percussion of biddle, gad and punch. Prospero's pillared cell, or Caliban's sty, is deserted; the mason's magic has gone. Amongst the unworked rubble at Winspit I once found a worked block with words cut into its face. When a shaper of stone shapes letters on his stone there is rough magic in it; but these told an old story. The memorial was set up once again in 1976, and commemorates a young man drowned here in 1935. When the ship broke up off Prospero's island, Gonzales cried, "Now would I give a thousand furlongs of sea for an acre of barren ground, long heath, broom, furze, anything. The wills above be done! but I would fain die a dry death." The stone is more fully reconciled to the nature of the place. It states: "He loved birds and green places and the wind on the heath. He saw the brightness of the skirts of God."

24

LYNCHETS, "VIA CRUCIS/LUCIS"

NARROW DEFILES BLASTED out of the rock, sheltered from the weather and lush with climbing growth, lead to barred caves which are the preserve of the mouse-eared bat and other species that hang themselves up to sleep on the pure left stone within. Winspit Bottom is itself an over-grown defile running up between the Scylla and Charybdis of East Man and West Man, two dome-shaped hills whose steep slopes ripple with strip-lynchets which, late in their life, were cropped with flax by order of Henry VIII. They are stippled with a miniature landscape of mole-hills. Mole-catching used to be more common than it is; the miners' runs were noosed and little gibbets of withy and wire swung with plush 'oonts. Ant-hills, or emmutt butts, are raided by green woodpeckers who find shelter in the dense valley-within-the-valley which brims with willow, hawthorn and ivy, full of blue-tits and great-tits, bullfinches and goldcrests.

Caught between the hills is Winspit Cottage, its garden and vegetable plot walled off from the rife streambed below. It is a grey quarrier's house, bearing the marks of that calling in its fabric, and a fisherman's cottage, for Bowers have followed both trades. A large Purbeck family, their different branches and distant connections were distinguished by nicknames or wives' maiden names, like Sugar Bower, Razorback Bower, Gad Bower, Whistler Bower and Frenchy Bower, or Chinchen Bower, Brown Bower, Corben Bower and Ivamy Bower. But one of the most celebrated Bowers, who lived for almost eighty years and boasted that he never slept out of this hollow, was hardly known as a Bower at all. William Jeremiah Bower was christened in Worth church with his grand-father William's name, while his grandfather Jeremiah had him registered at Swanage under his name, but all his life he was known as Billy Winspit. Despite the rigours of launching his boat and landing his catch on the treacherous rock shelves, and at least one close call with gelignite in the quarries, he survived until 1966, the namesake of the place where he lived and died.

A little further up, on the other side of the track, is the Old Quarry where the upper layers of the Purbeck Portland Beds were worked, and out of whose stone much of the village of Worth Matravers is built. The path winds up the valley, beside the steeper valley; and the hills step up towards more strip-fields on the east, sometimes overlaid with narrow-rig ploughing where, one day, I watched a man mending his fence along the skyline. As he drove each post in, distance, like time, blurred and dislocated his stroke, for he struck the timber soundlessly and only when the sledge was poised above his head did I hear its crack and its quick echo. That fence was a late imposition on the landscape, but the drystone boundaries of the manors here are still more or less continuously marked. Eastington Farm on the Priest's Way, Worth itself, and Weston Farm are named in the Domesday Book as Wirde, Wrde and Orde, from the Anglo-Saxon "worth" or enclosure, and "ord" or point; Renscombe Farm was Romescumbe. At Weston and Eastington, the platforms, plots and terraces of the settlements survive.

Worth, in its hollow at the head of Winspit valley, was the hamlet that, of these four, grew and prospered. The footpath up to it leaves the streambed and crosses pasture-land grazed by horses and donkeys and fringed by allotments. The newer cottages and bungalows are extrovert, facing southwards to the sea, but the core of the village is turned in upon itself, crowded at the foot of the church that, on its hill, was sea-mark and land-mark to sailors and smugglers. London Row signifies the quarry-men's link with the metropolis, and above it the spring which served the village has been transformed into a pond in an unnecessary attempt at the picturesque, while the traditional focus of the village, the green, has long been invaded by cottages. Seventeenth- and eighteenth-century cottages form the bones of the place, whose rubble walls, pierced by secretive, sometimes stone-mullioned, windows, support wavy roofs of stone tiles. Where the hill runs up towards Langton, the old smithy is tacked on to three cottages and, behind, Worth farmhouse bears the date 1847, when part of it became the schoolhouse. At that time the Winspit quarries, opened and intensively worked in the years following the Napoleonic Wars, had already begun their slow decline, and with them the quarrying community and the prosperity of the village declined too, until the place was valued for its remoteness and its situation, rather than its foundation stones. Workers' cottages have been transmuted into bijoux properties, priced way beyond the means of local young people. Their middle-class inhabitants have recently been demanding public lavatories to be erected in the village to serve the incontinent influx of trippers. Most native working people live outside the picturesque part, in Council houses or war-time barrack accommodation condemned years ago. Both settlers and tourists have become a vital and a sapping influence on the economy of the island. Praise or blame for the present state of villages like Worth cannot easily be apportioned; but it is certain that every day a little more of the islanders' birthright is bought up or trampled under foot.

Worth's inland quarries were important in the Middle Ages, and until 1506 the rector of Worth or his vicar served the chapelry of Swanage at the obscure end of the Priest's Way. After that, Worth was a vicarage in the gift of the rector of Swanage, which had made its way up in the world. Like those at Arne and Studland, the church is dedicated to St Nicholas of Myra, though the Saxon building that stood here must have had another patron saint, for Nicholas only came into vogue in 1087. The pyramidal roof of the tower is, as at Church Knowle and Kimmeridge, an addition of the latter half of the last century; the south porch was constructed at the same time from the fabric of a chapel that abutted on to the nave; and the chancel was rebuilt in the thirteenth century. Otherwise, tower and nave date from about 1100, and tiny lancet windows suit a defensible place rather than a church. The corbels are very French, and there is a mystery over the source of the chevron-carved south doorway, while its tympanum, showing the Coronation of the Virgin, is said to have been blasted by Parliamentary musketeers from Poole. Inside, the chancel arch with its squints and upper "windows" is thought by some to have been transferred here after the Dissolution, while others argue that it is original and that recessed side altars took up the apparent slack. Many details, both delicate and grotesque, are reflected in the *Halsewell*'s mirror which now serves the patron saint of sailors.

In the chancel and porch are coffin-lids of Purbeck marble, two of infants or burials of hearts or viscera, and part of one dug from a grave on St Aldhelm's Head. Bones in earlier cists of stone were uncovered in the churchyard in the 1850s, but it is two relatively modern headstones that catch the eye; those of Benjamin Jesty and his wife Elizabeth. His reads: "(Sacred) to the Memory of Benj.ᵐ Jesty. (of Downshay) who departed this Life, April 16ᵗʰ 1816. aged 79 Years. He was born at Yetminster in this *County*, and was an upright honest Man: particularly *noted* for having been the first Person (known) that *introduced* the Cow Pox by *Inoculation*, and who from his great *strength of mind made the Experiment from* the (*Cow*) *on* his Wife and two Sons in the Year 1774." That year there was a severe outbreak of the "flower disease" in Dorset and smallpox inoculation was introduced into Yetminster. But not far away, at Upbury Farm, Benjamin Jesty took matter from the infected udder of a cow and inoculated his family with a stocking-needle. The local doctor praised and reprimanded him at once for his boldness, and treated his patients as for a common fever, with success. But Jesty was abused and pelted for his cruelty whenever he attended market. He knew that any dairyman or maid who had, like him, suffered from cow pox, was immune to smallpox. By 1802, Andrew Bell, rector of Swanage, was a vaccinator himself and brought the achievement of his Downshay neighbour to the attention of the Vaccine Pock Institution. So it was that, in 1805, nine years after Jenner had made the procedure respectable, Jesty rode off to London with clean shirts in a borrowed portmanteau to describe and demonstrate his experiment to the learned men of the Institution. They protected their prodigy from the smears of the Royal Jennerian Society, had his portrait painted and presented him with a testimonial and a pair of gold lancets. The recognition pleased Jesty, but the city did not, although he appreciated the luxury of daily shaves, something he normally enjoyed only of a Saturday at Wareham market. Locally, it was a privilege to be vaccinated by Benjamin Jesty or by Benjamin, his son. Mary Brown's memorial tablet in Worth church notes with pride that her mother, Abigail, was personally inoculated for cow pox by Benjamin Jesty of Downshay. If his wife's headstone is anything to go by, Elizabeth valued her husband's action in extending her life-span to its eighty-four years, for its states:

> "The Time we have allotted here
> We highly ought to prize,
> And strive to make Salvation sure
> Ere Death doth close our eyes".

For Death was a busybody then at everybody's door, and might knock it early or late. Deaths by crushing in the quarries and by drowning added their quota to the usual tally of diseases. Doctors acted in the dark and, in Purbeck, might be called out at night by a masked escort and ridden blindfold to a house where a smuggler lay wounded. One such man, pierced by the coastguard's musket fire, died at the old public house. Ale was surely quaffed then, and sea-songs sung before his funeral, but more serious business was in hand, for his comrades swore at his graveside to avenge him. Informers might be intimidated or maimed, or might wisely flee the island when their bug-a-lug, or effigy, was burnt; but the coastguard in question was removed for his own safety. His successor, coming down to Winspit to creep up, the term used in depositions of the day, on an illicit cargo run ashore there, was ambushed, blindfolded, bound, gagged, pinned out face down in the time-honoured manner of pagan crucifixions, and beaten half to death.

The Square and Compass was, as the name indicates, a stonecutters' as well as a smugglers' house. Though it was enlarged in the last century, its narrow bar, its stony nooks and crannies and its warm, matter-of-fact parlour are thick, metaphorically speaking, with the stone dust and sea-spray of the village and the valley it overlooks. Billy Winspit, born of both, is here in spirit and in oil-paint to supervise, with bright eyes in a weathered face, the drinking and the songs. The soil also adds its mythology to that of rock and water. "Remember him," it begins, "tenant varmer, bin had up years afore if he hadn't kept up his 'osses. Inspector were keen on they, 'oss-ploughin', otherwise he'd a bin done fur bad husbandry long since. He'd be tacklin' up the leane, middle, flies undone, jacket undone, hanging off his shoulders, all of a caddle, shirt undone to here in all weathers; he'd do the milk roun' in the ol' days. See him now, flip up the churn lid, ketch'n under his arm, dip the measure. 'Twas alright so long as th'inspector sampled what wuz in the jug, not in the churn. Had up fur watering many a time. Bad as the beer . . ." Now the beer wets tourists' throats in the season, and slakes the thirsts of men from barracks or the Atomic Energy Research Establishment at Winfrith, as well as flushing stone dust from quarriers' gullets.

If the square and compass, along with the biddle and wedge, were tools of their trade, their faith was life and death to many of them. Purbeck's quarrymen never exhibited the fervour of Cornish miners, for it is not in their nature. But many attended the church down in the village or the chapel above the pub, and many stonecutters were preachers too. Trammelled lives often bequeath a breadth of vision, just as the narrow thorny streamed running down to Winspit Bottom opens out into the sea. They lived in shafts and underground lanes, or tunnels burrowed into the cliff; for them the grave was the last pit, the last defile through which they had to pass. The north door of St Nicholas' Church has a legend carved in its stone jamb: VIA $^{CR}_{L}$ UCIS, and a pointing hand that shows, through a pane of clear glass, a glimpse of the stone cross, now part of the war memorial, which stands at the head of the churchyard. The door opens between two buttresses that unite above it and hold off the sinister corbel heads under the eaves. The cross, for devout quarrymen, was the leg that bore the overburden of their lives, and death was an emergence from the sweaty darkness of the workings into the light.

25

COASTGUARD, CHANTRY AND TOUT

THE ROCKY PROMONTORY of St Aldhelm's, or St Alban's, Head is driven like a wedge against the wind and waves of the English Channel. Wild combes pierce the coast at either side of this, the southernmost outpost of Purbeck. Storms sing in the quarry caves of Winspit and slice between West and East Man up towards Worth, warping exposed trees inland and scorching their seaward shoots with spray. West of Worth, beyond Weston Farm, the Coastguard Station lines up southwards, but still almost a mile from the cliff-edge. The road passes the field that was called New Close early in the eighteenth century and where, more recently, a wireless transmitting station sprawled and tested radar systems developed, in part, in war-time Langton. Its masts used to throb and moan in the high winds; Renscombe Farm's seventeenth-century buildings still squat solid against their onslaught. Romescumbe may mean ram's valley, and below West Hill the gale is funnelled from Chapman's Pool, up past Hill Bottom with its plantation and sheep wash, and inland to Sheepsleights and Combe Bottom where wind and blasting whip stone dust from the floor of Swanworth Quarries.

There, pottery of the late Bronze and early Iron Ages, worked shale and flint, bones and a bronze razor have given glimpses of an earlier way of life, and quern-stones and spelt wheat embedded in ancient storage pits show what was harvested from the 150 acres of Celtic fields whose banks emboss Kingston Down and undulate brokenly across St Aldhelm's Plain. From Renscombe the road turns due south and runs, pocked with potholes, the mile to St Aldhelm's Head Quarry. The track's stone walls, hedged with crooked thorn, let fly with gusts of gale-crazed sparrows whose flocks take wing and alight ahead again and again, a staccato vanguard, a cloud of wings in the wind. To the left, barley beards flail in fields ploughed for centuries on the Lower Purbeck soils; to the right, Horse Croft, Middle Plain and Emmet's Hill are old pasture land on the

Portland Stone, with a dry, cattle-grazed combe running down into the Portland Sands and off the cliffs.

At the combe's head the quarry's raw stone gleams even under the eye of the storm. Shelves of Shrimp, Spangle and Pond Freestone incline gently upwards as far as the valley's edge. Joints are visible which quarrymen exploit in cleaving the blocks that dwarf them, and the pit's air shakes with pneumatic drills' stutter, while older implements tap out a calculated tattoo. Stacks of worked stones stand beneath the timbers of a spider-like derrick-crane, laced with cable, hand-driven by winch-gear at its base, the only survivor of a type introduced into Purbeck from Portland after the First World War. Its arm barely protrudes above the surrounding soil surface, and quarr-huts of dry stone, roofed with livid corrugated iron, nestle in the shelter of the gash from which they are built. Their yard grows, filled with rough rock, shaped blocks, slabs and beams of stone, as the earth's crust is unbuilt around them.

Pottery of the first four centuries A.D. has been found immediately east of the quarry, together with shale lathe-cores and a coin of Gallienus. To the south-west are the tatters of strip-fields; a bowl barrow, at the corner of a Celtic field, yielded seven or eight burials, one with four skulls and a bone pin at its feet. Upright slabs of stone were probably the remnants of a cist shaped by Bronze Age stonecutters. Under today's soil surface a two-foot layer of stone crowned the barrow, containing shale fragments, Romano-British sherds, coins spanning the Imperial reigns of Trajan to Tetricus, 98–273, and the shells of limpets and other sea-food gathered down below. If the modern quarry plumbs the ancient ocean bed, this barrow and the soil that ripples from its flanks is the modest meeting-place for British, Roman, medieval and recent man-marks which between them have weathered innumerable storms that swept, and still sweep St Aldhelm's treeless plain.

If you regain the path and press on, tilting against the wind, across the old sheep pasture which quilts long-fallow field-shapes, you come to a ruined settlement perched at Purbeck's extremity. There, rocks are hewn out, making a quarry-shelf on the cliff-top, rugged and raw where it steps down, but rich with vegetation in hollows and in the footings of the structures built into it. Some are complete but for their roofs, and the wind fills their shells, shrieking through vacant doorways and glassless windows from which a watch was kept in the last war, and wireless messages transmitted inland. A few yards westward the look-out with its mast is manned: a coastguard in its shelter continually scans the sea from the horizon to the skirts of the Head over three hundred feet below, where the waves crash soundlessly and devil-may-care gulls ride out the storm.

A blockhouse for a gunner stood here in the sixteenth century, one of a chain of fortifications which Elizabeth's obsessive grip upon the purse-strings of the Exchequer preserved in a condition of perilous dilapidation; so much so that the Deputy Admiral of the county had them put to rights out of his own pocket in 1588. On Tuesday 23 July of that year, look-outs on the Head were able to chart the manoeuvres of the English Fleet and the Spanish Armada as the Battle of Portland was waged, a battle with Portland Race in some phases of the engagement, as much as with the enemy. That night the opposing fleets passed Purbeck's snout, while infantry and cavalry on the march from Weymouth to Poole kept pace with them, a real army tramping over Flower's Barrow towards Corfe and across the heath to the causeway and Wareham. For a couple of hours the next day Drake engaged Medina Sidonia off Purbeck, a short but sharp battle with more casualties than all the previous day. Ships put out from Poole with provisions and volunteers, and even pirate vessels from Studland Bay weighed anchor for an officially sanctioned, if less profitable, attack on old rivals. A Portuguese carrack, the *San Salvador*, later sank in suspicious circumstances in Studland Bay when, as an Armada prize, she was on her way from Weymouth to Portland; but for the time being the ships moved east and north and nothing more was seen of the mariners until Dorset seamen, decimated by typhus, returned on foot from the south-eastern ports as licensed beggars.

The weather was relatively kind to the battle fleets and no-one suffered in the clutches of St Aldhelm's Race that day. Not so in January 1920, when the *Trevias*, on the return leg of her maiden voyage to Calcutta, ran aground. Heavy seas around the promontory foiled all attempts to relieve the crew, who abandoned ship in their boats and made for the hostile shore. Seven men reached it alive and were rescued by Frank Lander and the Revd Piercy, vicar of Worth. Thirty-six were drowned, and those that came ashore were laid out in the village's reading-room. It is said that a certain Norman native of Purbeck stood on this promontory, about the year 1140, with more than the wind bleeding tears from his eyes; for from here he witnessed his son—or his daughter and her bride-groom, according to the chronicler's taste—set sail and shortly perish in the treacherous eddies. He resolved then to erect a chapel, a chantry where candle-flames might flicker prayers and a sea-mark with a cresset whose burning beacon should warn against the seas beneath it.

GP

At the centre of encircling earthen banks whose turf is riffled by the boisterous air, the chapel still stands. If the church of St Martin, Wareham, at the northern end of our territory, owes its genesis to the Saxon bishop of Malmesbury, this chantry at the island's opposite pole is dedicated to him. Though folk call the place St Alban's Head more often than not, that saint had no known dealings with Purbeck, and Aldhelm claims the chapel unequivocally. Later buttresses shore its four-square walls and its roof rises to a cross of 1873, where the cresset may once have blazed, but its bulk is Norman through and through. Its quoins break the four winds. A stout door is set at the north-west beneath a Romanesque arch of two orders, whose jambs and voussoirs are mined by the weather. Miniature tunnels have been quarried in the masonry by wind-whipped particles of stone. The door opens into welcome shelter, though it is dank and dark inside. One lancet window at the south-eastern angle of the building focuses its light upon the altar there and dimly illuminates the massive central pier with its eight arches supporting the four vaults of the roof. The woodwork is weathered like ship's timbers and the walls gleam with moisture and with what green life can gain a hold. Here, founded on solid rock at 350 feet above the water, there is the sense of a subterranean, almost submarine place, appropriate enough as a chantry where sailors' masses could be sung and coastguard's Sunday services intoned. Medieval kings paid the chaplain here 50s a year a for his pains, and, southwards, signs of foundations are said to mark the site of a small cell where a holy man might bare his soul to the elements.

On Whit Thursday, Worth fair day, a two-mile pilgrimage from the village ended here; the chapel was gaudy and scented with flowers and music fanned the dance around earthworks that must have seen pagan rites, and around the great pillar of the small chapel that consecrated them. Then, when its paved floor rang with dance-steps and blossom brightened it, it plumbed its darker origins; for it was also a wishing-place, called Devil's Chapel. Seventeenth-century initials carved in its pier may belong to those who mouthed secret wishes here rather than breathed prayers, and pins dropped into a cavity in it by hopeful girls were charms towards the man of their dreams. Devil's Chapel or holy place, it was more recently used as a coastguards' store, but is now almost bare; a stolid, weather-beaten shelter with weeping walls, a twenty-five-foot-square ecclesiastical hut, a Norman survivor on the cliff-top.

On a good day, you may emerge from the dimness into sunlight of glaring clarity. The chapel's walls dry to pale greys and honeys; where they grow out of the ground, sea-kale and sorrel sprout or pitch on the buttresses. A few steps take you to the cliff-edge and a view down into the water's blue gradations. Natural buttresses shore the shivered rocks of the Head's brow, and between them the stone drops sheer away for a hundred feet or so to the dense green undercliff, speckled with fallen boulders, and the gentler slopes which meet and chivvy the calmest water to a fringe of foam. On a shelf of the chert vein, a little to the east, a pillar of Freestone stands like a neck for a crude head of Spangle whose beak points southwards to where schools of porpoise or common and bull-nosed dolphin sometimes play.

The coastguard's path linking look-outs at Peveril, Craig-y-don, Tilly Whim and Blacker's Hole with the one on the Head run along the quarried cliffs to the north-east which seemed lofty but, from this perspective, shelve almost to the sea. A short walk to the north-west brings you to the dry combe whose slopes fall steeply and climb up once more to Emmetts Hill's four hundred feet. There you can see clearly what you are standing on: a crown of limestone, like a fortress built on a foundation of Portland Sand which rests in turn upon a plinth of Kimmeridge Clay. Emmetts Hill breasts the prevailing winds and its name, for that reason, is a contraction of even-might. From its summit you look straight down into the grim, grey cove called Chapman's Pool whose clay cliffs demand the strongest sun to wake the blues that sleep in their darkness. Their rumpled and folded skirts rise up from Egmont Point and the under-cliff called Molly's Garden to the jagged limestone teeth of Hounstout. After a fine storm wreckers could lie in wait there and look out, or tout, for grisly custom. From there on, for nearly five miles the Portland Beds retreat inland, re-emerging beyond Broad Bench as the dramatically-serrated battlements of Gad Cliff. They fall back to sea-level as the Kimmeridge Clay submerges itself once more, and punctuate their last outcropping in Purbeck with Worbarrow Tout, final plosive in the wind's teeth.

Up here, though, the frontier is with limitless air, and in the distance, beyond boat and bird, sea-haze melds water and sky together into horizonless blue whose depth and heights are all the same. In his snug shelter, with binoculars and radar, with his cat and his tame gull to keep him company, the coastguard watches; in the chantry a man may pray. Whichever saint is patron of the place, St Aldhelm's or St Alban's Head is the island's look-out *par excellence*. It is Purbeck's Tout.

PART SIX

DRILL

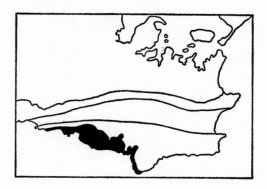

Limestone backs up inland; sublime viewpoints
supervise sea beyond deep seas of clay,
petrified, plundered swell; but carpeted
emerald and gold to the eye whose prey
is unspoilt beauty, nature out of joint.

Among the corn fox flaunts his flaming brush,
his earth the burning cliff whose brimstone breath
sours sea-mist; the grim shales' blackstone hoard
turned jet-like trinket on a flint-tooled lathe;
its fractions, gas-light, oil, tar, fertile ash.

Where small boats chart cement-stone's jagged hards
tarred pots net flesh in armour. Steened conduits
plumb the ground's wild water. Wire snares are laid
in tracks as lost as tramways to old adits.
Though leys from earth to quarry spurn man's roads,

both kinds in the keeper's mind intersect.
Prospecting eyes redraw the lines of sight;
the watchtower in decay, but at well-head
an iron donkey draws new tarmac to it.
Crude depths and refined distances connect.

26

HANT AND "HORTUS INCLUSUS"

ON HOT DAYS the little cove called Chapman's, or Shipman's, Pool bakes between the stony heights of Emmetts Hill and Hounstout. But the sun and the boat-house at its eastern lip do little to relieve the bleak wildness of the place, where Irish coastguards looking for a quiet life once asked smugglers if they wouldn't mind landing their contraband somewhere else. Its heated clays smell sulphurous and its air holds, in reserve, the sinister chill of a hant. Prehistoric farms covered Kingston Down behind, and who knows what trade the bay saw. Recently a gold solidus of Theodosius was found here, and one man recalls how, in his younger days, on some late-night, unnamed errand, he hid shivering as a band of men marched by. Perhaps he feared a squadron of Preventive men, but the moonlight showed him legionaries of the Roman army on an anachronistic mission. Not long ago a small boy saw the same sight in daylight; his mother, seeing nothing, asked him what had frightened him, and he described the soldiers in detail, down to the metal fringes on their tunics.

It is a treacherous place. The drought of 1976 opened clefts in the cliffs, and the torrential rain that followed swelled the clay and plummeted it to the shore. Years of normal erosion took place in a few months and Chapman's Pool, part of the Encombe Estate, had to be closed to the public because it was impossible to make the cliffs safe. When open, the climb up steps to Hounstout is a steep one. Below, rabbits run in Molly's Garden, while above, behind natural castellations, hares start from their forms, their black-tipped ears sensitive as antennae. To the east, streams run down from Westhill Farm and Sheepsleights, either side of the hill settlement of the past. To the west is the plush Vale of Encombe and the clayland's swell sweeping towards Tyneham Cap, a country of soft contours between the ragged cliffs and the rounded contortions of the limestone uplands. There are two routes to Kimmeridge: one, the coast path, and the other the high upland track that skirts Encombe and Smedmore, always looking down on the fifth province of Purbeck. For now we shall take the second.

On days when the sea-mist rises and the sun heats everything through its infinitesimal lenses, nothing can be seen except for the ground shelving away into whiteness, and sheep, black-faced and white, like boulders that bleat and stumble away into nothingness again. The bald path leads past a sheep wash, and soon the tree-shapes of Quarry Wood show up. Near both Kingston Plantation and Westhill Wood there were signs of the ancient Kimmeridge shale industry—blackstone waste from the lathes together with Romano-British pottery—and in Quarry Wood, near London Door Quarry where stone was dug for Kingston church, a skeleton was found interred between twin stones, along with a gallon pot full of lathe-cores. When the discovery was made, towards the end of the eighteenth century, these remnants were thought to be a form of currency, known as coal-money or Kimmeridge Pennies. Now that they are known to be industrial waste the value ascribed to them in this burial hoard is a puzzle, unless they were evidence of a shale-worker's industrious life.

The path turns south-westwards, crosses the driveway to Encombe beside sheep-pens and a derelict gateway, and follows The Belt and Polar Wood, from which pheasants' rasping cries cut through the mist and the shapes of roe deer nimbly clear the stone walls and merge into the undergrowth. On open pasture not far from the track, in the direction of Encombe Obelisk whose stone needle seems to sway in the eddying vapour, are the foundations of a stone-built, stone-flagged building of fifty by twenty feet or so containing shale debris and pottery of the first to fourth centuries, probably set in its own compound at the corner of a Celtic field. Now, the only buildings are in the valley beneath, and they are shrouded from view. Slowly but surely the path climbs, for it is approaching the highest point in all Purbeck. When the wind gets up, the curved prow of Swyre Head is engulfed by the mist's fine, flooding spray. Do not be misled into thinking that the breeze will clear it; rather, it feeds it and the battle between sun's heat and sea air may rage invisibly for hours. Ghostly jangling of chains turns out to be sheep rubbing and scratching and butting at an iron gate, when the mist evaporates at last. Beyond it a great tumulus is set on the head, and from the stone set in its crown almost all Purbeck may be surveyed.

Northwards, across the chalk ridge and Creech Barrow, the heaths stretch to Wareham and the coasts of the Harbour; Corfe Castle is humbled in its gap; ploughed chalk and raw chalk glisten on Ballard Down and the distant Needles of the Isle of Wight; the wooded, cropped valley suns itself, and the limestone of Acton shines; cottages, chapel and look-out are like warts on St Aldhelm's snout; and the claylands drop southwards to the sea and westwards towards Worbarrow Tout and the Isle of Portland. Swyre's promontory is Purbeck's sublimest view-point; and there are no tourist attractions here, no signs or exhortations carved in stone, no car-park or road.

The path doubles back in the direction of Kimmeridge village where half a mile or so of public road is all that penetrates the five square miles and more of this last province. Kimmeridge Clay nurtures the finest dairy pasture in the country, and in spring its emerald green is in vivid contrast to the black ploughed fields which still bear the shadows of nineteenth-century shale workings, and through which green-banked streams weave their way to the cliffs. Straighter hedge-lines mark the old manor boundaries of Little Kimmeridge, now occupied by Swalland Farm; of Smedmore, where an elegant manor house stands; and Kimmeridge itself. Smedmore Hill, along whose crest our path runs, screens them from the rest of the island. Large-scale remains of prehistoric occupation have been ploughed up long ago down there, but the gentle northern slopes of Smedmore Hill retain impressive settlement patterns, scarped enclosures and fields of Durotrigian and Roman date, despite some narrow-rig ploughing; with signs of Mesolithic flint-working and Iron Age shale-working towards West Orchard that, together, hint at the sort of enterprise that must have thrived on the Kimmeridge Clay, on richer land, nearer the blackstone's source. Our route drops down to an old stone quarry, which has bitten a picnic-area out of the hill's flank, and where roads from Blackmanston and Bradle join to run, dog-legged, into the village.

A Jacobean-style parsonage of 1837, built when Colonel John Mansel inherited Smedmore and Kimmeridge by marriage and installed a resident clergyman, stands amongst trees beside the little church which is now, once again, served by the rector of Church Knowle. Its dedication is unknown, and its homely, unaisled nave was rebuilt in 1872, retaining its thirteenth-century porch, its fifteenth-century bell-cote and its simplicity, though not its square, wood-framed windows. Many details and memorials were cleared out and fragments of the chancel arch still lie in the churchyard along with a curious line of coastguards' graves, though there is no sign of the most famous memorial of all: that to

William Clavell who died in 1644, on whose altar tomb were carved
the words:

> "Within this marble caskett lyes
> He who was learned stout and wise:
> Who would for no expense conceal
> His projects for the common weall:
> And when disloyall Irish did
> Rebell against the Queane their head,
> Approved valour then did gett
> Him the reward of Bannerett."

The twelfth-century font, a rough stone bowl, was recovered from a
ditch to the west where it served Kimmeridge Farm's cattle as a water
trough. The parsonage, church and farm, set at the head of the village
street, are all tiled with stone slatts, but most of the rubble cottages, of the
seventeenth and eighteenth centuries, have deep brows of thatch from
which dormer windows squint.

Beyond the village is a toll-hut which reaps a small harvest from those
who wish to park on the grassy cliffs of the bay. Ice-creams and postcards
must be purchased at the Post Office beforehand, for parking space and
discreet toilets are the only concessions to tourists down there. Trippers
have been known to return apoplectic at the lack of attractions, and
especially at the lack of sand for the children, which, presumably, Major
Mansel should have had the goodness to import and shovel on to the shale
beach and stone ledges at Gaulter Gap.

Kimmeridge belonged to Cerne Abbey until 1539. Sir William
Uvedale sold the manor to the Clavells of Smedmore in 1554. Walter de
Clavile had come to England with the Conqueror and his family held
property at Church Knowle, West Holme, Quarr and Leeson. In 1427
John Clavell added Smedmore when he married Joan, grand-daughter of
William Wyot who had purchased the manor from the De Smedmores
in 1391. Smedmore has not been sold for almost six centuries, but has
passed by inheritance and marriage to the Mansels of today. The road to
it runs from the village in the direction of Swyre Head, beside pasture-
land, barleyground and sweetcorn. A track branches right for
Kimmeridge Dairy, notable for an eighteenth-century barn almost thirty
yards long, and between Grange Plantation and The Rookery the for-
bidding front of Smedmore House shows up at the end of an unkempt
drive. Its bulbous, double-fronted Georgian façade, built by George

Clavell in the 1760s, set in rowaty grass, stands out, in the manner of a French château, an imposition on the landscape. There is little external evidence of Sir William Clavell's Jacobean house whose core survives within the present building. His valour brought glory to the family, but his projects, as we shall see, nearly ruined them.

The interior marries sanguine spaciousness with the warmer, darker intimacies of the previous century. Much of the furniture, which includes a chair that belonged to Napoleon, and most of the paintings were inherited from the Dutch Ginkel family in 1898, whose ancestor Godart Baron de Ginkel also won honour for his service in Ireland, and was created Earl of Athlone by William of Orange in 1691. Because part of the house is divided into flats, Major and Mrs Mansel are still able to show their visitors, one afternoon a week, around a lived-in home, an inheritance which they are pleased to share. The Major willingly unlocks the secrets of lacquered cabinets and brings down family papers and old books from the tall shelves of his library, while his wife talks gardening outside. The modest, classical façade of 1710 gives on to a secluded, cultured garden, in complete contrast to one's first impression of the house. There, visitors are invited to sit in chairs on the wide, shrub-bordered lawns, or to wander in the captive fragrance of the walled flower garden. Vigorous bushes of English lavender grow into the warm air and peaches colour up on espalier-trained trees; while in the larger walled kitchen-garden, ranks of vegetables are divided by box hedges, and an ancient mulberry, contorted and propped on a stout stilt, bears lush, scarlet fruit like crusty raspberries.

The old kitchen now houses a small exhibition of geological specimens, including the shale and oil that has so shaped the history of Kimmeridge and Smedmore; correspondence and patents relating to the works that Sir William Clavell gambled on; dolls from 1780 onwards; tapestry work and pottery made by members of the family. Across the courtyard, the brew-house was transformed, during army occupation, into a shower-room; but the large black boiler survives, with lead pipes running to where a vat was set into the floor. The lead pump, dated 1771, which pumped the wort up again for a second brew, is unused now, though the pump that lifted water from a crypt-like sump fed by springs under the courtyard's flags came into its own in the drought of 1976. It had not been used within living memory and its steel screws were rusted, but the original brass screws and taps were in perfect condition, the leather seals were mint and, once again, it tapped an unfailing supply of fresh water.

Despite disastrous speculation on the wealth of the treacherous cliffs and childlessness in several generations; despite having to bypass undesirable relatives, like the reformed highwayman of the seventeenth century, and by dint of foiling an attempt by the servants to forge the will of the intestate John Clavell and usurp the property in 1833, the manor has passed down by inheritance to its present inhabitants. It is impossible to feel for avaricious landowners who cared for nothing but self-enrichment and aggrandisement, but the name Mansel carries the reputation of a good landlord with tenant farmers and cottagers on the old Clavell estates. In Smedmore, a *hortus inclusus* sheltered from the grim coastline by the knoll behind Harry's Wood, it is easy to sympathise with those who wish to conserve and develop their heritage, so that it may survive, not merely as a museum-piece, but in organic relationship with those who continue to cherish it.

27

THE GOLDEN BOWL

VISITORS ARE NOT so welcome in Encombe Vale, but if you are fortunate to be granted the freedom of the estate you will find yourself surrounded by a landscape unlike any other. The road winds down beside Quarry Wood and curves quite steeply around the foot of a tall, flock-speckled hill whose brow is wrinkled with sheep-walks and pin-pointed by an obelisk of stone, quarried in the caves of Seacombe and erected to the memory of Baron Stowell, the first Earl of Eldon's elder brother. Then the private valley spreads itself wide before you and runs towards the sea, bounded on the east by the extended arm of Westhill whose knuckles are clenched above the sea at Hounstout, and protected to the west by the crook of Swyre Head which, from this perspective, rises tier on tier like a grassy ziggurat. Here is seclusion on a grand scale, untroubled by visitors except on special occasions, since, as Sir Frederick Treves explained in 1906, "I am unable to speak of this valley, because, owing to the atrocious conduct of the 'trippers', the road through it has been very properly closed by the owner".

The manors of Kingston and Encombe belonged to Shaftesbury Abbey until the Dissolution. The Protector, Edward Seymour, assumed posses-sion of Kingston until his downfall and beheading in 1552. Sir Thomas Arundel of Encombe shared the same fate. The Protector's son, Edward Seymour, married Lady Catherine Grey, sister of Lady Jane, without permission from Elizabeth and was incarcerated in the Tower for nine years. Eventually he sold Kingston to William Pitt of Westminster in 1604, while the Cullifords of Devonshire held Encombe until 1734, when George Pitt bought the estate for his son John, reuniting the manors once more. In the course of the next forty years, as well as establishing turnpike roads in Purbeck, John Pitt built Encombe House, probably to his own designs, around the core of the Culliford residence. It is an ambi-tious building faced in fine white ashlar, with porticoes and colonnades,

gables and chimneys, bays and wings, while its very breadth and the
weight of its cornice somehow prevent it from appearing overbearing and
set it firmly as the focus of the broad amphitheatre which it inhabits.
Backed by the trees of the North Gwyle, it faces on to two lakes,
embellished with a fountain, which extend down the valley towards a
third, beside Encombe Farm, and the South Gwyle whose woodland
stretches to the coast.

John's son, William Morton Pitt, was a man of many concerns, one of
which was not to consolidate the fortune left to him by his father. He was
a Member of Parliament for the county for thirty-six years, though he
was both more impatient with that institution and less ambitious than his
cousin William Pitt the Younger. Accordingly, he was deeply concerned
with local affairs, as a Justice of the Peace and a gaol visitor committed,
with John Howard, to the reform of prisons and asylums. He regarded
work-houses as places of confinement and campaigned for cottagers to
have their own smallholdings won from rough land, their own pigs and
home-brewed small beer. He initiated schemes to discourage the inhabitants of Purbeck from following their traditional illicit pursuits: in
Kingston's South Street he built a factory for rope and sailcloth manufacture from local hemp; in Langton his straw-plait industry flourished
for a time; in Corfe Castle similar ventures employed more than two
hundred people, although his herring-curing works in Swanage ran
into trouble and was succeeded by a brewery. In 1796, at the height of
the French wars, he and William Clavell produced elaborate plans for
the defence of the kingdom, and Dorset in particular. They surveyed the
state of the existing defences and put forward a scheme for raising the
posse comitatus. They recommended chains of command and evacuation
procedures in the event of invasion. The Government must have been
grateful for Pitt's patriotic endeavours, but not everyone was so interested
in his liberal philanthropic notions. In the last decades of the eighteenth
century he established Sunday Schools in Wareham, Poole and Purbeck
to teach the children of labourers and fishermen to read and write, and
later was president of the first branch of the National Society for the
Education of the Poor on the Principles of the Established Church in
Dorset.

His cousin's Chancellor, Lord Eldon, was by no means sympathetic to
his plans to improve the condition of the poor, and specifically objected
to the very idea of an enquiry into the penal system. Reform was as
repugnant to him as the idea of Wesley's "deeper work" was inimical.

But Pitt's philanthropy and his hopes for Swanage as a profitable watering-place had impoverished him, while Lord Eldon's rise to power had rapidly enriched him. In 1807, Encombe and Kingston passed from the reformer into the hands of the Lord Chancellor of England. John Scott, so the story goes, was born the son of a coal-trader in Love Lane, Newcastle; he ran away to marry Bessie Surtees, took to the law and made his name. He opposed the repeal of the Test Act, supported the Six Acts of 1819 and, in 1821, was raised to the condition of Earl. He was horrified by Morton Pitt's attempts to procure a satisfactory wages settlement for Dorset agricultural labourers. The militia were ready to defend Encombe against riotous assault when the Reform Bill was at first thrown out of Parliament, for the Earl opposed it and, later, must have found some comfort in the transportation of the Tolpuddle Martyrs. In his last Parliamentary speech he inveighed against the "dangerous innovation" of the Great Western Railway. In other words, he stood for all that Morton Pitt abhorred, and vice versa. The villagers of Kingston must have very quickly learnt to tug the forelock to their new landlord, but in a very different spirit to that with which they greeted the old one. He and his Bessie, Elizabeth, Countess of Eldon, are buried at the abandoned church which he had built in the village.

A few years after his purchase of Encombe, a fire sent him scurrying out into the night to bury the Great Seal for safety. By the next morning he had forgotten where he had hidden it, and employed the household in a desperate dig for its recovery. The fire forced him to refurbish much of the interior of the house, and he and his successor added to the buildings and improved the park. The pillared Temple now opens on to a swimming pool. Behind it, the stable block and cottages, built after John Pitt's style, form the east wall of a very large walled kitchen-garden, now mainly devoted to the rearing of pheasants. Luscious warm figs can still be plucked straight from the tree, but the weeds that thrive there would grieve the thirteen gardeners who tended the estate before the war. Then, three foresters managed the woodlands, now the province of Don Cannell, the gamekeeper, who raises game for the syndicate that shoots here.

Guns are stacked in a corner of his kitchen, complemented in the living-room by a fine collection of walking-sticks. One of yew, his favourite wood, is set with sixpences from every reign of his life, and others have handles in the form of lovingly shaped animal heads, growing out of the wood's grain. Both his carving and his keepering are in a long tradition; in outhouses, along with modern traps and nicklyvats, cages for catching pheasants, are disused traps of forged iron, with strong springs and vicious jaws hungry for vermin, and other exhibits from a bucolic chamber of horrors. While he will pamper nesseltripes, or weaklings, he will also lie in wait with his gun to pick off a young rogue pheasant that attacks and disembowels its fellows; his job is to produce 1,500 birds each season, including darknecks, whites, melanistic and Bohemian strains, to be flushed by beaters and bagged by the guns. His few chickens and partridges also scratch around together for the pellets that he distributes between rows of runs arrayed among lush dandelion and rusty dock in the kitchen-garden. Later, the game birds will find roosts in the woods which he and his two Labradors patrol for predators. There is no hunting because cliff-foxes have an unkind habit of luring hounds to their deaths on the shore beneath, but he has trapped up to 160 beasts in a season. He inspects wire nooses set in likely runs, and tunnel traps laid for stoat and grey squirrel. The dogs have an impeccable memory for hidden traps and will not pass that way again until they have seen them cleared. They alert their master to the presence of a creature in a thicket, or to its recent passage through the undergrowth where he can check the tracks and the droppings that signal a route or the bounds of a territory; while pellets regurgitated by raptors furnish a swift post-mortem of their victims. The dogs were equally inquisitive about the ice-well among the scrub on a bank near Long Wood; it is an immaculate flask of stone through whose opened dome we peered into perhaps eighteen feet of darkness, once the only source of refrigeration on the estate.

South of Long Wood, within Swyre Head's embrace, is the swollen, treeless mound, capped with plateau gravel whose name, the Golden Bowl, is often applied to the valley as a whole. The grass and woods and crops within it are extraordinarily rich, and the lakes, fringed with a superb variety of trees, survive the hottest summers; but here nature has been supplemented by art: underground works of stone beside which the ice-well is a mere trinket of convenience. In the middle of the last century the second Earl commissioned plans, for supplying the Mansion House and its lakes with water, from James Simpson, Civil Engineer, of Westminster, and contracts were drawn up with Thomas Isaac of Bristol to implement them. A tunnel, half a mile long, was mined through Westhill at a gradient of 1 in 866, lined with masonry and ventilated by three vertical shafts dug down from the hill-top. Reservoirs at either end were covered with stone landings; one hydraulic ram at Renscombe was to feed tanks and a weir there, while another at West Hill Farm supplemented springs which fed its tanks; over 4,000 yards of cast-iron pipe carried the water from these sources, through the hill, to the reservoir near the house. The supply also fed the upper and lower lakes whose clay beds and embankments were remade at the same time, and flowed beneath them in a stone-lined drain to an open culvert near Encombe Farm which completes the journey to the sea, running under a stone embankment above Freshwater Steps. All the masonry and ironwork were worked and installed to the highest specification and comprise a largely invisible feat of engineering as elegant as anything above ground in the estate. The Earl was not content with spring water alone, for a driftway was built, connected to a well sunk fifty feet deep near Freshwater from which sea-water could be pumped. Steps descend into the pump-house like a dome-shaped crypt, equipped with a great wheel by which the brine was raised. It is steened with foot-thick masonry as finely tooled and jointed as any on the façade of Encombe House itself.

The flow of water has carried us far beyond Encombe Farm, which faces the lower lake, or fish-pond, where boats are drawn up and horses drink. In the pastures around Big and Little Woods, which shelter the farm and climb towards Swyre, a dairy herd of Friesians cud. Barley beef and yearlings are reared there too, and on the slopes that hem the valley a thousand or so Dorset Down and Welsh sheep graze. The farm and dairy here are estate-managed, while tenants farm Colonel Scott's land across the length and breadth of Purbeck, at Arne and Blashenwell, Woodyhyde, Langton and Combe. More intimidating creatures used to tug at the turf and decimate the trees on the skirts of Westhill where the dense belt of Broadley Wood now stands. In the last century a deposit of mammaliferous drift was excavated beside the Golden Bowl; it contained bones of primeval elephant, rhinoceros, reindeer, ox and horse. Their presence in the past only emphasises the culture and nurture that has shaped the ancient swell and flux of Encombe's fabric.

The primitive has always had an appeal for the romantic mind and, despite the sophistication of the estate's buildings, someone, probably the second Earl, indulged in a little architectural primitivism down near the farm, having a rock bridge constructed of massive stones. The farm road runs over it, but passages within its rough-hewn bulk gave on to an alcove from which the fish-pond might be viewed in rugged splendour, at least in the days before it was choked by rather too undisciplined growth.

Evidence from an old print, and ancient remains built into the farm's garden wall, suggest the presence of that other *sine qua non* of a rustic estate—a ruined chapel. If no more than fragments survive, the Scott family made up for it by building two churches in quick succession up the hill at Kingston.

The prospect does grow wilder towards the coast, where the artificial water-channels and banks are overgrown; the chain of trees that link Quarry Wood at the valley's head with South Gwyle becomes more and more ragged and unkempt. Herons fly over the lakes to their roosts, and here in the thick underbrush is the cacophony, or charm, of small birds. The sea comes into view and the smell of shale greets the nostrils. Beyond the culvert, steps newly built into the shifting clay cliffs lead down on to a beach that sweeps greyly westwards. A small promontory at Freshwater Steps, tiny against the heights of Hounstout, spouts the gwyle's stream into the sea for gulls and cormorants to plunder; a sea whose extent, whose depths and shelving blues, make you feel that for all Encombe's expansiveness, you have emerged into reality once more from a private, other-worldly chamber.

28

SHALE, COAL AND OIL

WITH HOUNSTOUT'S BULK at your back and, on the right, the Kimmeridge claylands swelling up to the inland promontory of Swyre Head, the old coastguards' path runs up from Freshwater Steps and along the undulating tops of the grey cliffs. Fields of barley and of kale, beloved by pheasants, leave little enough living-room for the ruddy-stemmed wild cabbage and delicate early scurvy grass which thrive above the sea. Foundered fences dangle over the edge where cliff-falls have robbed good ground. Cracks open in the path at your feet where rain will abet the sun's treachery and send sodden clay to the shore. Down there a farmer's stock becomes beachcomber's spoil, and fishermen have been known to land a cow for their supper. Picknickers and bathers, unwisely seeking shelter from the wind, have had close calls with the cliffs.

Below Eldon Seat the path climbs to its highest point and the grey-blue shales fall away, layer upon lowering layer separated by stone-beds which climb westwards from the shore where they outcrop as successive ledges, jagged spines of rock bristling beneath the shallows, protruding far out to sea, boiling the water at low tide and conspiring to wreck more than a few vessels.

There are signs of the early Kimmeridge shale industry throughout the island, and here, near its source, is plentiful evidence of those who exploited the province's parent rock. It was no basic industry, but a luxury trade; clay hearths and floors of circular huts have been excavated between Freshwater and Eldon Seat, where craftsmen of about 400 B.C. cut bangles by hand, that are still worn by discerning Iron Age skeletons. Stone floors and walls nearby indicated a later phase of the industry, when flint tools were mounted on lathes from which armlets, cups and spindlewhorls were turned out in quantity. Another site spanning the period when the lathe revolution occurred lies between Swalland Farm and Rope Lake Head. Rope Lake is a synonym for waterfall, and streams diverted by later workings and erosion must have spilled on to the broad rock-blades below.

Between there and Clavell's Hard, rails run off the cliff and old tracks run in a zigzag path from adit to disused adit across the fields and up the valley below Kimmeridge Dairy. Nearly two miles of embankments and cuttings are now overgrown with golden crops, fragrant with clay flora and patrolled by crows, larks, redpolls and siskins. But on hot days, the air rising up the face of the cliffs near Clavell's Hard is pungent with the smell of bitumen and sometimes the rocks burn spontaneously; an ashen, evil-smelling, slow furnace above the sea, that last smouldered from 1972 to 1974. Remains of tunnels driven into the cliff were linked by a tramway on a shelf about thirty feet above the shore, where the seam of blackstone, or Kimmeridge coal, rises over a distance of half a mile from sea-level to the cliff-top above the Yellow Ledge at Cuddle. "Caddle" means a mess and "caudle" is a miner's term for mud. A tramway connected the workings at Cuddle with those north of D Plantation and ran down towards a wooden pier that stood off the old sea-wall beside Maple Ledge in Kimmeridge Bay. The shadow of an older tramway, which may have been the work of William Clavell, cuts a shadowy swathe through the corn-field between a notch in Cuddle's cliff-top and a platform above the Bay, beneath which Clavell's pier provided a sheltered quayside until high seas broke it up in 1745.

Today, the rocky shore is tamed only by a rough, stone hard where small fishing craft are beached before tar-black boat-houses piled with lobster pots, but in the early seventeenth century the Bay was the focus of ambitious hopes that were dashed as surely as the pier, and much more rapidly. Coker describes Sir William's enterprise as follows: "hee hath at his owne Charge, with great Rocks and Stones piled together, built a little Key in Imitation of that at Lime for small Barkes to ride, invironed on the East Side with an Hill yeelding Myne for the Allom Works and a kind of blueish Stones that serve to burne, for maintaineing Fire in the Glasse House; but in burneing yeelds such an offensive Savour and extraordinarie Blacknesse, that the people labouring about these Fires are more like Furies than Men". There was nothing new about the use of Kimmeridge coal, for cottages have burnt it on their hearths for centuries, a cheap source of fuel not to be sniffed at; but when Clavell, following Lord Mountjoy in 1600, employed it to keep his alum-pans bubbling he faced the Furies indeed. He had no royal patent and the Farmers of the Allom Works seized all his assets for the King's use. He agreed to royalties of £1,000 per annum, but later suffered the destruction of his works and the sale of his cattle, thus being deprived of both his means of profiting from the Kimmeridge clay. He invested money in litigation, in glassmaking, using the shale as a source of heat only, and in salt-boiling, but problems with his partner, the glassmaker Alexander Bigo, with royalties and concessions, led him to Marshalsea debtor's prison with losses exceeding £20,000, no small sum in the 1620s.

The most conspicuous landmark on Kimmeridge's cliffs is a more frivolous folly: the Clavel Tower on Hen Cliff, erected by the Revd John Richards, alias Clavell, after he came into the Smedmore Estate in 1817. Its basement and the Doric colonnade which surrounds the ground floor of the round tower are unsafe; grey stucco is flaking from its mellow brick and stone walls, revealing in decay a more attractive complexion, while the pierced parapet that tops its third storey is crumbling. It was used for a time as a coastguard's look-out, and there is talk of restoring it to its former glory. Meanwhile, a notice planted there reads, "Danger. Keep Out".

The example of their predecessor spelled out no such warning to nineteenth-century entrepreneurs lured to Kimmeridge by the promise of profits from the blackstone. No less than eight companies launched ventures here. In 1847 an Act of Parliament was passed to authorise the construction of tramways, and in January of the next year the Bituminous Shale Co was registered. The raw material was shipped to works at Weymouth where the French chemist Du Buisson supervised its distillation and transmutation into naphtha, varnish, lubricating grease, pitch, paraffin wax and dyes. They too ran into patent problems and their factory was patently offensive to its neighbours; the enterprise was wound up in 1854. Messrs Ferguson and Muschamp took over and built a works near Wareham to manufacture fertiliser. The inhabitants of Kimmeridge had long spread shale-ash, together with the contents of their cess-pits, on their plots with great success; the practice was called gaulting and gave Gaulter Gap, where the stream from Kimmeridge runs into the Bay, its name. Following this example, Ferguson and Muschamp produced 11½ cwts of fertiliser base, or Kimmeridge "guano", from each ton of shale, together with 10 gallons of oil and 7½ of naphtha, plus paraffin wax and gas; but not enough of anything to make money. However, in 1858, Messrs Wanostrocht obtained, through the influence of their partner, Duke Malakoff, the Marshal Pelissier of Sebastopol, a contract to light the city of Paris with Kimmeridge gas. They rehabilitated the Wareham works to this end, drove the later adits into the cliffs, constructed a stone pier and an iron jetty, from which they exported shale products to France and the United States at the rate of fifty tons of oil and two hundred tons of fertiliser a month; not counting gas, which was used to heat furnaces and light the factory. But cheaper oils, with less sulphur content, forced them to give up before the cottages which they built at Gaulter Gap were occupied by their workers. The Wareham Paraffin and Candle Manufactory took over and burnt down. Another company tried to refloat the industry, and in 1876 the Sanitary Carbon Co began to exploit the shale used in London and elsewhere for purifying sewage. It and two smaller successors also went bust. All that remained of their ambitions was pipework in the Sandford Pottery which used the works for many years, though derelict now; sketches in a Mansel's hand of miners wheeling loads of shale from the tunnels; ruins, ashes; and a few trucks which rusted for years on abandoned rails behind the proud, decaying Clavel Tower.

If alum, glass, salt and a spectrum of shale products must fail, what else could the malignant cliffs offer? What else but Medina Hydraulic Cement, made from the cement-stone beds at Cuddle promontory, and ideal for army installations at Lorient and Rochefort and breakwaters at Cherbourg and Alderney. Thus ended Kimmeridge's nineteenth-century French connection.

Beyond Gaulter Gap, the cliffs above Washing Ledge and The Flats are full of the remains of that much more successful and long-lived industry of Roman and pre-Roman times. Hutchins wrote of "coalmoney" found here in 1768, thought to be Phoenician dollars, treasuretrove hoarded against some hideous catastrophe; but their one square, or several round chuck-holes identified them, in William Barnes' eyes, as lathe discards thrown into waste pits. British craftsmen may have warmed themselves by burning the "coal", but they made more discriminating use of its 34-inch seam than their successors. Not only was it turned, but finely carved by hand and polished with beeswax to a dark, jet-like glow. They made dishes of it, tiles, plaques and trays, mace-heads and cunningly worked table-legs of Egyptian-inspired design, representing an abstract beast's head, fore-quarters and clawed foot, as produced at Norden for the Roman market. Like Purbeck marble, blackstone found its way to Silchester, Verulamium and many other towns. Floors and lathe-bases, daub and cobbles, troughs and props from salt-boiling, flint lathe-tools,

shale spindlewhorls, a marble mortar, Roman pottery and coins, female
burials with detached jaws, and a bullock sacrifice in a five-sided shale
cist, found above Kimmeridge Bay, all suggest a vigorous way of life, and
death, spanning as much as eight hundred years.

The grey shales of the cliff, sometimes rusty or yellow with sulphur,
are packed with the delicate, often crushed forms of a myriad ammonites
and other shells. Dark pools in the cement-stone ledges are rich with live
shellfish, with the frail fronds of red and green weed, with vivid anemones
and glassy, almost invisible crustaceans. The cliffs of the bleakly-named
Charnel are thinly laminated and multi-fractured, while the stone shelf of
the shore is scored with intricate patterns of intersecting lines mysteriously
chiselled by the sea and exactly inlaid with a pale precipitate, like the
negative of an ingrained palm whose fingers, elsewhere, reach out greedily
for prey.

The *Welfare* proved a tempting prize when it was driven ashore in the
Bay in 1371. It eluded the fingers of rock, but not the grasp of men. The
vessel was not abandoned but the the Abbot of Cerne's men, together with
local gentry, conspired to put that right by threats and intimidation. The
ship was soon relieved of its ballast of silks, cloth of gold and other
valuables. A commission of enquiry later convicted the Abbot, a monk,
John Russell of Tyneham, William Wyot of Kimmeridge and his son,
and other Purbeck worthies. In December 1872, seventeen mariners were
more mercifully removed from their ship, the *Straslund*, when she went
on to the Kimmeridge Ledges. The life-boat *Mary Heape*, manned by
Mr Stickland, a fisherman in his mid-fifties, battled gallantly to save
them. Now, only one fisherman works out of the Bay, mostly for
lobsters, supervised through binoculars from the seaward cottage at
Gaulter by his father, who communicates his knowledge of shoal and
wind and tide via a hand-cranked telephone to his son's boat-house.

In 1956 a converted corvette, S.S. *Seislim*, patrolled a nine-mile course
offshore, detonating charges as it went and recording seismographs in the
search for oil. Nineteen years earlier, the D'Arcy Exploration Co had
sunk an unsuccessful bore-hole on Broad Bench, but early in 1959 BP
drilled to a depth of 1,816 feet on the cliffs just west of Gaulter Gap and
struck oil in the Cornbrash strata. A second well sunk later that year hit
the jackpot a thousand feet lower still beneath Broad Bench, and four
times a day a blue tanker weaves its way down through Kimmeridge and
up again, each load contributing to the 18,000 tons of crude produced
each year.

Broad Bench is a wide platform of cement-stone whose ragged edges chafe the sea into a fringe of spume. It forms a plinth for the blunt snout of the promontory, vantage-point from which to read the remains of the clay country. To either side of it the cliffs of Charnel and of Hobarrow Bay, where the lowest Kimmeridge strata are exposed, conceal more evidence of the early shale and salt-boiling industries. Beyond the ledges of Long Ebb is the long, bleak sweep of Brandy Bay, where the blackstone outcrops again and which saw settlement long before barrels of spirits were surreptitiously put ashore there. Above Wagon Rock the shales climb, give way to Portland sands and are crowned by sheer stone. From the green peak of Tyneham Cap, Gad Cliff falls away and outcrops as jagged fortifications which, above their clay buttresses, drive their wedges, gad after gad, against the sky. Turf-capped limestone rises from the water at Worbarrow Tout, and between that and the Mupe rocks, the western boundary of Purbeck meets the sea at Arish Mell, hidden from view within the larger curve of Worbarrow and Mupe Bays. Hidden and inaccessible, for it lies within army territory never open to the public. From its deserted, magical shores a pipeline thrusts invisibly out to sea, carrying the out-fall from the Winfrith Atomic Energy Establishment; but that, and all that lies beyond, is another story.

Inland from Broad Bench, the woods and springs of Egliston Gwyle run down from South Egliston Farm towards Stickland's cottage and the ruined Black Cottage which stands not far from the fenced enclosure of the well-head. Offshore drilling rigs may spring up in the sea during the next few years. Meanwhile, on the platform of Broad Bench and on the cliff above The Flats, small iron donkeys nod monotonously, drawing black gold up through the blackstone, a leisurely gesture to industry, opposite the Clavel Tower on Hen Cliff which oversaw so much sweated endeavour.

PART SEVEN

THE OLD ROAD NORTH

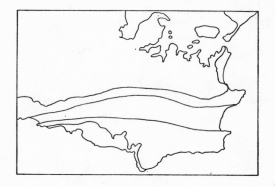

29

THE OLD ROAD NORTH

THE OIL TANKER weaves its way north from Kimmeridge, for changing
economic demands and the brief reign of the railway meant the reorienta-
tion of the island's old roads. But the busy shale industry of Iron Age and
Romano-British times must have demanded as easy outlet by land as
well as by sea, and it is still possible to tread a direct route back through
the provinces of fragments of ancient tracks.

From Gaulter Cottages a right-of-way makes up beside the stream,
through fields thick with wheat and beside productive cottage-gardens to
Kimmeridge Farm. It runs around the anonymous church and climbs the
steep slope of Smedmore Hill, where the strip-fields of three manors once
pushed arable land to its limit, to the Old Quarry. Where the rock-face
is now weathered and colonised by hardy saplings, workings disinterred
nine or ten Bronze Age skeletons in cists of shale and limestone. From near
the Telephone Exchange a path leads down again to Hyde Wood and a
richly-turfed ride through dark oak and alder where, at almost every
other wary step, you may flush pheasants and partridges with their
young, and, serenaded by the coarse cries of rooks and the genteel sighing
of doves, glimpse a shy treecreeper or send magnificent hares thumping
and drumming their warning through the undergrowth.

At Hurpston Coppice, a neck of the woods running due north turns
out to be an impenetrable hollow-way, dense with vicious thorn and
bramble and trammelled by almost invisible stone walls. Perhaps a track
from the prehistoric settlement above Bradle Barn joined the road here,
swelling the tide of blackstone merchandise that flowed out of Purbeck,
but it is certain that no-one passes this way now. The air trapped in the
highway's thickets is disturbed only by the reverberating clap and roll of
guns on the army ranges that penetrate here from an alien world.

On the hollow-way's left side, at the field's edge, the Harp Stone stands
framed by hawthorn and elder, like a sentinel on a road overtaken by time.

What must have been a landmark is all but hidden, a rugged limestone monolith, magnificent in obscurity. The seven feet and more of its southern face is hardly weathered, while its less durable northern portion is pocked and ribbed, and the whole is vivid with liverwort and lichen. Perhaps its grooves are aboriginal, the strings from which its name was plucked; or possibly, contrary to feeling, nearby Hurpston gave its name to the way-mark. We cannot tell whether the shadow it casts is long or short, sacred or profane, for no-one knows when or why it was bedded here.

A short way on, the old walls peter out at the Corfe River, known also as Steeple Brook, the Wicken or the Lake, which pursues a serpentine course, through the Wealden clays it once shifted, to Corfe Gap. To the right, Hurpston Mill harnessed its flow, but only traces of the mill-race survive. The public right-of-way up to Whiteway Farm no longer follows the old route which linked Herpstone Lane and the White Way itself; but two gates face each other on the Steeple to Church Knowle road, and from there you can climb, beside chalk-pits at the bends of the hairpin ascent, on to Ridgeway Hill where the green road makes a cross-roads with the old road north.

The view back across the valley takes in the familiar chimney-stacks of Clavell's Barnston and the squat tower of St Peter's, Church Knowle. In that tower, and in the chimney-breast and stack of Church Farm, are set stones inscribed with black lettering which must have been part of the same, long-lost fabric. Words but no sense emerge; they are divorced, dislocated, symbolic of all that, from this distance, we can never decipher. Beyond, at Cooper's Bridge, Bucknowle, a tessellated pavement with slabs and footings of limestone has recently been unearthed; the ground-work of the first villa found south of the ridge, and one more evidence of a densely populated Roman Purbeck.

Our road continues northwards, past more chalk-workings which nudge at the ditch of an infinitely older tumulus, past old lime kilns, across the metalled road where the pit-head of the clay mine stands, and up on to the unfathomable summit of Creech Barrow. In less than two-and-a-half miles as the crow flies we have travelled the two hundred and more millennia of Purbeck's geological past. Behind, the stubborn, treacherous shale, polished once to fine, worked blackness, still muddies the blues of a translucent, shifty sea. Next, cliff-stone, whose tunnels and man-mined caves make space within it for the darkness; and Purbeck stone, cleft for generations, from which fresh surfaces are born to outface the weather every day. Then the sheltered valley where, at one end, the evidence of husbandry survives in its friable flesh despite its abandonment to the army, and, at the other, more or less transitory dwellings of brick and canvas are raised to house a new population. The hills' chalk marled the land down there, was burnt to make mortar for its masonry and lime-wash for its walls, pastured thousands of its sheep and served as a green highway from Flower's Barrow to Corfe, and Corfe to Ballard Head. Northwards from Creech Barrow is the intractable heath, ever claimed and reclaimed, tamed and wild, shot through with tracks and tramways, and plumbed for its blue clays whose wounds fill or subside, and for its oil. Beyond is the water of the Frome and of the island-spotted Harbour, while to the east the sea continuously spawns the fine, white and sometimes singing sands of Studland and Shell Bay.

The old road did not run up on to the cone of Creech, but the Barrow is the place from which to take a long view, to take stock and admit to all the loose ends. The lanes which undermine this look-out drive out to the extremities on the lenses, and the blue clay is dug out in retreat. It is not possible to exploit every ounce of the white earths, and my roads too have had to bypass rich seams. Much that I have seen and heard has had, in the end, to be left in the ground.

The old road skirted Creech Barrow's flank and made for Grange Gate. From there the causeway runs to Stoborough and Wareham, while neglected tracks stretch away into the darklands of Holme Heath; across Luckford Lake to Bindon Abbey; over Battle Plain to West Holme and the old bridge across the Frome, where a handful of Royalists once barred the island against a Parliamentary force; and to Holme Mount, from which sandstone was quarried for Nathaniel Bond's church of 1866 beside Holme Priory, where his wife, Lady Selina, daughter of the second Earl of Eldon, "with her own hands adorned these walls" with murals. In Edward I's reign, William de Clavell complained against Elyas de Rabayne, the Constable of Corfe, who took unwarranted liberties on Ingelram de Walley's estate and infringed the Abbot of Cerne's right of wreck at Kimmeridge, for filching sandstone from Holme for the castle; but much of the fabric, including marble pillars, for East Holme church and the chapel at Creech Grange, was lifted from the ruins of the Cluniac Priory which Robert de Lincoln founded early in the twelfth century. Neither complaints about the misuse of resources, nor the destruction of ancient monuments are anything new.

Today's road makes straight for Stoborough, whose name, Coker tells us, means "Place of the Towne or Burrough, and well may it be called soe, for onlie the Place remaines, the Burrough being gone to Wareham." Stoborough is recorded as a settlement in Domesday Book, and grew up into a solid place, though hated by some because it harboured radicals and dissenters. The freshly-thatched King's Arms and cottages there are none of them older than the eighteenth century, and a number of houses have been demolished or rebuilt in recent years; its lineage has been violently disrupted for, in 1655, its inhabitants petitioned Parliament in these terms: "in 1643 we willingly permitted our town of 100 families to be burned to preserve the Parliament garrison at Wareham". Across alluvial meadows from the little hamlet, Wareham still squats within its walls.

Old elms on the town walls have been decimated by Dutch Elm disease, and carefully felled to preserve fortifications consolidated by their roots. The Abbess of Shaftesbury arraigned Elyas de Rabayne for cutting down oaks, ashes, maples and thorns on her land, whereas today the Forestry Commission are given stick for planting monotonous forests on tracts of Purbeck's rich waste. East of Frome-mouth is Arne's plantation where, concealed in a clearing among the conifers, Arne Number 1 Well's bright new nodding donkey pumps oil into storage tanks. From it, the chimney of Sandford's old shale works and pottery can be seen as a reminder of earlier ventures.

Our road north started from the Kimmeridge wells, and it is fitting that we should finish by surveying an oil-field in the process of development. Early in January 1974, Gas Council (Exploration) Ltd struck black gold trapped at the top of a dome of porous Bridport sandstone, 3,000 feet below Wytch Creek. Seismic surveys and the drilling of step-out wells—at the north-west corner of Wytch Heath plantation, at Fitzworth Coppice and beside Ower Lake—delineated the four- by half-mile Wytch Farm Field and gave the oil-men confidence that it is a rich one, capable of giving up 1,500,000 barrels of light, good quality crude, worth £11 million, per annum for the next fifteen years or so. Coniferous ranks now shield four well-heads which some conservationists see as a greater threat to the heath than the Forestry Commission's plantations. The Gas Council has immediate plans for eight more wells and may drill up to twenty-two altogether, including injection wells. As far as possible they will be inclined outwards from the existing sites, for at that depth deviated drilling can tap the reservoir 1,000 feet away from the well-head in any direction. Water, probably drawn from the stream that runs out into Ower Bay,

will be injected to drive the oil from the edge of its zone, inwards to the
well-shafts. Four-inch flowlines, buried beneath fields to the north of the
plantations, will link the wells to a gathering station, covering up to ten
acres, whose storage tanks and separators will be buried in trees at the
corner of Wytch Fir Pound. There, water and gas will be removed from
the crude oil; the water to be pumped back into the injection system,
and the gas processed so that about 400,000 cubic feet per day may be fed
directly into Southern Gas's mains. Lower quality gas will be used for
process heating on site, the remainder will be incinerated, and ten tons of
liquid petroleum gas will be exported from the rail terminal by lorry. The
gathering station and the well-sites will be served by the Wytch Farm
road, and a planned causeway across Wytch Creek would relieve the road
from Bushey to Fitzworth of all oil traffic.

It is the passage of the six-inch, buried pipeline across the heath to
Furzebrook which causes most concern. Though the first part of it, in
Corfe River's alluvium, will cross agricultural land, it will impinge upon
the Hartland Moor National Nature Reserve, so recently ravaged by fire,
and may disrupt the ecology of Stoborough Heath. The Nature Conservancy are concerned to prevent the destruction of a disused quarry
which harbours reptiles, birds and mammals on the proposed route. So
old scars are defended against new ones. Others will be employed: part
of Fayle's tramway will soon carry oil beneath it, existing firebreaks will
be used where possible, and the Gas Council have pledged themselves to
consult the Nature Conservancy in detail when the time comes to lay the
pipe. Botanical advice is being sought so that heathland may be regenera-
ted above the new artery implanted in the heath's flesh, and where a gas
main has already been diverted around the Furzebrook site, heather roots
and litter have been transplanted. If necessary, heather seeds collected
locally will be broadcast on the disturbed ground.

The oil's immediate destination will be a rail terminal to be built
opposite the clay-works at Furzebrook; one more nail, according to local
pressure groups, in the heath's coffin. Storage tanks, administrative
buildings, processing units and safety systems will be erected. These will
certainly add to the present blot beside the curtailed main-line, and two
new sidings will be laid to serve the six trains that will take up to 36,000
barrels of oil to the refinery each week. But four or five of the site's
eighteen acres will be left undisturbed, managed by the Nature Conservancy, and another four will be landscaped and replanted. Major
Ryder, who owns the land at Wytch and Ower, but receives modest

rents rather than royalties, regards the enterprise as a necessary nuisance; while, for the Swanage Railway Society, it means a set-back to their plans for returning Purbeck to the age of steam.

Oil is in a long tradition, for men have always valued Purbeck for what she will give up to them. It will pulse beneath the heath's skin for a while, but I hope to see the day when the industry's bones will be only another shadow on the face of the wilderness, and passions which rage today will have been long forgotten. Hunting and mining, farming and tourism have always staked claims here, sometimes opposed and sometimes in bizarre concert. Purbeck is a dense, compact place whose small compass fills infinite space in the mind; its swell and solidity, its flux and permanence continually vie with one another. Men enter it as invaders or are thrust into its heritage from the womb, to live at one with it, to take up a stance of arrogant insularity, or to prey upon it—to come and see, if not to conquer. In turn, they leave it once again, with spoils or souvenirs, with four horses instead of one over Wareham's south bridge, or, empty-handed, via the grave. Trampled by trippers as it is, it is still a haven for dissenters, for nonconformists and for those who claim ancient rights upon its soil. Some campaign for jobs, and some for the wildlife of its provinces. Of all the creatures that inhabit the island it is man who can make irretrievable choices, who may brand the landscape with his ambition; with the fine tool-marks of a craftsman's care, or with the destructive mark of the beast.

Conservation for its own sake is absurd. It is like wishing eternal youth upon the woman you love, sparing her the travail of child-bearing, to end up a beautiful old maid in a museum. But progress as an end in itself is as gross a nonsense; it is right that the oil-men have had to wait two years before their plans can go ahead. What might have been rape may grow into a marriage of convenience. It is not all drilling-rigs and well-heads, or fish bars and amusement arcades yet. There are miles and miles of perfect Purbeck between the sea, the Harbour and Luckford Lake. There is good, sensitive building and restoration, and a vocal population well aware of its legacy and its responsibility; though one of the saddest results of the island's attractions is that while outsiders are free to colonise it, those who should inherit them are priced out of the market. But emigration, like exploitation, is an old story.

Purbeck's charms are its trap. Tourism feeds on uniqueness and gnaws it away. Distant boardroom decisions may end in the wresting of her vitals from her soil. But none of this should happen. Hoteliers and

landladies live in the island; men of clay and families of stonecutters have
worked it for generations; and its farmers have to live with the fruits of
their husbandry. The inhabitants of Purbeck must decide; her left hand
must know what her right is doing. The one is scrubbed, manicured and
richly decked, extended in welcome to the furriner. The other is
work-worn, clenched around its ingrained dirt; the clean dirt of pit and
quarry, the dark dirt of her cropped soils, and of her shale and oil. I came,
by main roads, as an admirer to grasp the first; and then, through old,
secretive ways, to woo and prise the second open; to read and record a
little of what I saw in it.

Beside the drive to his new house at Rempstone, Major Ryder has
erected a new sandstone stone circle, a whole reflection of the Bronze
Age monument across the road in the withy bed, a gesture towards the
past. While at Studland, on the massive heathstone base of the medieval
cross—akin to the circle and the Agglestone—is a plinth of thornback
from Acton, the base of a modern village cross. For a year after the un-
carved shaft of pond freestone from St Aldhelm's Head Quarry had been
dedicated by the Bishop of Salisbury, the marbler Treleven Haysom
worked it, after designs found on the Saxon cross-shafts of Dorset, until
it was ready to be returned from his quarr-hut and erected in July 1976.

On its west side the vine, symbol of fruitfulness, twines up from an
insoluble knot; birds roost and feed in it, and man the hunter, with his
bow, is poised above it, at once dependent and predatory. On the east side
the double helix of inheritance, a DNA molecule, grows out of ears of
primitive spelt wheat and entwines in its spiral a violin, a bomb, delta-
winged Concorde and a butterfly. Christ surmounts the chemistry, which
resolves itself into a crux. The north side is hellish, while runes on the
south, reminiscent of the inscribed stones in Lady St Mary's, Wareham,
spell out the text, "I created this world and I sustain this world". Studland
Cross's fine detail grows out of a rich tradition. It looks backwards and
forwards at once. Day after day, the sun rises to illuminate its helix and
sets behind its vine. It is a self-conscious gesture towards continuity. That
is how it must be.

NOTE   As this book goes to press, it has been announced that the largest
ever British onshore oil strike has been made at 8,500 feet beneath Wytch
Farm. The potential oil yield is probably double the earlier estimates.

HP

BIBLIOGRAPHY

ACKNOWLEDGEMENTS

INDEX

BIBLIOGRAPHY

ARKELL, W. J. *Geology of the Country around Weymouth, Swanage, Corfe and Lulworth* (H.M.S.O., 1947)

BENFIELD, E. *Southern English* (Eyre & Spottiswoode, 1942)

—— *Purbeck Shop* (Cambridge University Press, 1940)

BOND, L. M. G. *Tyneham* (Friary Press, 1955)

BOND, T. *Corfe Castle* (1883)

CALKIN, J. B. *Ancient Purbeck* (Friary Press, 1968)

COCHRANE, C. *Poole Bay and Purbeck, vols I and II* (Friary Press, 1970/1)

COKER, J. (THOMAS GERARD) *Survey of the Counties of Dorset* (1732)

DACOMBE, M. *Dorset Up Along and Down Along* (Dorset Women's Institute, 1951)

DARTON, F. J. H. *Marches of Wessex* (Nisbet, 1922)

DENSHAM, W. and OGLE, J. *The Story of the Congregational Churches of Dorset* (1899)

DORSET COUNTY COUNCIL EDUCATION COMMITTEE. *Environmental Studies Booklets* (Globe Education, 1976)

GARDINER, D. *Companion into Dorset* (Methuen, 1932)

HUTCHINS, J. *History & Antiquities of the County of Dorset, 3rd ed.* (1861–73)

KERR, B. *Bound to the Soil* (Baker, 1968)

LEGG, R. *Purbeck Island* (Dorset Publishing Company, 1972)

LELAND, J. *Itinerary in England and Wales* (c. 1535/43)

LEWER and CALKIN. *Curiosities of Swanage* (Friary Press, 1971)

LLOYD, R. *Dorset Elizabethans* (Murray, 1967)

LOCK, H. O. *Dorset* (Black, 1925)

POOLE FRIENDS OF THE EARTH. *Mining in Dorset* (1975)

ROBINSON, C. E. *A Royal Warren, or Picturesque Rambles in the Isle of Purbeck* (1882)

ROYAL COMMISSION FOR HISTORICAL MONUMENTS. *Dorset, vol II* (H.M.S.O., 1970)

SHORT, B. S. *The Isle of Purbeck* (Looker, 1967)

TAYLOR, C. *Dorset* (Hodder & Stoughton, 1970)

TENNENT, R. J. *A Purbeck Parish* (Friary Press, 1967)
TREVES, F. *Highways and Byways in Dorset* (Macmillan, 1906)
VICTORIA COUNTY HISTORY. *Dorset, vols II and III* (1908, 1968)

ACKNOWLEDGEMENTS

I am indebted to articles published in:
   The Proceedings of the Dorset Natural History & Archaeological Society
   Somerset and Dorset Notes and Queries
   Dorset (ed. Rodney Legg)
and grateful to the staffs of the following libraries for the use of mss., newspaper cuttings and other material:
   Dorset Record Office
   Dorset County Museum Library
   Poole Library—Local Collection
   Guildhall Museum Library, London.
Also, thanks are due to Peter Mitchell of the National Trust, Michael Wilton of the British Gas Corporation and Alan Williamson of English China Clays for their co-operation; to my wife for compiling the index and for her steadfast encouragement; and to all the people of Purbeck who knowingly and unknowingly contributed to this book.

INDEX

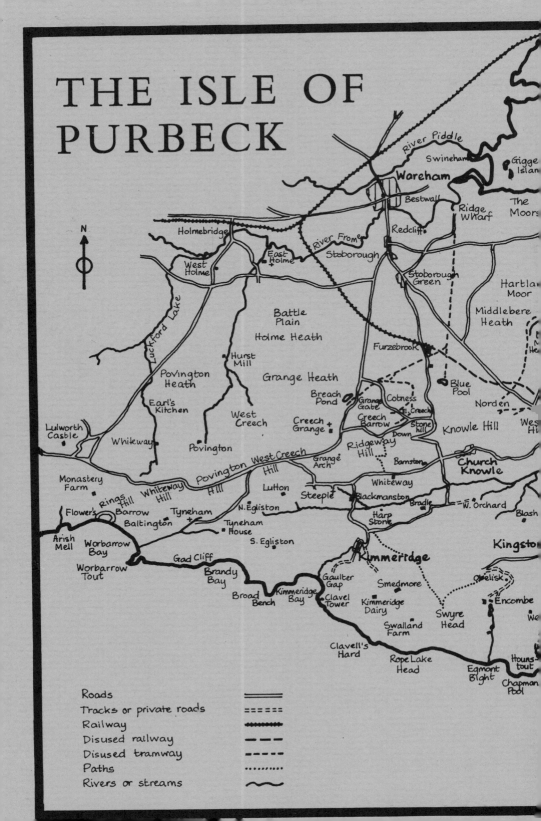

THE ISLE OF PURBECK

N

River Piddle

Swineham

Gigge
Island

Wareham

Bestwall

The
Moors

Holmebridge

East
Holme

River Frome

Redcliff

Ridge
Wharf

West
Holme

Stoborough

Stoborough
Green

Hartla
Moor

Battle
Plain

Holme Heath

Furzebrook

Middlebere
Heath

Hurst
Mill

Grange Heath

He

Povington
Heath

Breach
Pond

Grange
Gate

Cotness

Blue
Pool

Earl's
Kitchen

West
Creek

Creech
Grange

Creech
Barrow

Creech

Stone
hill

Norden

Down

Lulworth
Castle

Whiteway

Povington

Ridgeway
Hill

Knowle Hill

West
Hi

Povington West Creech
Hill

Grange
Arch

Bamston

Church
Knowle

Monastery
Farm

Rings
Hill

Whiteway
Hill

Hill

Lutton

Steeple

Whiteway

Bradle

W. Orchard

Blash

Flower's

Barrow
Baltington

Tyneham

N. Egliston

Blackmanston

Harp
Stone

Kingston

Arish
Mell

Worbarrow
Bay

Tyneham
House

S. Egliston

Kimmeridge

Worbarrow
Tout

Gad Cliff

Brandy
Bay

Gaulter
Gap

Smedmore

Obelisk

Broad
Bench

Kimmeridge
Bay

Clavel
Tower

Kimmeridge
Dairy

Encombe

We

Swalland
Farm

Swyre
Head

Clavell's
Hard

Rope Lake
Head

Egmont
Bight

Houns
tout

Chapman
Pool

Roads	————
Tracks or private roads	=====
Railway	•••••••
Disused railway	– – –
Disused tramway	- - -
Paths	·········
Rivers or streams	∿∿∿